A Stanley G.
Thematic Cat

COLLECT
MAMMALS ON STAMPS

Hanne and Jens Eriksen

First Edition, 1986

Stanley Gibbons Publications Ltd.
London and Ringwood

By Appointment to Her Majesty The Queen
Stanley Gibbons Ltd., London
Philatelists

Published by **Stanley Gibbons Publications Ltd**
Editorial, Sales Offices and Distribution Centre:
5 Parkside, Christchurch Road, Ringwood,
Hants BH24 3SH

First Edition – January 1986

© Stanley Gibbons Publications 1986

ISBN: 0 85259 123 3

Item No. 2852

Printed in Great Britain by Pardy Printers, Ringwood, Hampshire

A Helping Hand

Much interest was aroused in June 1983 by the publication of the first Stanley Gibbons thematic catalogue, *Collect Birds on Stamps*. Its revolutionary approach to stamp listing was intended to provide an essential tool for the thematic collector.

Unlike other branches of philately, thematic collecting places much emphasis on the design of the stamp, and it is our hope that the SG thematic catalogues will, by providing the basic information in an easily accessible form, allow collectors to spend more time on the fascinating factual research needed to sustain this aspect of the hobby.

Many collectors have, in recent months, enquired about further volumes in the series and we are now very pleased to present *Collect Mammals on Stamps*.

The same authors, Hanne and Jens Eriksen, have provided a similar framework of Country and Species Sections, but the Index has been extended beyond the style used in the first catalogue so that it now covers the English and both components of the zoological names of all the mammals listed.

Wild animals, not forgetting marine mammals, have become one of the most popular subjects for stamp issues and many fine examples of the designer's art are represented. We are sure that this second thematic catalogue will be as popular as the first!

Thematic collecting is a fascinating hobby and, for those needing a concise introduction to it, James Watson has written a skilful guide *Stamp Collecting – Collecting by Theme* (available from Stanley Gibbons Publications at £1.25 plus postage).

David J. Aggersberg

About This Book

This catalogue is a listing of stamps depicting wild mammals issued by countries throughout the world. It is based on the Stanley Gibbons *Stamps of the World Simplified Catalogue*, published annually in two volumes. This first edition contains over 5,000 stamps depicting almost 600 species of mammals. It has been updated so that it includes all mammal stamps which have appeared in the *Gibbons Stamp Monthly* Catalogue Supplements up to and including the September 1985 issue.

What is included

All issues, including overprints and surcharges, depicting wild mammals as listed in the *Stamps of the World Catalogue*. Miniature sheets are included when they contain stamps different from those in the regular stamp sets.

What is excluded

All stamp variations of watermark and perforation which are outside the scope of the *Stamps of the World*. The lists also exclude mammals forming part of a coat of arms, symbolic mammals and those too stylised to be identified. Prehistoric animals are excluded, but mammals that have become extinct during historic times are

included. Excluded also are domesticated mammals which deserve a catalogue of their own. This domestic category includes Indian Elephants, used for labour, and Camels, used for riding. South American Guanacos and Vicunas have, of course, been included, but their relatives, the Llamas and Alpacas, which have never lived in the wild, are excluded from this catalogue. Stamps listed in the Appendix of *Stamps of the World* are found under similar headings in the Country Section.

Country Section

This section lists in alphabetical order, with prices, the various countries and territories that have issued mammal stamps. Within each country the stamps are listed in chronological order with the year of issue and catalogue number taken from the *Stamps of the World Catalogue*.

Each mammal has been given a recognised English name (see also under Mammal Names) and the listing also includes, in brackets, the mammal name which actually appears on the stamp. The following order has been adopted for quoting these inscriptions: (1) English name, if this differs from the recognised name, (2) systematic, in italic, (3) local name. The inscriptions are shown exactly as on the stamps, even if erroneous.

Species Section

This section lists all species which have appeared on stamps in systematic order. Subspecies are not dealt with. Under each entry are given, in alphabetical order, the countries and catalogue numbers of the stamps which depict that particular mammal.

Mammal Names

The recognised English and systematic names follow the order proposed by G. B. Corbet and J. E. Hill, *A World List of Mammalian Species*, British Museum (Natural History), 1980. When English names were not given there we have consulted Desmond Morris, *The Mammals. A Guide to Living Species*, Hodder and Stoughton, London 1965. Many other books have been used for identification purposes and a selection of the most useful is given below.

Acknowledgements

We would like to thank the many fellow stamp collectors who have kindly made their collections available to us. We also thank Birger Jensen, Curator of the Natural History Museum at Aarhus University, for his encouragement and his help in the identification of certain difficult bat and rodent species. Special thanks to Editor David Aggersberg and Deputy Editor Pam Basley of Stanley Gibbons Publications Ltd., who kindly made the Gibbons Reference Collection available to us and without whose assistance this catalogue would not have had its present shape or value.

Great pains have been taken to keep both identification and typographical errors to a minimum. We would be grateful to hear of any corrections which may be discovered so that these may be amended in a future edition.

Hanne and Jens Eriksen
Aarhus, September 1985

Books on Mammals

A large number of books on mammals are available. In addition to several popular books and encyclopediae we have found the following most useful.

W. H. Burt and R. P. Grossenheider *A Field Guide to the Mammals* (of North America), Houghton Mifflin Co., Boston, 1964.
G. Corbet and D. Ovenden *The Mammals of Britain and Europe*, Collins, London, 1980.
J. Dorst and P. Dandelot *A Field Guide to the Larger Mammals of Africa*, Collins, London, 1983.
T. Haltenorth and H. Diller *A Field Guide to the Mammals of Africa including Madagascar*, Collins, London, 1980.
R. M. Nowak and J. L. Paradiro *Walker's Mammals of the World*, 4th Ed., The John Hopkins University Press, Baltimore and London, 1983.

The Authors

Hanne and Jens Eriksen live in Aarhus, Denmark. Hanne (30) is secretary to the Marketing Director of the Danish Dairy Federation and Jens (35) is Professor of Chemistry at Aarhus University. They are both devoted wildlife photographers and have given numerous talks and slide presentations. The search of wildlife in their natural habitats has taken the Eriksens all over Europe and North America in addition to visits to Africa, South-East Asia and Central America. The Eriksens both enjoy stamp collecting and they are the authors of the similar catalogue *Collect Birds on Stamps* (1983) and its *Supplement* (1984).

Stanley Gibbons Ltd.

Head Office, Auction Room, Shop and Rare Stamp Departments
399 Strand, London WC2R 0LX.
Offices open Monday – Friday 9.30 a.m. to 5 p.m. and Saturday by appointment only.
Shop open Monday – Friday 9.30 a.m. to 5.30 p.m. and Saturday 10 a.m. to 12.30 p.m.
Telephone 01-836 8444 and Telex 28883 for all departments.

Stanley Gibbons Publications Ltd: Mail Order and Editorial Departments: 5, Parkside, Christchurch Road, Ringwood, Hants BH24 3SH.
Telephone 04254 2363 and Telex 41271.

Countries Section

Arrangement
The various countries and territories are listed in the same order as in *Stamps of the World*. Those few which are not in alphabetical order are covered by cross-references. Each entry includes the geographical location and details of the currencies used. The dates quoted against these currencies are those on which they were first used for stamps in this catalogue.

Illustrations
These are three-quarters of actual size. One design from each issue is depicted, but only those overprints and surcharges required for identification are included.

Listings
These are divided into years by dates and into individual issues by the illustrations.

For philatelic details the *Stamps of the World*, or the 22 volume standard catalogue, should be consulted.

A † against the catalogue number indicates an issue where unlisted stamps in the set depict designs other than mammals.

Miniature sheets are indicated by a MS prefix.

Prices
Those in the lefthand column are for unused stamps and those in the righthand column are for used.

Issues where all the designs depict mammals are priced as sets only; single stamps and those from "broken" sets are priced individually.

Our prices are for stamps in fine average condition, and in issues where condition varies we may ask more for the superb and less for the sub-standard.

The prices of unused stamps are for lightly hinged examples for those issued before 1946, thereafter for examples unmounted mint.

Prices for used stamps refer to postally used examples, though for certain issues it is for cancelled-to-order.

The minimum price quoted is 5p which represents a handling charge rather than a basis for valuing common stamps.

The prices quoted are generally for the cheapest variety of stamps but it is worth noting that differences of watermark, perforation, or other details, outside the scope of this catalogue, may often increase the value of the stamp.

All prices are subject to change without prior notice and we give no guarantee to supply all stamps priced. Prices quoted for albums, publications, etc. advertised in this catalogue are also subject to change without prior notice.

Guarantee
All stamps supplied by us are guaranteed originals in the following terms:

If not as described, and returned by the purchaser in the original transaction, we undertake to refund the price paid to us. If any stamp is certified as genuine by the Expert Committee of the Royal Philatelic Society, London, or by B.P.A. Expertising Ltd., the purchaser shall not be entitled to make any claim against us for any error, omission or mistake in such certificate.

Consumers' statutory rights are not affected by the above guarantee.

ABU DHABI
Arabian Peninsula
1964 100 naye paisa = 1 rupee
1966 1000 fils = 1 dinar

1964

5†	40np Mountain Gazelle	.. ..	1.75	20
6†	50np Mountain Gazelle	.. ..	1.50	30
7†	75np Mountain Gazelle	.. ..	1.75	60

1966
Nos. 5/7 surcharged in new currency

19†	40f on 40np Mountain Gazelle	.. ..	1.50	55
20†	50f on 50np Mountain Gazelle	.. .. ..	6.00	8.00
21†	75f on 75np Mountain Gazelle	.. .. ..	6.00	8.00

1967

34†	125f Mountain Gazelle	.. ..	2.00	1.10

STANLEY GIBBONS
STAMP COLLECTING SERIES
Introductory booklets on *How to Start*, *How to Identify Stamps* and *Collecting by Theme*. A series of well illustrated guides at a low price.

Write for details.

1970

65† 150f Mountain Gazelle 2.50 1.00

1972
No. 65 overprinted UAE *and Arabic inscription*
93† 150f Mountain Gazelle 17.00 17.00

ADEN PROTECTORATE STATES
Seiyun
Appendix
The following stamps have either been issued in excess of postal needs, or have not been made available to the public in reasonable quantities at face value. Miniature sheets, imperforate stamps etc., are excluded from this section.

1967
Gazelle. 20f.

AFGHANISTAN
Central Asia
100 poul = 1 afghani

1964

520 25p Snow Leopard
521 50p Ibex
522 75p Argali
523 5a Yak
              Set of 4 2.50 1.50

1967

600 2a Rhesus Macaque (*Macaca mulatta*)
601 6a Striped Hyena (*Hyaena*)
602 12a Goitred Gazelle (*Gazella subgut turosa*)
              Set of 3 2.50 1.50

1969

673 1a Indian Crested Porcupine (*Hystrix jndica*)
674 3a Wild Boar (*Sus scrofa*)
675 8a Red Deer (*Cervus elaphus bactrianus*)
              Set of 3 2.00 1.50

1972

724† 12a Lynx (*Lynx lynx*) 1.25 1.00

1974

761† 5a Asiatic Black Bear (*Selenarctos thibetanus*) .. .. 30 - 15
763† 10a Goitred Gazelle (*Gazella subgutturosa*) 50 40
764† 12a Leopard (*Phanthera pardus*) 50 50
              (761/4 *Set of* 4) 1.50 1.00

1981

864 12a Urial 75 50

1982

888† 3a Brandt's Hedgehog ('Le Herisson') .. 25 15

899 2a Lion
900 7a Asiatic Wild Ass
901 12a Sable
Set of 3 1.40 75

1984

959 1a Hunting Dog (*Lycaon pictus*)
960 2a Argali (*Ovis ammon*)
961 6a Wild Horse (*E. przewalskii*)
962 8a Wild Boar (*Sus scrofa*)
963 17a Snow Leopard (*Panthera uncia*)
964 19a Tiger (*P. tigris*)
965 22a Indian Elephant (*Elephas maximus*)
Set of 7 4.00 3.00

AJMAN

Arabian Peninsula
1964 100 naye paise = 1 rupee
1967 100 dirhams = 1 riyal

1964

3† 3np Dromedary 10 10
12† 70np Dromedary 25 25

1965
As No. 3 but inscribed "AIR MAIL"
57† 35np Dromedary 25 10

1967
Nos. 3, 12 and 57 with currency names changed by overprinting to **Dh**
101† 3d on 3np Dromedary 10 10
110† 70d on 70np Dromedary 25 20
119† 35d on 35np Dromedary 25 10

OFFICIAL STAMPS

1965
As No. 3 additionally inscribed "ON STATE'S SERVICE"
O66† 50np Dromedary 15 15

1967
No. O66 with currency names changed by overprinting to **Dh**
O128† 50d on 50np Dromedary 15 15

Appendix
The following stamps have either been issued in excess of postal needs, or have not been made available to the public in reasonable quantities at face value. Miniature sheets, imperforate stamps etc., are excluded from this section.

1969
Wild Animals (Zebra, Dromedary, Brown Bear, Rhinoceros, Lion, African Elephant). Postage 1r × 6; Air 5r.

1972
Wild Animals (Tiger, Elephant, Zebra, Cheetah, Lion, Gibbon, Rhinoceros, Gazelle), 5, 10, 15, 20, 25, 30, 35, 40d.
African Animals (Cheetah, Lion, Gnu, Kongoni, Elephant, Rhinoceros). Postage 5, 10, 15, 20, 25d; Air 5r.

ALBANIA

South-east Europe
100 qint = 1 lek

1961

673 2 lek European Otter ('Vider')
674 6 lek 50 Eurasian Badger ('Baldose')
675 11 lek Brown Bear ('Ari')
Set of 3 16.00 6.00

1962

724 0 lek 50 Chamois (*Rupicapra r.*)

725	1 lek Lynx (*Lynx l.*)				
726	1 lek 50 Wild Boar (*Sus scrofa*)				
727	15 lek Roe Deer (*Capreolus*)				
		Set of 4	16.00	3.00	
MS727a	20 lek Roe Deer	. . . .	30.00	30.00	

1964

810 1 lek Eurasian Red Squirrel (*Sciurus vulgaris*)
811 1 lek 50 Beech Marten (*Martes foina*)
812 2 lek Red Fox (*Canis vulpes*)
813 2 lek 50 East European Hedgehog (*Erinaceus rumunicus*)
814 3 lek Brown Hare (*Lepus europaeus*)
815 5 lek Golden Jackal (*Canis aureus*)
816 7 lek Wild Cat (*Felis silvestris*)
817 8 lek Wolf (*Canis lupus*)

Set of 8 7.50 3.00

1965

882 1 lek Water Buffalo
883 2 lek Water Buffalo
884 3 lek Water Buffalo
885 7 lek Water Buffalo
886 12 lek Water Buffalo

Set of 5 10.00 2.00

943† 20q Roe Deer 25 15
946† 50q Wild Boar 70 30
947† 1 lek Brown Hare 1.40 55

970 10q Brown Bear

971 20q Brown Bear
972 30q Brown Bear
973 35q Brown Bear
974 40q Brown Bear
975 50q Brown Bear
976 55q Brown Bear
977 60q Brown Bear

Set of 8 9.00 2.50

1967

Inscribed "*Capreolus capreolus*—Sorkadhe"
1129 15q Roe Deer (fawn)
1130 20q Roe Deer (head of buck)
1131 25q Roe Deer (head of doe)
1132 30q Roe Deer (doe and fawn)
1133 35q Roe Deer (doe and new-born fawn)
1134 40q Roe Deer (young buck)
1135 65q Roe Deer (buck and doe)
1136 70q Roe Deer (running deer)

Set of 8 7.50 2.00

1155† 25q Brown Hare (*Lepus europaeus*) . . 25 10
1157† 40q Common Rabbit (*Oryctolagus cuniculus*) 60 10
Six other stamps in this set depict domesticated hares and rabbits

ALGERIA
North Africa
1957 100 centimes = 1 franc
1964 100 centimes = 1 dinar

1957

373† 12f + 3f Fennec Fox 1.75 1.75

STAMP MONTHLY
– finest and most informative magazine for all collectors. Obtainable from your newsagent or by postal subscription – details on request

1965

450† 5d Sand Gazelle 6.00 3.00

1967

489† 40c Sand Gazelle (*Gazella leptoceros*) . . 75 55
490† 70c Fennec Fox (*Fennecus zerda*) 1.25 75

1968

520 40c Barbary Sheep (*Ammotragus lervia*)
521 1d Red Deer (*Cervus elaphus barbarus*)
                                    Set of 2   2.00   75

1981

800 60c Mediterranean Monk Seal (*Monachus monachus*)
801 1d40 Barbary Ape (*Macaca sylvanus*)
                                    Set of 2   1.10   50

ANDORRA
Pyrenees Mountains between France and Spain

French Post Offices
100 centimes = 1 franc

1950

F143 100f Chamois 45.00 32.00

1971

F230† 80c Brown Bear ('Ours') 1.75 1.10

1977

F279 1f Stoat ('Hermine') 85 70

1978

F286 1f Eurasian Red Squirrel 60 45

1979

F293 1f Chamois ('Isard') 25 25

1982

F325† 1f80 Wild Cat (*Felix sylvestris sylvestris*) 50 40

Spanish Post Offices

100 centimos = 1 peseta

EXPRESS LETTER STAMP

1949

E54 25c Eurasian Red Squirrel 6.50 2.00

ANGOLA

South-west Africa
1953 100 centavos = 1 angolar
1977 100 lweis = 1 kwanza

1953

487 5c Leopard (*Pathera pardus shortridgei*)
488 10c Sable Antelope (*Hippotragus niger variani*)
489 20c African Elephant (*Loxodonta africana*)
490 30c Eland (*Taurotragus oryx livingstonii*)
492 50c Impala (*Aepyceros melampus petersi*)

493 1a Mountain Zebra (*Equus (Hippotigris) hartmannae*)
494 1a50 Sitatunga (*Limnotragus spekii selousi*)
495 2a Black Rhinoceros (*Diceros bicornis*)
496 2a30 Gemsbok (*Oryx gazella blainei*)
497 2a50 Lion (*Felis leo bleyenberghi*)
498 3a African Buffalo (*Syncerus caffer caffer*)
499 3a50 Springbok (*Antidorcas marsupialis angolensis*)
500 4a Blue Wildebeest (*Gorgon taurinus*)
501 5a Hartebeest (*Alcelaphus caama evalensis*)
502 7a Warthog (*Phacocherus aethiopicus shortridgei*)
503 10a Waterbuck (*Kobus defassa penricei*)
504 12a50 Hippopotamus (*Hippopotamus amphibius capensis*)
505 15a Greater Kudu (*Strepsiceros strepsiceros zambeziensis*)
506 20a Giraffe (*Giraffe camelopardalis angolensis*)

Set of 20 32.00 15.00
The set of 20 includes a 40c value which shows a crocodile.

1984

833 1k Greater Kudu (*Tragelaphus strepsicerus*)
834 4k Springbok (*Antidorcas marsupialis angolensis*)
835 5k Chimpanzee (*Pan troglodytes*)
836 10k African Buffalo (*Synceros caffer*)
837 15k Sable Antelope (*Hippotragus niger variani*)
838 20k Aardvark (*Orycteropus afer*)
839 25k Spotted Hyena (*Crocuta crocuta*)

Set of 7 4.25 3.50

ANGUILLA

West Indies
100 cents = 1 West Indian dollar

1972

145 25c Common Dolphin
146 40c Common Dolphin

Set of 2 3.25 5.00

1984

611†   10c Eastern Grey Kangaroo (on Australia
No. 2d)   10   5

ANTIGUA
West Indies
100 cents = 1 West Indian dollar

1982

744†   50c Small Indian Mongoose ('Golden
Spotted Mongoose')   30   30
746† $3 Mexican Bulldog Bat ('Bulldog Bat') ..   1.75   1.75
MS747 $5 Caribbean Monk Seal 3.00   3.25

1983

788   15c Bottle-nosed Dolphin ('Bottlenose
Dolphin')
789   50c Fin Whale ('Finback Whale')
790   60c Bowhead Whale
791   $3 Spectacled Porpoise
    Set of 4   2.25   2.40
MS792 $5 Narwhal ('Unicorn Whale (Narwhal)')   2.75   3.00

ARGENTINE REPUBLIC
South America
100 centavos = 1 peso

1951

829†   25c Common Dolphin   25   10

1959

948†   50c Puma   15   15
1032†   500p Red Deer 1.00   30

1970

As No. 1032 *but currency revalued*
1325†   5p Red Deer   40   10

1977
As No. 1325, *but colours changed, surcharged*
**100 PESOS 150 ANNIV. DEL CORREO NATIONAL DEL
URUGUAY**
1566   100p on 5p Red Deer 1.00   20

1980

MS1687 Two sheets of twelve stamps, one with
the centre two stamps depicting South
Orkney Naval Station and the other two
stamps depicting 'Puerto Soledad,
Falkland Islands, 1829'. Other stamps
are common to the two sheets 15.00   15.00
(e)†   500p Southern Elephant-Seal (*Mirounga leonina*)
(f)†   500p Kerguelen Fur Seal (*Arctocephalus tropicalis gazella*)

1981

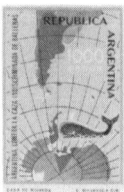

1718   1000p Sperm Whale   75   40

1983

AGUARA GUASU-LOBO DE CRIN
Chrysocyon brachyurus (Illiger)

$a 1,00

REPUBLICA ARGENTINA

1815   1p Maned Wolf (*Chrysocyon brachyurus*)
1816   1p50 Pampas Deer (*Ozotocerus bezoarticus*)
1817   2p Giant Anteater (*Myrmecophaga tridactyla*)
1818   2p50 Jaguar (*Leo onca*)
                                  Set of 4   1.00   60

LEOPARDO MARINO
Hydrurga leptonyx $ 2.-
REPUBLICA ARGENTINA

MS1858 Sheet of twelve stamps
(j)   2p Leopard Seal (*Hydrurga leptonyx*)
(k)   2p Crabeater Seal (*Lobodon carcinophagus*)
(l)   2p Weddell Seal (*Leptonychotes weddelli*) . .   2.40   2.40
      No. **MS**1858 contains a total of 12 stamps, the remaining nine depict birds and explorers.

1984

VICUÑA – Vicugna vicugna (Molina) $. 20

REPUBLICA ARGENTINA

1886†   20p Vicuna (*Vicugna vicugna*)
1887†   20p Chilean Guemal (*Hippocamelus bisulcus*) 2.50   2.50

OFFICIAL STAMPS

1960

No. 948 overprinted **S. OFICIAL**
O957†   50c Puma   10   10

No. 1032 overprinted **SERVICIO OFICIAL**
O1049†   500p Red Deer 2.75   50

ASCENSION
South Atlantic
100 pence = 1 pound

1983

ASCENSION

15ᵖ   INTRODUCED SPECIES · THE RABBIT

346†   15p Common Rabbit ('The Rabbit')   30   35

AUSTRALIA
Oceania
1913 12 pence = 1 shilling
20 shillings = 1 pound
1966 100 cents = 1 dollar

1913

1	½d Eastern Grey Kangaroo	. . . .	7.00	1.50
2	1d Eastern Grey Kangaroo	. . . . . .	6.00	30
35b	2d Eastern Grey Kangaroo	. . . .	20.00	3.50
36	2½d Eastern Grey Kangaroo	. . . .	20.00	6.00
37	3d Eastern Grey Kangaroo	. . . . . .	22.00	2.75
6	4d Eastern Grey Kangaroo	. . . . . .	75.00	27.00
8	5d Eastern Grey Kangaroo	. . . . . .	60.00	28.00
38	6d Eastern Grey Kangaroo (blue)	. . . .	45.00	7.50
73	6d Eastern Grey Kangaroo (brown)	. . . .	15.00	2.50
133	9d Eastern Grey Kangaroo	. . . . . .	18.00	1.75
40	1s Eastern Grey Kangaroo	. . . . . .	32.00	2.75
41	2s Eastern Grey Kangaroo (brown)	. . . .	£150	25.00
212	2s Eastern Grey Kangaroo (red)	. . . .	4.75	1.75
135	5s Eastern Grey Kangaroo	. . . . . .	£175	17.00
136	10s Eastern Grey Kangaroo	. . . . . .	£450	£120

44	£1 Eastern Grey Kangaroo (brown and blue)	£1400	£600
137	£1 Eastern Grey Kangaroo (grey)	£650	£225
138	£2 Eastern Grey Kangaroo	£1800	£350

1937

228†	½d Wallaroo	20	5
188†	4d Koala	75	5
190†	9d Platypus	1.50	5

1959

316†	6d Numbat ('Banded Anteater')	1.75	5
317†	8d Tiger Cat	1.25	5
318†	9d Eastern Grey Kangaroo	3.50	30
319†	11d Common Rabbit-Bandicoot ('Rabbit Bandicoot')	1.75	15
320†	1s Platypus	4.75	20
321†	1s2d Thylacine ('Tasmanian Tiger') ..	2.00	25

1971

492†	18c Red Kangaroo	1.50	50

1974

561	20c Common Wombat ('Wombat')		
562	25c Short-nosed Echidna ('Spiny Anteater')		
563	30c Brush-tailed Possum ('Brushtail Possum')		
564	75c Pygmy Glider ('Feather-tailed Glider')		
	Set of 4	4.00	2.00

1981

784†	5c. Queensland Hairy-nosed Wombat ..	10	5
788†	24c Thylacine ('Tasmanian Tiger')	35	30
789†	25c Common Rabbit-Bandicoot ('Greater Bilby')	35	30
792†	30c Bridle Nail-tailed Wallaby ('Bridled Nail-tailed Wallaby')	40	30
796†	50c Leadbeater's Possum	60	50
797†	55c Stick-nest Rat	70	55

1982

838	24c Sperm Whale		
839	35c Black Right Whale ('Southern Right Whale')		
840	55c Blue Whale		
841	60c Humpback Whale		
	Set of 4	3.00	2.75

1984

944	30c. Eastern Grey Kangaroo (on stamp No. 2d)	35	40

960†	30c Leadbeater's Possum	30	35

AUSTRALIAN ANTARCTIC TERRITORY

Antarctica
100 cents = 1 dollar (Australian)

1966

11†	5c Southern Elephant-Seal	2.75	1.50

1973

27†	9c Leopard Seal	45	30
28†	10c Killer Whale	6.50	1.25
34†	$1 Sperm Whale	3.75	2.75

1983

57†	27c Southern Elephant-Seal ('Elephant Seal')	40	40

STANLEY GIBBONS
STAMP COLLECTING SERIES

Introductory booklets on *How to Start, How to Identify Stamps* and *Collecting by Theme*. A series of well illustrated guides at a low price.
Write for details.

AUSTRIA

Central Europe
100 groschen = 1 schilling

1959

1339†	1s50 Roe Deer		70	10
1340†	2s40 Wild Boar		50	50
1341†	3s50 Red Deer		40	25
	(1338/41 *Set of* 4)		1.90	1.00

1960

1361	3s + 70g Red Deer (on stamp No. 1341)	90	90

1969

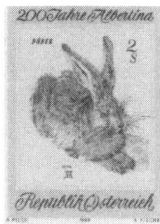

1560†	2s Brown Hare	25	25

1982

1943†	4s Eurasian Beaver ('Biber')	20	20

BAHAMAS

West Indies
100 cents = 1 dollar

1982

626	10c Buffy Flower Bat ('Bat')			
627	16c Bahaman Hutia ('Hutia')			
628	21c Common Racoon ('Racoon')			
629	$1 Common Dolphin ('Dolphin')			
		Set of 4	2.00	2.25

BAHAWALPUR

Indian sub-continent
12 pies =1 anna
16 annas =1 rupee

OFFICIAL STAMPS

1945

O2†	1a Dromedary	.. ..	1.60	1.50
O3†	2a Blackbuck	.. ..	2.50	2.50

Nos. O2/3 overprinted **SERVICE** and Arabic inscription

O15†	1a Dromedary	.. ..	1.75	2.50
O16†	2a Blackbuck ..	.. ..	3.50	7.50

BAHRAIN

Arabian Peninsula
1000 fils = 1 dinar

1982

296†	100f Goitred Gazelle	.. ..	70	70
297†	100f Dorcas Gazelle	.. ..	70	70

299†	100f Brown Hare	.. ..	70	70
300†	100f Arabian Oryx ..	.. ..	70	70
301†	100f Addax	.. ..	70	70
		(296/301 Set of 6)	3.75	3.75

The remaining design depicts a lizard.

BANGLADESH

Indian sub-continent
100 paisa = 1 taka

1973

Size 21 × 28 mm

27†	25p Tiger	.. ..	35	10

1974

52	25p Tiger ('Our National prowess')			
53	50p Tiger ('Save the Tiger')			
54	2t Tiger ('Stop Hunting Tiger')			
		Set of 3	3.25	3.25

1976
As No. 27, but size 18 × 23 mm

67†	25p Tiger	.. ..	10	5

1977

101	40p Sloth Bear ('Bear')			
102	1t Spotted Deer			
103	2t25 Leopard			
104	3t50 Gaur ('Goyal')			
105	4t Indian Elephant ('Elephant')			
106	5t Tiger			
		Set of 6	2.00	1.60

1981

167 50p Spotted Deer
168 5t Spotted Deer

Set of 2   45   50

1984

234† 2t Tiger ('Royal Bengal Tiger')   15   15

OFFICIAL STAMPS

1973
No. 27 overprinted SERVICE

O6† 25p Tiger   15   8

1974
No. 67 overprinted SERVICE

O17† 25p Tiger   10   5

BARBUDA
West Indies
100 cents = 1 West Indian dollar

1977

379† $5 Lion 2.75   2.50
380† $5 Lion 2.75   2.50
381† $5 Lion 2.75   2.50
382† $5 Lion 2.75   2.50

1983
Nos. 788/92 of Antigua overprinted BARBUDA MAIL

667 15c. Bottle-nosed Dolphin ('Bottlenose
     Dolphin')
668 50c Fin Whale ('Finback Whale')
669 .60c Bowhead Whale
670 $3 Spectacled Porpoise
                                Set of 4   1.75   2.00
MS671 $5 Narwhal ('Unicorn Whale (Narwhal)')   2.50   2.75

BECHUANALAND
Southern Africa
100 cents = 1 rand

1961

180† 1r Lion 4.50   4.50

BELGIAN CONGO
Central Africa
100 centimes = 1 franc

1894

Inscribed "ETAT INDEPENDANT DU CONGO"
22† 1f African Elephant (black and mauve) ..   16.00   7.25
35† 1f African Elephant (black and red) 90.00   1.50

1909
No. 35 overprinted CONGO BELGE

42† 1f African Elephant 17.00   1.40

1910
As No. 35 but inscribed "CONGO BELGE – BELGISCH-CONGO"

66† 1f African Elephant 2.40   1.90

1915
As No. 66, but colours changed

76† 1f African Elephant (black and olive) 1.50   60

1918

As No. 66, but blue centre, surcharged with red cross and premium

84† 1f + 1f African Elephant (blue and olive) .. 1.25 1.50

1921

No. 66 overprinted 1921

97† 1f African Elephant 75 65

1922

No. 76 surcharged

110† 10c on 1f African Elephant 30 30

1923

140† 10f African Elephant 14.00 4.25

1931

191a† 2f50 Okapi 30 15
192† 3f25 Okapi 50 30

1939

227† 1f25 + 1f25 Kob 3.25 3.25
228† 1f50 + 1f50 Chimpanzee 5.00 5.00
230† 5f + 5f Lion 3.50 3.50

1942

Inscribed "CONGO BELGE BELGISCH CONGO", or vice versa
261† 1f75 Leopard 50 40
262† 2f Leopard 50 15

263† 2f50 Leopard 50 10
269† 20f Okapi 2.25 65

1944

No. 261 surcharged **Au Profit de la Croix Rouge +100 Fr. Ten voordeele van het Roode Kruis**

269c 1f75 + 100f Leopard 1.60 1.90

1959

339 10c Roan Antelope (*Hippotragus equinus*)
340 20c White Rhinoceros (*Ceratotherium simum*)
341 40c Giraffe (*Giraffa*)
342 50c Demidoff's Galago (*Galago*)
343 1f Gorilla
344 1f50 African Buffalo (*Bubalus*)
345 2f Eastern Black-and-White Colobus (*Colobus*)
346 3f African Elephant (*Loxodonta africana*)
347 5f Okapi (*Okapia*)
348 6f50 Impala
349 8f Giant Ground Pangolin (*Smutsia gigantea*)
350 10f Eland (*Taurotragus oryx*), Common Zebra (*Hippotigris*)
Set of 12 4.75 2.00

BELGIUM

Western Europe
100 centimes = 1 franc

1961

1778 40c + 10c White Rhinoceros ('Rhinoceros Blanc – Witte Neushoorn')
1779 1f + 50c Wild Horse ('Przewalskipaard – Cheval de Przewalski')
1780 2f + 50c Okapi
1781 2f50 + 1f Giraffe ('Giraffe – Girafe')
1782 3f + 1f Lesser Panda ('Panda – Panda')
1783 6f + 2f Elk ('Eland – Elan')
Set of 6 10.00 8.00

1974

2367   3f Wild Boar   20   10

2373†   5f + 2f50 Eurasian Badger (*Meles meles*)   50   50

BELIZE
Central America
100 cents = 1 dollar

1973
Nos. 257/67 of British Honduras overprinted **BELIZE**
349†	2c White-lipped Peccary ('Warree')	10	8
351†	4c Collared Anteater ('Ant Bear') (latin name wrong)	10	8
353†	10c Paca ('Gibnut')	15	15
355†	25c Kinkajou ('Night Walker')	35	35
357†	$1 Tayra ('Bush Dog')	90	1.25
359†	$5 Puma ('Mountain Lion')	4.50	7.00

1974

364†	2c White-lipped Peccary ('Warree')	10	5
366†	4c Collared Anteater ('Ant Bear')	10	8
368†	10c Paca ('Gibnut')	15	15
370†	25c Kinkajou ('Night Walker')	35	35
372†	$1 Tayra ('Bush Dog')	1.50	1.90
374†	$5 Puma ('Mountain Lion')	6.50	8.00

1981

660†   85c Baird's Tapir ('Tapir')   55   60

1983

756	5c Jaguar	
757	10c Jaguar	
758	85c Jaguar	
759	$1 Jaguar	
	Set of 4	1.40 1.40
MS760	$3 Jaguar	2.10 2.25

BENIN
West Africa
100 centimes = 1 franc

1976

624†   210f Lion 1.40   1.10

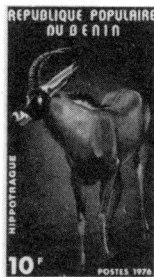

635	10f Roan Antelope ('Hippotraque')	
636	30f African Buffalo ('Buffle')	
637	50f Hippopotamus ('Hippopotome')	
638	70f Lion	
	Set of 4	2.25 1.50

STAMP MONTHLY

– finest and most informative magazine for all collectors. Obtainable from your newsagent or by postal subscription – details on request

1978

730† 100f African Buffalo 1.00 90

1979

759 5f Roan Antelope ('Antelope Cheval')
760 10f Giraffe ('Girafe')
761 20f Chimpanzee ('Chimpanzee')
762 50f African Elephant ('Elephant')
Set of 4 1.40 1.00

1981
No. 624 surcharged
835† 50f on 210f Lion 30 15

BERMUDA
North Atlantic Ocean
100 cents = 1 dollar

1978

401† $2 Humpback Whale 3.00 3.25

COLLECT BIRDS ON STAMPS
The first Stanley Gibbons thematic catalogue – a few
copies still available at £4.95 (p.+p. £1.30) plus FREE
1983–84 Supplement from:
Stanley Gibbons Publications Ltd, 5, Parkside,
Christchurch Road, Ringwood, Hants BH24 3SH.

BHOPAL
Central Asia
12 pies = 1 anna
16 annas = 1 rupee

OFFICIAL STAMPS

1940

O344 ½a Tiger
O345 1a Spotted Deer
Set of 2 4.50 1.00

BHUTAN
Central Asia
100 chetrum = 1 ngultrum

1962

3† 5c Yak ('Wild Yak') 55 55
7† 1n30 Yak 1.10 1.10

1965
No. 7 surcharged
61† 15c on 1n30 Yak 2.00 2.00

1966

68 1c Asiatic Black Bear (*Selenarctos
tibetanus*)
69 2c Snow Leopard (*Panthera uncia*)
70 4c Pygmy Hog (*Sus salvanius*)
71 8c Tiger (*Panthera tigris*)
72 10c Dhole (*Cuon alpinus*)
73 75c Tiger
74 1n Takin
75 1n50 Dhole

76	2n Pygmy Hog		
77	3n Snow Leopard		
78	4n Asiatic Black Bear		
79	5n Takin		
	Set of 12	7.50	7.50

1967
No. 75/9 overprinted AIR MAIL

112†	1n50 Dhole	35	35
113†	2n Pygmy Hog	40	40
114†	3n Snow Leopard	55	55
115†	4n Asiatic Black Bear	70	70
116†	5n Takin	90	90

1970
Nos. 77/9 surcharged 20 CH

204†	20c on 3n Snow Leopard	70	70
205†	20c on 4n Asiatic Black Bear	70	70
206†	20c on 5n Takin	70	70

1972
Nos. 75/6 surcharged 20 CH

224†	20c on 1n50 Dhole	1.50	1.50
225†	20c on 2n Pygmy Hog	1.50	1.50

Nos. 77/8 surcharged

255†	55c on 3n Snow Leopard	50	50
256†	90c on 4n Asiatic Black Bear	75	75

1984

521	50c Golden Langur		
522	1n Golden Langur		
523	2n Golden Langur		
524	4n Golden Langur		
	Set of 4	2.25	2.00
MS525	Set of three sheets	14.00	14.00
	20n Snow Leopard		
	25n Yak		
	25n Bharal ('Blue Sheep')		

Appendix
The following stamps have either been issued in excess of postal needs, or have not been made available to the public in reasonable quantities at face value. Miniature sheets, imperforate stamps etc., are excluded from this section.

COLLECT BIRDS ON STAMPS
The first Stanley Gibbons thematic catalogue – a few copies still available at £4.95 (p.+p. £1.30) plus FREE 1983–84 Supplement from:
Stanley Gibbons Publications Ltd, 5, Parkside, Christchurch Road, Ringwood, Hants BH24 3SH.

1970
Wild Animals (African Elephant, Leopard, Ibex, Tiger, 'Abominable Snowman', Gaur, Rhinoceros, Giant Panda, Snow Leopard, Spotted Deer, Wild Boar, Asiatic Black Bear, Takin). Postage 5, 10, 20, 25, 30, 40, 65, 75, 85c; Air 2, 3, 4, 5n.

BIAFRA
West Africa
12 pence = 1 shilling
20 shillings = 1 pound

1968
No. 172/85 of Nigeria overprinted SOVEREIGN BIAFRA

4†	½d Lion	35	60
5†	1d African Elephant ('Elephants')	1.25	1.75
8†	4d Leopard	13.00	18.00
13†	2s6d Kob	1.50	3.00
14†	5s Giraffe	2.00	3.50
15†	10s Hippopotamus	9.00	20.00
16†	£1 African Buffalo ('Buffalos')	10.00	20.00

1968
Nos. 4/5 surcharged BIAFRA–FRANCE FRIENDSHIP 1968

16b	½d + 5s Lion		
16c	1d + £1 African Elephant		
	Set of 2	20.00	

BOLIVIA
South America
1939 100 centavos = 1 boliviano
1963 100 centavos = 1 peso boliviano

1939

349†	10c Vicuna	70	50
350†	15c Vicuna	70	55
351†	20c Vicuna	70	35
356†	60c Mountain Viscacha ('Chinchilla')	1.40	70
357†	75c Mountain Viscacha	1.40	70
362†	4b Jaguar	4.00	1.40
363†	5b Jaguar	5.00	1.60

1947
No. 357 surcharged 1947 Habilitada Bs. 1.40

452†	1b40 on 75c Mountain Viscacha	10	10

1951

511†	20c Guanaco (green)	10	10
521†	20c Guanaco (red) (air)	15	15

BOPHUTHATSWANA
Southern Africa
100 cents = 1 rand

1977

| 2† | 10c Leopard | 1.00 | 1.00 |

5†	1c African Buffalo	10	5
6†	2c Bush Pig	10	5
7†	3c Chacma Baboon	10	5
8†	4c Leopard	10	5
10†	6c Savanna Monkey	10	5
11†	7c Lion	10	5
12†	8c Spotted Hyena	10	10
13†	9c Cape Porcupine	10	10
14†	10c Aardvark	15	15
16†	20c Hunting Dog	25	25
17†	25c Common Duiker	30	30
18†	30c African Elephant	35	35
20†	1r Hippopotamus	90	90
21†	2r Greater Kudu	1.75	1.75
	(5/21 Set of 17)	4.50	4.50

1983

100 8c White Rhinoceros (*Ceratotherium simum*)
101 20c Common Zebra (*Equus burchelli*)
102 25c Sable Antelope (*Hippotragus niger*)
103 40c Hartebeest (*Alcelaphus caama*)

| | Set of 4 | 1.00 | 1.00 |

BOTSWANA
Southern Africa
1966 100 cents = 1 rand
1976 100 thebe = 1 pula

1966
No. 180 *of Bechuanaland overprinted* REPUBLIC OF BOTSWANA
| 218† | 1r Lion | 2.25 | 3.50 |

1967

238†	3c Bushbuck ('Chobe Bush Buck')	10	5
239†	7c Sable Antelope	15	15
	(238/40 Set of 3)	90	60

1969

| 253† | 3c Lion | 30 | 5 |

1971

| 282† | 7c Common Zebra | 35 | 35 |

1975

| 347† | 10c White Rhinoceros | 80 | 35 |
| 348† | 25c Spotted Hyena | 2.00 | 85 |

1977

394 3t African Clawless Otter ('Clawless Otter')

395   4t Serval
396   10t Bat-eared Fox
397   25t Temminck's Ground Pangolin
        ('Pangolin')
398   40t Brown Hyena

                              Set of 5   5.00   3.50

1983

543†   35t Roan Antelope   45   50

POSTAGE DUE STAMPS

1971

D16   1c African Elephant
D17   2c African Elephant
D18   6c African Elephant
D19   14c African Elephant

                              Set of 4   2.50   4.25

1977

D20   1t Common Zebra
D21   2t Common Zebra
D22   4t Common Zebra
D23   10t Common Zebra
D24   16t Common Zebra

                              Set of 5   35   45

STANLEY GIBBONS
STAMP COLLECTING SERIES

Introductory booklets on *How to Start, How to Identify
Stamps* and *Collecting by Theme.* A series of well illustrated guides at a low price.

                              Write for details.

BRAZIL
South America
100 centavos = 1 cruzeiro

1973

1479†   70c Jaguar (*Panthera onca*) 1.40   70

1975

1546†   1cr Giant Otter (*Pteronura brasiliensis*)   70   25

1976

1589†   1cr Golden Lion Tamarin (*Leontopitecus
           rosalia*)   25   25

1977

1663   1cr30 Blue Whale (*Balaenoptera
           musculus*)   20   10

1979

1767† 12cr Amazon Manatee (*Trichechus inunguis*) 95 50

1982

1958 17cr Giant Anteater (*Priodontes giganteus*)
1959 21cr Maned Wolf (*Chrysocyon brachyurus*)
1960 30cr Pampas Deer (*Ozotoceros bezoarticus*)
Set of 3   60   40

1984

2083† 65cr Marsh Deer 15 10
2084† 65cr Jaguar, Capybara 15 10
(2083/5 Set of 3)   50   20

2089 65cr Woolly Spider Monkey (*Brachyteles arachnoides*)
2090 80cr Woolly Spider Monkey (*Brachyteles arachnoides*)
Set of 2   40   30

2091 65cr Water Buffalo ('Bufalos')
2092 65cr Water Buffalo ('Bufalos')
2093 80cr Water Buffalo ('Bufalos')
Set of 3   60   20

BRITISH ANTARCTIC TERRITORY
Antarctica
100 pence = 1 pound

1971

40† 5p Weddell Seal 7.50 4.75

1972

42 5p Kerguelen Fur Seal
43 10p Kerguelen Fur Seal
Set of 2   4.50   3.00

1977

79 2p Sperm Whale ('Sperm')
80 8p Fin Whale ('Fin')
81 11p Humpback Whale ('Humpback')
82 25p Blue Whale ('Blue')
Set of 4   12.50   9.25

1981

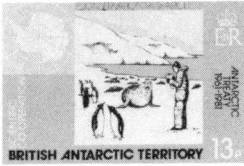

100† 13p Kerguelen Fur Seal 45 45

1983

113 5p Leopard Seal
114 10p Weddell Seal
115 13p Southern Elephant-Seal ('Elephant Seal')
116 17p Kerguelen Fur Seal ('Fur Seal')
117 25p Ross Seal
118 34p Crabeater Seal

Set of 6 1.90 2.10

1984

137† £1 Crabeater Seal (Lobodon carcinophagus) 1.75 1.90
138† £3 Blue Whale ('Antarctic Marine Food Chain') 5.50 5.75

BRITISH HONDURAS

Central America
100 cents = 1 dollar

1953

180a† 2c Baird's Tapir ('Mountain Cow') 12 5
188† $1 Nine-banded Armadillo ('Armadillo') 3.50 3.50

1961

No. 180a overprinted NEW CONSTITUTION 1960
194† 2c Baird's Tapir 8 10

1967

247† 10c Red Brocket ('Deer') 10 10
248† 22c Jaguar 15 10

1968

257† 2c White-lipped Peccary ('Warree') 10 5
259† 4c Collared Anteater ('Ant Bear') (latin name wrong) 10 15
261† 10c Paca ('Gibnut') 15 15
263† 25c Kinkajou ('Night Walker') 30 30
265† $1 Tayra ('Bush Dog') 2.00 1.60
267† $5 Puma ('Mountain Lion') 9.50 6.50

1970

Nos. 261 and 263 overprinted POPULATION CENSUS 1970
284† 10c Paca 10 10
286† 25c Kinkajou 15 20

1971

No. 261 overprinted RACIAL EQUALITY YEAR – 1971
313† 10c Paca 10 5

BRITISH OCCUPATION OF JAPAN

East Asia
12 pence = 1 shilling
20 shillings = 1 pound

1946

No. 228 of Australia overprinted B.C.O.F. JAPAN 1946
B1† ½d Wallaroo 2.00 2.00

BRUNEI

South-east Asia
100 cents = 1 dollar

1984

352† $1 Several tiny animals 75 80

BULGARIA
South-east Europe
100 stotinki = 1 lev

1957

1065†	12s Red Deer	10	10

1958

1091 2s Brown Hare
1092 12s Roe Deer
1093 16s Red Deer
1094 44s Chamois
1095 80s Brown Bear
1096 1 lev Wild Boar

Set of 6   3.00   1.00

1961

1251†	2s Mediterranean Monk Seal (*Pelagius monachus*)	10	10
1253†	16s Common Dolphin (*Delfinus delfis*)	10	10

1963

1373 1s Eurasian Red Squirrel
1374 2s East European Hedgehog
1375 3s Marbled Polecat
1376 5s Beech Marten
1377 13s Eurasian Badger
1378 20s European Otter

Set of 6   2.40   80

1966

1610 1s Indian Elephant
1611 2s Tiger
1612 3s Chimpanzee
1613 4s Ibex
1614 5s Polar Bear
1615 8s Lion
1616 13s American Bison
1617 20s Eastern Grey Kangaroo

Set of 8   3.00   1.25

1967

1685†	5s Brown Hare	25	10
1686†	8s Roe Deer	75	20
1687†	13s Red Deer	1.10	40

1968

1815†	3s Common Zebra	20	10
1816†	5s Leopard	40	10

1973

2243 1s Muskrat (*Ondatra zibethica*)
2244 2s Racoon-Dog (*Nyctereutes procyonoides*)
2245 3s Mouflon (*Ovis musimon*)
2246 12s Fallow Deer (*Dama dama*)
2247 18s European Bison (*Bison bonasus*)
2248 40s Elk (*Alces alces*)

Set of 6   4.50   2.50

1977

2575 1s Wolf (*Canis lupus*)
2576 2s Red Fox (*Vulpes vulpes*)
2577 10s Weasel (*Mustela nivalis*)
2578 13s Wild Cat (*Felis silvestris*)
2579 23s Golden Jackal (*Canis aureus*)
Set of 5   1.25   50

1979

MS2761 80s Indian Rhinoceros ('Rhinocervs') .. 1.50 1.50

1980

2902† 3s Wild Horse 15   10

1981

2942 5s Wild Cat
2943 13s Wild Boar
2944 23s Mouflon
2945 25s Chamois

2946 35s Roe Deer
2947 53s Fallow Deer
Set of 6   3.25   1.50
MS2948 1 lev Red Deer 2.25   2.25

1983

3128 12s Eurasian Common Shrew (*Sorex araneus*)
3129 13s Greater Horseshoe Bat (*Rhinolophus ferrum equinum*)
3130 20s Common Long-eared Bat (*Plecotus auritus*)
3131 30s Forest Dormouse (*Dryomys nitedula*)
3132 42s Fat Dormouse (*Glis glis*)
Set of 5   2.25   1.50

BURUNDI
Central Africa
100 centimes = 1 franc

1962

Nos. 203/30 of Ruanda–Urundi overprinted **Royaume du Burundi**
9   10c Gorilla
10   20c African Buffalo (*Bubalus*)
11   40c Eastern Black-and-White Colobus (*Colobus*)
12   50c Impala
13   1f Gorilla
14   1f50 African Buffalo
15   2f Eastern Black-and-White Colobus
16   3f African Elephant (*Loxodonta africana*)
17   3f50 on 3f African Elephant (No. 16)
18a 4f on 10f Eland, Common Zebra (No. 23)
19   5f Eland (*Taurotragus oryx*), Common Zebra (*Hippotigris*)
20   6f50 Impala
21   8f African Elephant
23   10f Eland, Common Zebra
24   20f Leopard (*Panthera pardus*)
25   50f Lion (*Felis leo*)
Set of 16   5.00   4.00

1964

77   50c Impala
78   1f Hippopotamus
79   1f50 Giraffe (*Giraffa*)

80	2f African Buffalo (*Bubalus*)		
81	3f Common Zebra (*Hippotigris*)		
82	3f50 Waterbuck (*Kobus defassa*)		
83	4f Impala		
84	5f Hippopotamus		
85	6f50 Common Zebra		
86	8f African Buffalo		
87	10f Giraffe		
88	15f Waterbuck		
89	20f Cheetah (*Acinonyx jubatus*)		
90	50f African Elephant (*Loxodonta africana*)		
91	100f Lion (*Felis leo*)		
92	6f Common Zebra (air)		
93	8f African Buffalo		
94	10f Impala		
95	14f Hippopotamus		
96	15f Waterbuck		
97	20f Cheetah		
98	50f African Elephant		

Set of 22   18.00   4.00

1970

534†	7f Bactrian Camel ('Chameau')	50	25
534†	7f Dromedary ('Dromadaire')	50	25
534†	7f Okapi	50	25
534†	7f White Rhinoceros ('Rhinoceros')	50	25
534†	7f Addax	50	25
535†	14f Bactrian Camel (air)	50	30
535†	14f Dromedary	50	30
535†	14f Okapi	50	30
535†	14f White Rhinoceros	50	30
535†	14f Addax	50	30

Nos. 534 and 535 each cover 18 different designs forming a map of the Nile.

1971

613†	1f Lion (*Panthera leo*)	8	5
614†	1f African Buffalo (*Syncerus caffer*)	8	5
615†	1f Hippopotamus (*Hippopotamus amphibius*)	8	5
616†	1f Giraffe (*Giraffa camelopardalis*)	8	5
617†	2f Topi (*Damaliscus lunatus topi*)	15	15

618†	2f Black Rhinoceros (*Diceros bicornis*) . .	15	15
619†	2f Common Zebra (*Equus quagga boemi*)	15	15
620†	2f Leopard (*Panthera pardus*)	15	15
621†	3f Grant's Gazelle (*Gazella granti*)	25	25
622†	3f Cheetah (*Acinonyx jubatus*)	25	25
624†	3f Okapi (*Okapia johnstoni*)	25	25
625†	5f Chimpanzee (*Pan troglodytes*)	30	25
626†	5f African Elephant (*Loxodonta africana*)	30	25
627†	5f Spotted Hyena (*Crocuta crocuta*) . .	30	25
628†	5f Gemsbok (*Oryx beisa*)	30	25
629†	6f Gorilla (*Gorilla gorilla*)	40	25
630†	6f Blue Wildebeest (*Connochaetes taurinus*)	40	25
631†	6f Warthog (*Phacochoerus aethiopicus*) . .	40	25
632†	6f Hunting Dog (*Lycaon pictus*)	40	25
633†	11f Sable Antelope (*Hippotragus niger*) . .	70	30
634†	11f Caracal (*Lynx caracal*)	70	30
636†	11f Bongo (*Boocercus eurycerus*)	70	30
637†	10f Lion (air)	50	25
638†	10f African Buffalo	50	25
639†	10f Hippopotamus	50	25
640†	10f Giraffe	50	25
641†	14f Topi	60	30
642†	14f Black Rhinoceros	60	30
643†	14f Common Zebra	60	30
644†	14f Leopard	60	30
645†	17f Grant's Gazelle	70	30
646†	17f Cheetah	70	30
648†	17f Okapi	70	30
649†	24f Chimpanzee	90	40
650†	24f African Elephant	90	40
651†	24f Spotted Hyena	90	40
652†	24f Gemsbok	90	40
653†	26f Gorilla	1.00	40
654†	26f Blue Wildebeest	1.00	40
655†	26f Warthog	1.00	40
656†	26f Hunting Dog	1.00	40
657†	31f Sable Antelope	1.25	50
658†	31f Caracal	1.25	50
660†	31f Bongo	1.25	50

(613/60 *Set of* 48) 25.00   12.00

Nos. 637/40 overprinted
**LUTTE CONTRE LE RACISME ET LA DISCRIMINATION
RACIALE**

668†	10f Lion	25	10
669†	10f African Buffalo	25	10
670†	10f Hippopotamus	25	10
671†	10f Giraffe	25	10

Nos. 641/4 surcharged
UNESCO LUTTE CONTRE L'ANALPHABETISME

672†	14f + 2f Topi	35	15
673†	14f + 2f Black Rhinoceros	35	15
674†	14f + 2f Common Zebra	35	15
675†	14f + 2f Leopard	35	15

COLLECT BIRDS ON STAMPS

The first Stanley Gibbons thematic catalogue – a few
copies still available at £4.95 (p.+p. £1.30) plus FREE
1983–84 Supplement from:
Stanley Gibbons Publications Ltd, 5, Parkside,
Christchurch Road, Ringwood, Hants BH24 3SH.

Nos. 645/8 *surcharged* **AIDE INTERNATIONALE AUX REFU-**
GIES

676†	17f + 1f Grant's Gazelle	50	25
677†	17f + 1f Cheetah	50	25
679†	17f + 1f Okapi	50	25
	(668/79 *Set of* 12)	4.00	1.75

Nos. 653/6 *surcharged* **75eme ANNIVERSAIRE DES JEUX**
OLYMPIQUES MODERNES (1896–1971), *Olympic rings and pre-*
mium

680†	26f + 1f Gorilla	90	35
681†	26f + 1f Blue Wildebeest	90	35
682†	26f + 1f Warthog	90	35
683†	26f + 1f Hunting Dog	90	35

Nos. 657/60 *surcharged* **JEUX PRE-OLYMPIQUES MUNICH**
1972

684†	31f + 1f Sable Antelope	1.75	1.00
685†	31f + 1f Caracal	1.75	1.00
687†	31f + 1f Bongo	1.75	1.00
	(680/7 *Set of* 8)	9.50	5.00

1975

Republique du Burundi

1028	1f Addax (*Addax nasomaculatus*)
1029	1f Roan Antelope (*Hippotragus equinus*)
1030	1f Nyala (*Tragelaphus angasi*)
1031	1f White Rhinoceros (*Ceratotherium simun*)
1032	2f Mandrill (*Papio mandrilus*)
1033	2f Eland (*Taurotragus oryx*)
1034	2f Salt's Dik-Dik (*Madoqua saltiana*)
1035	2f Thomson's Gazelle (*Gazella thomsoni*)
1036	3f African Clawless Otter (*Aonyx capensis*)
1037	3f Bohar Reedbuck (*Redunca redunca*)
1038	3f African Civet (*Viverra civetta*)
1039	3f African Buffalo (*Syncerus caffer manus*)
1040	5f Black Wildebeest (*Connochaetes gnou*)
1041	5f African Ass (*Equus asinus*)
1042	5f Angolan Black-and-White Colobus (*Colobus angolensis*)
1043	5f Gerenuk (*Litocranius walleri*)
1044	6f Addra Gazelle (*Gazella dama*)
1045	6f Black-backed Jackal (*Canis mesomelas*)
1046	6f Sitatunga (*Tragelaphus spekei*)
1047	6f Banded Duiker (*Cephalophus zebra*)
1048	11f Fennec Fox (*Fennecus zerda*)
1049	11f Lesser Kudu (*Tragelaphus imberbis*)
1050	11f Blesbok (*Damaliscus dorcas phillipsi*)
1051	11f Serval (*Felis serval*)
1052	10f Addax (air)

1053	10f Roan Antelope
1054	10f Nyala
1055	10f White Rhinoceros
1056	14f Mandrill
1057	14f Eland
1058	14f Salt's Dik-Dik
1059	14f Thomson's Gazelle
1060	17f African Clawless Otter
1061	17f Bohar Reedbuck
1062	17f African Civet
1063	17f African Buffalo
1064	24f Black Wildebeest
1065	24f African Ass
1066	24f Angolan Black-and-White Colobus
1067	24f Gerenuk
1068	26f Addra Gazelle
1069	26f Black-backed Jackal
1070	26f Sitatunga
1071	26f Banded Duiker
1072	31f Fennec Fox
1073	31f Lesser Kudu
1074	31f Blesbok
1075	31f Serval
	Set of 48 15.00 6.00

Nos. 1052/9 *overprinted*
ANNEE INTERNATIONALE DE LA FEMME

1076	10f Addax
1077	10f Roan Antelope
1078	10f Nyala
1079	10f White Rhinoceros
1080	14f Mandrill
1081	14f Eland
1082	14f Salt's Dik-Dik
1083	14f Thomson's Gazelle
	Set of 8 2.75 2.00

Nos. 1068/75 *overprinted*
30eme ANNIVERSAIRE DES NATIONS UNIES

1084	26f Addra Gazelle
1085	26f Black-backed Jackal
1086	26f Sitatunga
1087	26f Banded Duiker
1088	31f Fennec Fox
1089	31f Lesser Kudu
1090	31f Blesbok
1091	31f Serval
	Set of 8 5.00 3.50

1977

REPUBLIQUE DU BURUNDI

1178†	2f Kob (*Adenota kob*)	25	25
1180†	2f Blue Wildebeest (*Connochaetes albojubatus*)	25	25
1181†	2f Bush Pig (*Potamochoerus porcus*)	25	25
1182†	5f Grevy's Zebra (*Equus grevyi*)	30	25
1184†	5f Striped Hyena (*Hyaena hyaena*)	30	25

1185†	5f Pygmy Chimpanzee (*Pan troglodytes paniscus*)	30	25
1189†	8f Greater Kudu (*Tragelaphus strepsiceros*)	35	25
1190†	11f Large-toothed Rock Hyrax (*Procavia johnstoni*)	40	30
1192†	11f Golden Jackal (*Canis aureus*)	40	30
1194†	21f Ratel (*Mellivora capensis*)	50	40
1195†	21f Bushbuck (*Tragelaphus scriptus*) . .	50	40
1197†	21f Klipspringer (*Oreotragus oreotragus*)	50	40
1198†	27f Bat-eared Fox (*Otocyon megalotis*)	70	45
1199†	27f African Elephant (*Loxodonta africana cyclotis*)	70	45
1201†	27f Impala (*Aepyceros melampus*) . .	70	45
1202†	9f Kob (air)	30	25
1204†	9f Blue Wildebeest	30	25
1205†	9f Bush Pig	30	25
1206†	13f Grevy's Zebra	50	30
1208†	13f Striped Hyena	50	30
1209†	13f Pygmy Chimpanzee	50	30
1213†	30f Greater Kudu	75	50
1214†	35f Larged-toothed Rock Hyrax	85	60
1216†	35f Golden Jackal	85	60
1218†	54f Ratel	1.10	75
1219†	54f Bushbuck	1.10	75
1221†	54f Klipspringer	1.10	75
1222†	70f Bat-eared Fox	1.75	90
1223†	70f African Elephant	1.75	90
1225†	70f Impala	1.75	90

1979

REPUBLIQUE du BURUNDI

1348†	31f Lion (on stamp No. 25)	50	30

1982

REPUBLIQUE DU BURUNDI

1385   2f Lion (*Panthera leo*)
1386   3f Giraffe (*Giraffa c. reticulata*) (name of subspecies wrong!)
1387   5f Black Rhinoceros (*Diceros bicornis*)
1388   10f African Buffalo (*Syncerus c. caffer*)
1389   20f African Elephant (*Loxodonta africana*)
1390   25f Hippopotamus (*Hippopotamus amphibius*)
1391   30f Common Zebra (*Equus burchelli*)
1392   50f Warthog (*Phacochoerus aethiopicus*)

1393   60f Eland (*Taurotragus oryx*)
1394   65f Black-backed Jackal (*Canis mesomelas*)
1395   70f Cheetah (*Acinonyx jubatus*)
1396   75f Blue Wildebeest (*Connochaetes t. albojubatus*)
1397   85f Spotted Hyena (*Crocuta crocuta*)

         Set of 13   12.00   6.50

1983

Nos. 1385/97 overprinted with WWF Panda emblem

1398   2f Lion
1399   3f Giraffe
1400   5f Black Rhinoceros
1401   10f African Buffalo
1402   20f African Elephant
1403   25f Hippopotamus
1404   30f Common Zebra
1405   50f Warthog
1406   60f Eland
1407   65f Black-backed Jackal
1408   70f Cheetah
1409   75f Blue Wildebeest
1410   85f Spotted Hyena

         Set of 13   12.00   8.00

CAICOS ISLANDS
West Indies
100 cents = 1 dollar

1984

58†	10c American Manatee	15	20

CAMBODIA
South-east Asia
100 cents = 1 riel

1964

159   50c Kouprey
160   3r Kouprey
161   6r Kouprey

         Set of 3   1.75   1.50

1967

208	3r Wild Boar		
209	5r Hog-Deer		
210	7r Indian Elephant		
	Set of 3	1.75	1.50

CAMEROUN

West Africa
100 centimes = 1 franc

1916

Nos. 1/4 of Middle Congo and No. 41 of French Congo overprinted
Occupation Francaise du Cameroun

16†	1c Leopard	22.00	22.00
17†	2c Leopard	28.00	25.00
18†	4c Leopard	28.00	25.00
19†	5c Leopard	8.00	7.00
22†	15c Leopard	17.00	17.00

Nos. 1/7 of Middle Congo overprinted **CAMEROUN Occupation Francaise**

30†	1c Leopard	10	10
31†	2c Leopard	10	10
32†	4c Leopard	10	10
33†	5c Leopard	10	10
34†	10c Leopard	25	15
34a†	15c Leopard	25	15
35†	20c Leopard	15	10

1921

As Nos. 1/7 of Middle Congo, but colours changed, overprinted **CAMEROUN**

46†	1c Leopard	10	10
47†	2c Leopard	10	10
48†	4c Leopard	10	10
49†	5c Leopard	10	10
50†	10c Leopard	10	10
51†	15c Leopard	10	10
52†	20c Leopard	10	10

1924
No. 51 surcharged
| 63† | 25c on 15c Leopard | 25 | 25 |

1939

133†	80c African Elephant	40	35
134†	90c African Elephant	20	15
135†	1f African Elephant (red)	25	25

135a†	1f African Elephant (brown)	30	15
136†	1f25 African Elephant	55	50
137†	1f40 African Elephant	25	20
138†	1f50 African Elephant	20	20
139†	1f60 African Elephant	50	45
140†	1f75 African Elephant	15	15
141†	2f African Elephant	25	25
142†	2f25 African Elephant	15	15
143†	2f50 African Elephant	25	20
144†	3f African Elephant	15	10

1940
Nos. 133/4, 136/40 and 142/3 overprinted **CAMEROUN FRANCAIS 27.8.40**

167†	80c African Elephant	80	70
168†	90c African Elephant	20	20
170†	1f25 African Elephant	25	20
171†	1f40 African Elephant	45	35
172†	1f50 African Elephant	15	15
173†	1f60 African Elephant	30	30
174†	1f75 African Elephant	30	30
176†	2f25 African Elephant	20	20
177†	2f50 African Elephant	20	15

1953

| 261† | 100f Giraffe | 1.50 | 25 |

1961
No. 261 surcharged **REPUBLIQUE FEDERALE** *and value*
| 295a† | 5s on 100f Giraffe | 5.00 | 5.00 |

1962

309†	50c Moustached Monkey ('Cercopitheque Moustac')	10	5
310†	1f African Elephant ('Elephant')	10	5
311†	1f50 Kob ('Cobe de Buffon')	10	5
312†	2f Hippopotamus ('Hippopotame')	15	5
313†	3f Kob	15	5
314†	4f African Elephant	15	5
315†	5f Hippopotamus	20	8
316†	6f Moustached Monkey	25	12
317†	8f African Manatee ('Lamantin')	20	35
319†	15f Moustached Monkey	30	20
320†	20f Giraffe ('Girafes')	60	20
322†	30f African Manatee	2.00	70
323†	40f Giraffe	2.50	1.00

1964

357 10f Lion
358 25f Lion

Set of 2   1.10   50

372† 250f Black Rhinoceros ('Rhinoceros') .. 5.00 1.75

1979

856 50f Black Rhinoceros ('Rhinoceros')
857 60f Giraffe ('Girafe')
858 60f Gorilla ('Gorille')
859 100f African Elephant ('Elephant')
860 100f Leopard ('Panthere')

Set of 5   2.75   2.25

1980

892† 300f Kob ('Cobe de Buffon') 1.40 90

1981

904† 50f African Buffalo ('Moutourou') (forest
race) 35 20

906† 100f Long-tailed Pangolin ('Pangolin') .. 60 40
(904/06 Set of 3) 1.10 75

1982

928 90f Giraffe 75 50

939 200f Bongo (Boocercus euryceros)
940 300f Black Colobus (Colobus satanas)

Set of 2   3.00   2.00

1983

975† 200f African Civet ('La Civette') 1.10 65
976† 200f Gorilla ('Le Gorille') 1.10 65
(975/7 Set of 3) 3.25 2.25

1984

1007 250f Antelope sp.
1008 250f Wild Boar

Set of 2   2.50   2.00

CANADA

North America
1851 12 pence = 1 shilling
20 shillings = 1 pound
1859 100 cents = 1 dollar

1851

10	3d American Beaver (imperf)	£750	£140

1858

26	3d American Beaver (perf) (as No. 10) ..	£1700	£400

1859

As No. 10, but face value in cents

31	5c American Beaver	£140	10.00

1951

439	15c American Beaver (on stamp No. 10) ..	90	12

1953

447	2c Polar Bear		
448	3c Elk		
449	4c American Bighorn		
	Set of 3	45	15

1954

472	4c Walrus		
473	5c American Beaver		
	Set of 2	30	8

STAMP MONTHLY

– finest and most informative magazine for all collectors. Obtainable from your newsagent or by postal subscription – details on request

1955

478†	4c Musk Ox	20	5

1956

486	4c Reindeer ('Caribou')		
487	5c Mountain Goat		
	Set of 2	30	8

1968

622	5c Narwhal	25	8

1972

703†	15c American Bighorn	45	10
705†	25c Polar Bear	50	12

1977

886	12c Puma (*Felis concolor cougar*)	20	20

1979

937†	35c Bowhead Whale (*Balaena mysticetus*)	40	60

1981

1006　17c Vancouver Marmot (*Marmota vancouverensis*)
1007　35c American Bison (*Bison bison athabascae*)

Set of 2	45	55

1982

1037†　30c American Beaver (on stamp No. 10)　25　25

CANAL ZONE
Central America
100 cents = 1 dollar

1924
No. 700 of the United States overprinted **CANAL ZONE**
95†　30c American Bison　.. .. ..　22.00　14.00

1948

194　10c Northern Coati ('Coati-Mundi')　.. ..　2.00　1.10

CAYMAN ISLANDS
West Indies
100 cents = 1 Jamaican dollar

1980

522†　50c Waterhouse's Leaf-nosed Bat　.. ..　90　95

CENTRAL AFRICAN EMPIRE
Central Africa
100 centimes = 1 franc

1977
Nos. 390/3 of Central African Republic overprinted
EMPIRE CENTRAFRICAIN
459　10f Kob
460　15f Warthog
461　20f Waterbuck
462　30f Lion

Set of 4	1.25	1.00

505†　100f Diana Monkey　.. .. ..　1.00　50

1978

550†　40f Black Rhinoceros ('Rhinoceros')
552†　60f Leopard
553†　100f Giraffe ('Girafe')
554†　200f African Elephant ('Elephant')
555†　300f Gorilla ('Gorille')

(550/55 Set of 6)	5.00	2.00

CENTRAL AFRICAN REPUBLIC
Central Africa
100 centimes = 1 franc

1966

113　5f Congo Forest Mouse (*Deomys ferrugineus*)
114　10f Back-striped Mouse (*Hybomys univittatus*)
115　20f Dollman's Tree Mouse (*Prionomys batesi*)

Set of 3	1.00	75

1971

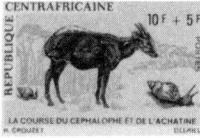

230†	10f + 5f Common Duiker ('La Course du Cephalophe')	3.50	2.25
231†	20f + 5f Hippopotamus ('L'Hippopotame'), African Elephant ('L'Elephant')	4.00	2.50
233†	50f + 20f Monkey sp. ('Le Singe'), Leopard ('La Panthere')	9.00	8.50

252	30f Lesser Bushbaby ('Galago Gris')	
253	40f Western Needle-clawed Bushbaby ('Galago Elegant')	
254	100f Angwantibo ('Potto de Calabar')	
255	150f Potto ('Potto de Bosman')	
256	200f Red Colobus ('Colobe d'Oustalet')	
	Set of 5	9.00 5.50

1975

390	10f Kob ('Cob de Buffon')	
391	15f Warthog ('Phacochere')	
392	20f Waterbuck ('Cob Defassa')	
393	30f Lion	
	Set of 4	1.00 75

STANLEY GIBBONS
STAMP COLLECTING SERIES

Introductory booklets on *How to Start, How to Identify Stamps* and *Collecting by Theme*. A series of well illustrated guides at a low price.
Write for details.

1982

820	60f African Elephant ('Elephant')
821	90f Giraffe ('Girafe Reticulee')
822	100f Addax
823	110f Okapi
824	300f Mandrill (air)
825	500f Lion
	Set of 6 6.50 4.50

1983

971	10f Black Rhinoceros ('Rhinoceros Noir')
972	40f Black Rhinocerus ('Rhinoceros Noir')
973	70f Black Rhinoceros ('Rhinoceros Noir')
974	180f Black Rhinoceros ('Rhinoceros Noir')
975	400f Black Rhinoceros ('Rhinoceros Noir'), Common Zebra (air)
976	500f Lion, Grant's Gazelle, African Elephant
	Set of 6 6.00 3.00
MS977	600f Cheetah ('Guepard') 4.50 4.50

1984

990	30f African Elephant, Black Rhinoceros, Giraffe, Common Zebra, Warthog, Gazelle sp, Hare sp
991	130f African Elephant, Common Zebra, Giraffe, African Buffalo, Waterbuck
	Set of 2 1.00 80

Appendix

The following stamps have either been issued in excess of postal needs, or have not been made available to the public in reasonable quantities at face value. Miniature sheets, imperforate stamps etc., are excluded from this section.

1982

Leopard 1500f

CEYLON

Indian Ocean
100 cents = 1 rupee

1935

| 377† | 50c Indian Elephant ('Wild Elephants') | .. | 5.00 | 65 |

1938

As No. 377, but with portrait of King George VI

| 394d† | 50c Indian Elephant | .. .. | 1.25 | 15 |

1951

Inscribed "Ruhuna National Park"

| 419† | 2c Sambar | .. .. | 10 | 5 |

1958

As No. 419, but with Sinhalese inscriptions

| 448† | 2c Sambar | .. .. | 10 | 5 |

1963

| 480 | 5c Indian Elephant | .. .. | 10 | 5 |

COLLECT BIRDS ON STAMPS

The first Stanley Gibbons thematic catalogue – a few copies still available at £4.95 (p.+p. £1.30) plus FREE 1983–84 Supplement from: .
Stanley Gibbons Publications Ltd, 5, Parkside, Christchurch Road, Ringwood, Hants BH24 3SH.

1970

561	5c Water Buffalo ('Wild Buffalo')
562	15c Slender Loris
563	50c Spotted Deer
564	1r Leopard

Set of 4   1.60   2.25

CHAD

Central Africa
100 centimes = 1 franc

1922

As Nos. 1/7 of Middle Congo, but colours changed, overprinted
TCHAD

1†	1c Leopard	.. ..	10	10
2†	2c Leopard	.. ..	10	10
3†	4c Leopard	.. ..	15	15
4†	5c Leopard	.. ..	20	20
5†	10c Leopard	.. ..	30	30
6†	15c Leopard	.. ..	35	35
7†	20c Leopard	.. ..	95	95

1924

Nos. 1/7 further overprinted **AFRIQUE EQUATORIALE FRANCAISE**

19†	1c Leopard	.. ..	10	10
20†	2c Leopard	.. ..	10	10
21†	4c Leopard	.. ..	10	10
22†	5c Leopard	.. ..	15	15
23†	10c Leopard (green)	.. ..	15	10
24†	10c Leopard (red and grey)	.. ..	15	15
25†	15c Leopard	.. ..	15	15
26†	20c Leopard	.. ..	15	15

1964

129	5f Barbary Sheep ('Mouflon a Manchettes')
130	10f Addax
131	20f Scimitar Oryx ('Oryx')
132	25f Giant Eland ('Eland de Derby')
133	30f Giraffe, African Buffalo, Lion
134	85f Greater Kudu ('Grand Koudou')

Set of 6   4.50   2.00

1972

377† 25f Dromedary ('Dromadaire')   30   20

1973

No. 377 surcharged **SECHERESSE SOLIDARITE AFRICAINE**
and value

401 100f on 25f Dromedary 1.00   55

1976

482† 125f Polar Bear   65   25

1978

536† 100f Black Rhinoceros 1.10   80

1979

555 40f Sand Gazelle (*Gazella leptoceros*)
556 50f Addax (*Addax nasomaculatus*)
557 60f Scimitar Oryx (*Oryx dammah*)
558 100f Cheetah (*Acinonyx jubatus*)
559 150f African Ass (*Equus asinus*)
560 300f Black Rhinoceros (*Diceros bicornis*)
Set of 6   4.75   2.00

Appendix

The following stamps have either been issued in excess of postal needs, or have not been made available to the public in reasonable quantities at face value. Miniature sheets, imperforate stamps etc., are excluded from this section.

1972

African Animals (Zebra, Mandrill, Elephant, Gazelle, Hippopotamus) 20, 30, 100, 130, 150f.

CHILE

South America
1948 100 centavos = 1 peso
1960 100 centesimos = 1 escudo
1975 100 centesimos = 1 peso

1948

381a†	60c Huidobria Otter (*Lutra huidobria*) . .		40	25
381d†	60c Striped Skunk (*Mephitis chilensis*) . .		40	25
381f†	60c South American Fur Seal ('Otaria Ursina de Magellanes')		40	25
381i†	60c Red Fruit Bat (*Stenoderma chilensis*)		40	25
381j†	60c Long-tailed Chinchilla (*Chinchilla laniger*)		40	25
381r†	60c Chilean Guemal (*Hippocamelus bisulcus*)		40	25
382a†	2p60 Huidobria Otter		60	30
382d†	2p60 Striped Skunk		60	30
382f†	2p60 South American Fur Seal		60	30
382i†	2p60 Red Fruit Bat		60	30
382j†	2p60 Long-tailed Chinchilla		60	30
382r†	2p60 Chilean Guemal		60	30
383a†	3p Huidobria Otter		60	60
383d†	3p Striped Skunk		60	60
383f†	3p South American Fur Seal		60	60
383i†	3p Red Fruit Bat		60	60
383j†	3p Long-tailed Chinchilla		60	60
383r†	3p Chilean Guemal		60	60

Nos. 381/3 each cover 25 stamps of different designs.

STANLEY GIBBONS
STAMP COLLECTING SERIES

Introductory booklets on *How to Start, How to Identify Stamps* and *Collecting by Theme*. A series of well illustrated guides at a low price.
Write for details.

1974

733† 200e Eastern Grey Kangaroo 25 15

1984

993 9p Blue Whale (*Balaenoptera musculus*)
994 9p Juan Fernandez Fur Seal
(*Arctocephalus philippi*)
995 9p Chilean Guemal (*Hippocamelus bisulcus*)
996 9p Long-tailed Chinchilla (*Chinchilla lanigera*)

Set of 4 1.50 1.25

1985

1000† 10p Andean Hog-nosed Skunk
(*Conepatus chinga*) 30 20
1003† 10p Marine Otter (*Lutra felina*) 30 20
1006† 10p Southern Pudu (*Pudu pudu*) 30 20
1009† 10p Argentine Grey Fox (*Dusicyon griseus*) 30 20

CHINA

Chinese People's Republic

East Asia
100 fen = 1 yuan

1959

1812 4f Giant Panda
1813 8f Giant Panda

Set of 2 50 25

1963

2116 8f Giant Panda (facing right)
2117 8f Giant Panda (eating bamboo shoots)
2118 10f Giant Panda (two pandas)

Set of 3 12.00 2.50

2121 8f Snub-nosed Monkey
2122 10f Snub-nosed Monkey
2123 22f Snub-nosed Monkey

Set of 3 5.00 1.00

1973

2498 4f Giant Panda
2499 8f Giant Panda (panda and cub)
2500 8f Giant Panda (two pandas)
2501 10f Giant Panda
2502 20f Giant Panda
2503 43f Giant Panda

Set of 6 7.50 7.50

1979

2866 4f Tiger
2867 8f Tiger
2868 60f Tiger
                              Set of 3   1.10   1.10

1980

2968 8f Bear Macaque 1.00   1.00

2995 4f Sika Deer
2996 8f Sika Deer
2997 60f Sika Deer
                              Set of 3   1.10   1.10

3016 8f Bactrian Camel   25   25

3030 8f White Flag Dolphin (*Lipotes vexillifer*)
3031 60f White Flag Dolphin (*Lipotes vexillifer*)
                              Set of 2   1.00   1.00

1981

3062† 8f Giant Panda (on stamp No. 2116) . .   15   15

1982

3185 8f Sable (*Martes zibellina*)
3186 80f Sable (*Martes zibellina*)
                              Set of 2   1.10   1.00

Taiwan

100 cents = 1 new taiwan yuan

1960

365† $2 Sika Deer   80   40

1970

766 $1 Tiger   25   10

1971

807 $1 Taiwan Macaque (*Macaca cyclopis*)
808 $2 Red and White Flying Squirrel
    (*Petaurista alborufusiena*)
809 $3 Chinese Pangolin (*Manis pentadactyla*
    pentadactyla)
810 $5 Sika Deer (*Cervus taiouanus*)
                              Set of 4   1.75   1.40

1973

975 50c Tiger
976 $4.50 Tiger
                              Set of 2   80   40

1974

1035 50c Chinese Hare
1036 $4.50 Chinese Hare
                              Set of 2   50   30

1975

1067† $5 Tiger   50   20

1976

1117† $8 Sika Deer   45   30

1979

1278 $1 Taiwan Macaque
1279 $6 Taiwan Macaque
                              Set of 2   40   30

CHRISTMAS ISLAND
Indian Ocean
100 cents = 1 dollar

1983

175† 24c Eastern Grey Kangaroo   20   25

STANLEY GIBBONS
STAMP COLLECTING SERIES
Introductory booklets on *How to Start, How to Identify
Stamps* and *Collecting by Theme.* A series of well illus-
trated guides at a low price.
Write for details.

CISKEI
Southern Africa
100 cents = 1 rand

1982

30	8c Brown Hare (*Lepus capensis*)			
31	15c Cape Fox (*Vulpes chama*)			
32	20c Cape Ground Squirrel (*Xerus inaurus*)			
33	25c Caracal (*Felis caracal*)			
		Set of 4	80	80

COLOMBIA
South America
100 centavos = 1 peso

1960

1005†	5c Two-toed Sloth ('Unau')		20	10
1007†	20c Long-haired Spider Monkey			
	('Marimba')		20	10
1008†	35c Giant Anteater ('Oso Hormiguero')			
	(air)		1.00	10
1009†	1p30 Nine-banded Armadillo ('Armadillo')		1.60	1.50

1961
Nos. 1005 and 1007 overprinted **AEREO** *or surcharged also*

1078†	5c Two-toed Sloth		10	10
1079†	10c on 20c Long-haired Spider Monkey		10	10
	(1077/79 Set of 3)		25	20

COLLECT BIRDS ON STAMPS
The first Stanley Gibbons thematic catalogue – a few copies still available at £4.95 (p.+p. £1.30) plus FREE 1983–84 Supplement from:
Stanley Gibbons Publications Ltd, 5, Parkside, Christchurch Road, Ringwood, Hants BH24 3SH.

COMORO ISLANDS
Indian Ocean
100 centimes =1 franc

1976

208†	20f Tiger Cat ('Martre Marsupiale')		25	15
209†	35f Leopard		30	15
210†	40f White Rhinoceros ('Rhinoceros			
	Blanc')		35	15
211†	75f Mountain Nyala ('Nyala')		60	15
212†	400f Orang-Utan ('Orang-Outan') (air) . .	3.00	1.25
	(207/12 Set of 6)	4.50	2.10
MS213	500f Indri ('Indri Lemurien')	4.00	3.50

1977

214†	10f Wolf ('Loup des Rocheuses')		10	10
215†	30f Aye-Aye ('Aye-Aye-Lemurien')		20	10
216†	40f Banded Duiker ('Cephalopode Zebre')		25	15
218†	200f Ocelot		1.40	55
MS220	500f Tiger ('Tigre de Sumatra')		3.00	1.25

1980
Nos. 209/10 overprinted **REPUBLIQUE FEDERALE ISLAMIQUE DES COMORES**

401†	35f Leopard		30	20
402†	40f White Rhinoceros		40	25

CONGO (BRAZZAVILLE)
Central Africa
100 centimes = 1 franc

1965

62†	15f Bushbuck ('Antilope')		35	25
63†	20f African Elephant ('Elephant')		40	30
	(62/4 Set of 3)		2.10	1.60

1972

333 1f Lion (*Panthera leo*)
334 2f African Elephant (*Loxodonta africana*)
335 3f Leopard (*Panthera pardus*)
336 4f Hippopotamus (*Hippopotamus amphibius*)
337 5f Gorilla (*Gorilla beringei*)
338 20f Potto (*Perodicticus potto*)
339 30f De Brazza's Monkey (*Cercopithecus neglectus*)
340 40f Pygmy Chimpanzee (*P. paniscus*)

Set of 8   2.00   1.25

1973

363† 250f Lion 2.75 1.75
364† 300f Tiger, Lion ('Tigre et Lion') 3.25 2.00
(362/64 Set of 3) 6.50 4.50

385† 100f Lion, Leopard 1.50 75
386† 100f Indian Elephant 1.50 75
(384/86 Set of 3) 4.00 2.00

1974

436† 100f Serval ('Serval Africain') 1.00 50

1975

452 40f Indian Elephant
453 50f Tiger

Set of 2   1.00   80

1976

529 5f Kob ('Antilope')
530 10f African Buffalo ('Buffles')
531 15f Hippopotamus ('Hippopotames')
532 20f Warthog ('Phacochere')
533 25f African Elephant ('Elephants')

Set of 5   1.00   75

1978

620 35f Okapi
621 60f African Buffalo ('Buffle d'Afrique')
622 85f Black Rhinoceros ('Rhinoceros')
623 150f Chimpanzee ('Chimpanze')
624 200f Hippopotamus ('Hippopotame')
625 300f Kob ('Cobe de Buffon')

Set of 6   5.50   2.75

1968

655	2k Leopard		
656	9.6k Leopard		

		Set of 2	80	25

644†	100f Leopard	1.00	65

1984

962	30f Giant Ground Pangolin ('Le Pangolin')
963	70f Bat sp. ('Chauve-souris')
964	85f African Civet ('Civette')

		Set of 3	1.25	80

Nos. 962/4 are inscribed "1983"

CONGO (KINSHASA)
Central Africa
1960 100 centimes = 1 franc
1967 100 sengi = 1 kuta

1960

Nos. 339/50 of Belgian Congo overprinted CONGO *or surcharged
also*

378	10c Roan Antelope
379	20c White Rhinoceros
380	40c Giraffe
381	50c Demidoff's Galago
382	1f Gorilla
383	1f50 African Buffalo
384	2f Eastern Black-and-White Colobus
385	3f50 on 3f African Elephant
386	5f Okapi
387	6f50 Impala
388	8f Giant Ground Pangolin
389	10f Eland, Common Zebra

		Set of 12	2.75	1.25

1964
Nos. 340 and 348 of Belgian Congo surcharged
REPUBLIQUE DU CONGO

519†	1f on 20c White Rhinoceros	10	10
521†	5f on 6f50 Impala	30	20

Nos. 379 and 387 surcharged

523†	1f on 20c White Rhinoceros	10	10
526†	5f on 6f50 Impala	30	20

1971

773	10s Savanna Monkey (*Cercopithecus aethiops*)
774	20s Moustached Monkey (*Cercopithecus cephus*)
775	70s De Brazza's Monkey (*Cercopithecus neglectus*)
776	1k Yellow Baboon (*Papio cynocephalus*)
777	3k Pygmy Chimpanzee (*Pan paniscus*)
778	5k Black Mangabey (*Cercocebus*)
779	10k Owl-faced Monkey (*Cercopithecus hamlyni*)
780	15k Diana Monkey (*Cercopithecus diana d.*)
781	25k Western Black-and-White Colobus (*Colobus polykomos*)
782	40k L'Hoest's Monkey (*Cercopithecus l'hoesti*)

		Set of 10	14.00	12.00

COOK ISLANDS
South Pacific
100 cents = 1 dollar

1984

946	10c Cuvier's Beaked Whale
947	18c Risso's Dolphin
948	20c True's Beaked Whale
949	24c Long-finned Pilot Whale
950	30c Narwhal

951 36c White Whale ('Beluga')
952 42c Common Dolphin
953 48c Commerson's Dolphin
954 60c Bottle-nosed Dolphin
955 72c Sowerby's Beaked Whale ('Sowerby's Whale')
956 96c Common Porpoise
957 $2 Boutu

Set of 12   5.50   6.00

COSTA RICA
Central America
100 centimes = 1 colon

1963

648 5c Paca (*Cuniculus paca virgatus*)
649 10c Baird's Tapir (*Tapirella bairdii*)
650 25c Jaguar (*Felis onca centralis*)
651 30c Ocelot (*Felis pardalis aequatorialis*)
652 35c White-tailed Deer (*Odocoileus virginianus chiriquensis*)
653 40c American Manatee (*Trichechus manatus*)
654 85c White-throated Capuchin (*Cebus capucinus imitator*)
655 5col White-lipped Peccary (*Tagassu pecari spiradens*)

Set of 8   8.00   6.00

Unissued stamps surcharged
670 10c on 1c Tamandua (*Tamandua tetradactyla chiriquensis*)
671 25c on 2c Grey Fox (*Urocyon cinereoargentateus costarricensis*)
672 35c on 3c Nine-banded Armadillo (*Dasypus novemcinctus fenestratus*)
673 85c on 4c Giant Anteater (*Myrmecophaga tridactyla centralis*)

Set of 4   1.00   50

1980

1211† 3col Puma (*Felis concolor*)   55   40
1212† 5col50 Black-handed Spider Monkey (*Ateles geoffrovi*) 1.00   1.75

CUBA
West Indies
100 centavos = 1 peso

1962

1054† 10c Jamaican Long-tongued Bat (*Monophyllus cubanus*) 2.00   1.00
1057a† 10c Desmarest's Hutia (*Capromys piloridls*) 2.00   1.00
1057b† 10c Prehensile-tailed Hutia (*Capromys prehensilis*) 2.00   1.00
1057c† 10c Cuban Solenodon (*Solenodon cubanus*) 2.00   1.00
1057d† 10c Desmarest's Hutia (*Capromys pilorides*) (white race) 2.00   1.00

Nos. 1054 and 1057a/d were printed in sheets of 25, containing four examples of each stamp and five labels.

1964

1157 1c Leopard ('Leopardo')
1158 2c Indian Elephant ('Elefante')
1159 3c Red Deer ('Gamo')
1160 4c Eastern Grey Kangaroo ('Canguro')
1161 5c Lion ('Leones')
1162 6c Eland
1163 7c Common Zebra ('Cebra')
1164 8c Striped Hyena ('Hiena')
1165 9c Tiger ('Tigre')
1166 10c Guanaco

1167 13c Chimpanzee ('Chimpance')
1168 20c Collared Peccary ('Pecari')
1169 30c Common Raccoon ('Mapache')
1170 40c Hippopotamus ('Hipopotamo')
1171 50c Brazilian Tapir ('Tapir')
1172 60c Dromedary ('Dromedario')
1173 70c American Bison ('Bisonte')
1174 80c Asiatic Black Bear ('Oso')
1175 90c Water Buffalo ('Bufalo')
1176 1p Roe Deer
Set of 20   25.00   12.00

1969

1678† 13c Night Monkey 1.50   75

1720† 4c Dwarf Hutia (Capromys nana)   15   20

1970

1800† 13c Wild Boar (Sus scrofa) 1.50   70
1801† 30c White-tailed Deer (Odocoileus
       virginianus) 2.50   1.00

1806† 3c Common Zebra   35   15

1977

2416† 2c Leopard (Panthera pardus) (black
       race)   5   5
2417† 8c Puma (Felis concolor)   15   8
2418† 10c Leopard (Panthera pardus)   60   15

2419† 13c Tiger (Panthera tigris) (air)   70   15
2420† 30c Lion (Panthera leo) 1.00   40
       (2415/20 Set of 6)   2.00   80

1978

2504 1c White Rhinoceros (Cerototherium
      simun)
2505 4c Okapi (Okapia johnstoni)
2506 6c Mandrill (Mandrillus sphinx)
2507 10c Giraffe (Giraffa camelopardalis)
2508 13c Cheetah (Acinonyx jubatos) (air)
2509 30c African Elephant (Loxodonta
      africana)
      Set of 6   1.75   85

1979

2596 1c Chimpanzee ('Chimpance')
2597 2c Leopard ('Leopardo')
2598 3c Fallow Deer ('Corzo')
2599 4c Lion ('Leon')
2600 5c Brown Bear ('Oso Pardo')
2601 13c Eurasian Red Squirrel ('Ardilla')
2602 30c Giant Panda ('Oso Panda')
2603 50c Tiger ('Tigre')
      Set of 8   2.25   1.25

1980

2640 1c Bottle-nosed Dolphin (*Tursiops truncatus*)
2641 3c Humpback Whale (*Megaptera novaeangliae*)
2642 13c Cuvier's Beaked Whale (*Ziphius cavirostris*)
2643 30c Caribbean Monk Seal (*Monachus tropicalis*)

Set of 4   1.00   50

1981

MS2717 50c Red Deer (on Austria stamp No. 1341) 1.10   1.10

2765† 5c Desmarest's Hutia ('Jutia')   15   15
2766† 20c Cuban Solenodon ('Almiqui')   50   15
2767† 35c American Manatee ('Manati')   90   20

1983

MS2897 1p Stoat 2.25   2.25

1984

2984 1c Risso's Dolphin (*Grampus griseus*)
2985 2c Common Dolphin (*Delphinus delphis*)
2986 5c Sperm Whale (*Physeter catodon*)
2987 6c Spotted Dolphin (*Stenella plagiodon*)
2988 10c False Killer Whale (*Pseudorca crassidens*)
2989 30c Bottle-nosed Dolphin (*Tursiops truncatus*)
2990 50c Humpback Whale (*Megaptera novaeangliae*)

Set of 7   2.40   1.10

1984

3043† 2c Cuban Solenodon (*Solenodon cubanus*)   8   5
3047† 10c Bushy-tailed Hutia (*Capromys melanurus*)   30   15

CYPRUS
Mediterranean
1000 milliemes = 1 pound

1962

222† 500m Mouflon 32.00   15.00

1963

231† 150m Mouflon 3.50 3.25

CZECHOSLOVAKIA

Central Europe
100 haleru = 1 koruna

1955

892† 1k50 Brown Hare 1.00 25

1957

993† 20h Chamois (*Rupicapra rupicapra*) . . 75 50
994† 30h Brown Bear (*Ursus arctos*) 50 10

1959

1112 30h Alpine Marmot (*Marmotta marmotta*)
1113 40h European Bison (*Bison bonassus*)
1114 60h Lynx (*Lynx lynx*)
1115 1k Wolf (*Canis lupus*)
1116 1k60 Red Deer (*Cervus elaphus*)
                                    Set of 5 5.00 1.10

1962

1291 20h Polar Bear (*Thalarctos maritimus*)
1292 30h Chimpanzee (*Pan troglodytes*)
1293 60h Bactrian Camel (*Camelus bactrianus*)
1294 1k Indian Elephant (*Elaphus maximus*),
     African Elephant (*Loxodonta africana*)
1295 1k40 Leopard (*Felis pardus*)
1296 1k60 Wild Horse (*Equus caballus
     przewalskii*)
                                    Set of 6 4.75 1.40

1963

1394 30h Chamois (*Rupicapra rupicapra*)
1395 40h Ibex (*Capra ibex ibex*)
1396 60h Mouflon (*Ovis musimon*)
1397 1k20 Roe Deer (*Capreolus capreolus*)
1398 1k60 Fallow Deer (*Dama dama*)
1399 2k Red Deer (*Cervus elaphus*)
                                    Set of 6 10.00 3.75

1966

1588† 1k American Bison 30 10

STANLEY GIBBONS
STAMP COLLECTING SERIES

Introductory booklets on *How to Start, How to Identify
Stamps* and *Collecting by Theme*. A series of well illus-
trated guides at a low price.
Write for details.

1975

1612 30h Eurasian Badger (*Meles meles*)
1613 40h Red Deer (*Cervus elaphus*)
1614 60h Lynx (*Lynx lynx*)
1615 80h Brown Hare (*Lepus europaeus*)
1616 1k Red Fox (*Vulpes vulpes*)
1617 1k20 Brown Bear (*Ursus arctos*)
1618 2k Wild Boar (*Sus scrofa*)

Set of 7   5.00   2.00

On No. 1615 the inscription is incorrectly shown as "euiopaens" on 40 out of the 50 stamps in each sheet.

2202†	60h Brown Hare	25	10
2203†	1k Lion	35	20
2204†	1k60 Red Deer	50	30
	(2202/5 Set of 4)	2.25	95

1967

1682 30h Eurasian Red Squirrel (*Sciurus vulgaris*)
1683 60h Wild Cat (*Felis silvestris*)
1684 1k Stoat (*Mustela erminea*)
1685 1k20 Hazel Dormouse (*Muscardinus avellanarius*)
1686 1k40 West European Hedgehog (*Erinaceus europaeus*)
1687 1k60 Pine Marten (*Martes martes*)

Set of 6   5.50   1.25

1976

2307 10h Common Zebra ('Zebra Stepni')
2308 20h African Elephant ('Slon Africky')
2309 30h Cheetah ('Gepard')
2310 40h Giraffe ('Zirafa')
2311 60h Black Rhinoceros ('Nosorozec Tuponosy')
2312 3k Bongo ('Bongo (Antilopa)')

Set of 6   2.50   70

1981

2595 50h Gorilla
2596 1k Lion
2597 7k Wild Horse

Set of 3   3.50   1.50

1971

1969†	80h Mouflon (*Ovis musimon*)		25	10
1970†	1k Chamois (*Rupicapra rupicapra*)		25	10
1971†	2k Red Deer (*Cervus elaphus*)		55	15
1972†	2k60 Wild Boar (*Sus scrofa*)		3.00	65

1983

2678†	5k Lynx (*Lynx lynx*)	1.75	70
2679†	7k Red Deer (*Cervus elaphus*)	2.25	80

COLLECT BIRDS ON STAMPS

The first Stanley Gibbons thematic catalogue – a few copies still available at £4.95 (p.+p. £1.30) plus FREE 1983–84 Supplement from:
Stanley Gibbons Publications Ltd, 5, Parkside, Christchurch Road, Ringwood, Hants BH24 3SH.

DAHOMEY
West Africa
100 centimes = 1 franc

1968

318†	15f African Buffalo (*Syncerus caffer*) ..	25	15
319†	30f Lion (*Panthera leo*)	45	25
320†	45f Kob (*Adenota kob*)	80	40
322†	100f Hippopotamus (*Hippopotamus*		
	amphibius*)	2.25	1.10
	(318/22 *Set of* 5)	4.50	2.10

1969

353	5f Warthog (*Phacochoerus aethiopicus*)		
354	30f Leopard (*Panthera pardus*)		
355	60f Spotted Hyena (*Crocuta crocuta*)		
356	75f Olive Baboon (*Papio anubis*)		
357	90f Hartebeest (*Alcelaphus buselaphus*)		
	Set of 5	4.50	2.00

1974

530†	5f African Elephant ('L'Elephant')	15	10

DENMARK
Northern Europe
100 ore = 1 krone

1970

516	60ore Red Deer	20	10

1975

613†	70ore West European Hedgehog		
	('Pindsvin')	30	10
616†	200ore European Otter ('Odder')	50	10

DJIBOUTI REPUBLIC
East Africa
100 centimes = 1 franc

1977

718†	50f Klipspringer (*Oreotragus oreotragus*)	65	45

1978

740†	250f Brown Hare	2.50	2.00

747†	90f Caracal	1.00	80

1981

820 60f Tree Hyrax
821 105f Greater Kudu

Set of 2   1.50   1.25

1984

913† 2f Klipspringer   10   10
918† 45f Warthog 1.00   45

DOMINICA

West Indies
100 cents = 1 West Indian dollar

1972

352† ½c Common Opossum ('Manicou')   10   5
353† 35c Brazilian Agouti ('Agouti')   40   25

1975

501†   30c Common Opossum ('Manicou')   ..   40   20

1978

No. 501 overprinted INDEPENDENCE 3rd NOVEMBER 1978
643†   30c Common Opossum   25   20

1979

661†   30c Striped Dolphin ('Spotted Dolphin') ..   25   15
664† $1 Long-finned Pilot Whale ('Pilot Whale')   70   45

1983

839   45c Cuvier's Beaked Whale ('Goosebeak Whale')
840   60c Humpback Whale
841   75c Black Right Whale ('Great Right Whale')
842   $3 Melon-headed Whale ('Melonhead Whale')

  Set of 4   2.50   2.75
MS843 $5 Pygmy Sperm Whale 3.00   3.25

859†   45c Jaguar   20   25
862†   90c Red Deer   40   45

DOMINICAN REPUBLIC

West Indies
100 centavos = 1 peso

1977

1306†   6c Haitan Solenodon (Solenodon paradoxus)   15   10

1980

REPUBLICA DOMINICANA

1410†	10c Hispaniolan Hutia (*Plagiodontia aedium*)		25	15
1411†	25c American Manatee (*Trichechuf manatus*)		65	35

1984

1580†	25c White-lipped Peccary (*Dominicus iabati*)		15	12
1581†	35c Haitian Solenodon (*Solenodon paradoxus*)		25	20

EAST GERMANY
See under Germany

ECUADOR
South America
100 centavos = 1 sucre

1956

1057†	1s90 Guanaco ('Llamincos')		25	25

1960

1160	20c Giant Anteater (*Myrmecophaga tridactyla*)		

1161	40c Mountain Tapir (*Tapirus villosus*)		
1162	80c Spectacled Bear (*Tremarctos ornatus*)		
1163	1s Puma (*Puma concolor*)		
	Set of 4	1.75	50

1961

1202	10c Collared Peccary (*Pecari tajacu*)			
1203	20c Kinkajou (*Potos flavus*)			
1204	80c Jaguar (*Panthera onca*)			
1205	1s Little Coatimundi (*Nasua olivacea*)			
		Set of 4	1.75	50

No. 1 of Galapagos Islands overprinted UNESCO 1961 Estacion de Biologia Maritima de Galapagos

1207†	20c Californian Sealion		15	10

1965

1291†	20c Nine-banded Armadillo (*Dasypus novemcynetus*)		10	10
1292†	30c Eurasian Red Squirrel (*Sciurus vulgaris*)		10	10
1293†	40c Peruvian Guemal (*Hippocamelus antisionsis*)		20	10
1295†	80c Two-toed Sloth (*Choloepus didactylus*)		40	10
	(1291/95 *Set of* 5)		1.00	40

1968
No. 1057 overprinted

1346	1s30 on 1s90 Guanaco		20	15

1973

1527†	60c Galapagos Fur Seal		25	10
1529†	1s Californian Sealion		25	10

1983

1883† 3s Californian Sealion 35 10

EL SALVADOR
Central America
100 centavos = 1 colon

1963

1180†	1c Coyote (*Thos latrans*)	25	10
1181†	2c Black Spider Monkey (*Ateles neglectus*)	25	10
1182†	3c Common Racoon (*Procyon lothor*) . .	25	10
1184†	6c Northern Coati (*Nasua narica*)	25	10
1185†	10c Kinkajou (*Pottus flavus*)	25	10

1981

1662† 25c Black-handed Spider Monkey
(*Ateles geoffroyi*) 15 10

1983

1810† 25c Paca (*Cuniculus paca*) 20 15

EQUATORIAL GUINEA
West Africa
1968 100 centimos = 1 peseta
1973 100 centimos = 1 ekuele (plural = bikuele)

1982

60	40b Gorilla (*Gorilla gorilla*)		
61	60b Hippopotamus (*Hippopotamus amphibius*)		
62	80b African Brush-tailed Porcupine (*Atherurus africanus*)		
63	120b Leopard (*Felis pardus*)		
		Set of 4 2.25	1.25

1984

72† 125b Sperm Whale 60 45

Appendix
The following stamps have either been issued in excess of postal needs, or have not been made available to the public in reasonable quantities at face value. Miniature sheets, imperforate stamps etc., are excluded from this section.

1974
Australian Animals (Dingo, Tiger Cat, Koala, Thylacine, Grey Kangaroo, Tree Kangaroo, Marsupial Wolf). Postage 80, 85, 90, 95c, 1e; Air 15, 40e.

African Animals (Dromedary, Mongoose, Lion, Giraffe, Chimpanzee, Eland, Gnu). Postage 55, 60, 65, 70, 75c; Air 10, 70e.

Endangered Species (European Wolf, Polecat, European Lynx, Kob, Caracal, Okapi, Arctic Fox, American Black Bear, Paca, Pampas Deer, Wallaby, Numbat, Argali, Sumatran Rhinoceros, Tiger). Postage 10, 15, 20, 25, 30, 35, 40, 45, 50, 55, 60c, 1e; Air 2, 10, 70e.

1975
Monkeys (Various species). Postage 5, 10, 15, 20, 25, 30, 40, 45, 50, 55, 60c, 1, 2e; Air 10, 70e.

1976
European Animals (Wild Boar, Marmot, Porcupine, Brown Bear, Genet, Wild Cat, Ibex). Postage 5, 10, 15, 20, 25c; Air 5, 70p.

Asian Animals (Arctic Fox, Tiger, Macaque, Lesser Panda, Giant Panda, Snow Leopard, Loris). Postage 30, 35, 40, 45c, 8p; Air 50c, 60p.

1977

North American Animals (Polar Bear, Wolf, Reindeer, Walrus, Puma, Black Bear, Lynx). Postage 1e25, 1e50, 1e75, 2e, 2e25; Air 20, 50e.

South American Animals (Armadillo, Llama, Pampas Deer, Paca, Sloth, Ocelot, Giant Anteater). Postage 2e50, 2e75, 3e, 3e50, 4e; Air 25, 35e.

ERITREA

North-east Africa
100 centesimi = 1 lira

1922

Nos. 10/16 *of Somalia overprinted* ERITHREA

57	2c on 1b African Elephant	
58	5c on 2b African Elephant	
59	10c on 1a Lion	
60	15c on 2a Lion	
61	25c on 2½a Lion	
62	50c on 5a Lion	
63	1li on 10a Lion	

Set of 7   6.00   5.00

1933

199†	2c Dromedary	. . . .	25	25
201†	10c Dromedary	. . . .	25	25
206†	2li African Elephant	. . . .	1.50	50

1934

As Nos. 201 *and* 206, *but colours changed, overprinted*
ONORANZE AL DUCA DEGLI ABRUZZI

209†	10c Dromedary	. . . .	1.00	1.50
213†	2li African Elephant	. . . .	1.00	2.00

216†	5c Grant's Gazelle	. . . .	1.00	1.50
217†	10c Grant's Gazelle	. . . .	1.00	1.50
218†	20c Grant's Gazelle	. . . .	1.00	1.50
219†	50c Grant's Gazelle	. . . .	1.00	1.50
220†	60c Grant's Gazelle	. . . .	1.00	1.50
221†	1li25 Grant's Gazelle	. . . . . .	1.00	1.50
222†	25c Dromedary (air)	. . . .	1.00	1.50
223†	50c Dromedary	. . . .	1.00	1.50
224†	75c Dromedary	. . . .	1.00	1.50

ETHIOPIA

North-east Africa
1919 16 guerche = 1 menelik dollar
1946 100 cents = 1 Ethiopian dollar
1978 100 cents = 1 birr

1919

181†	½g Gerenuk	. . . .	15	10
182†	½g Giraffe	. . . .	15	10
183†	½g Leopard	. . . .	15	10
188†	8g Black Rhinoceros	. . . .	40	40
190†	$1 African Elephant	. . . .	1.00	85
191†	$2 African Buffalo	. . . .	2.50	2.00
192†	$3 Lion	. . . .	3.75	3.50

1921

Stamps of 1919 *surcharged*

197†	½g on ½g Gerenuk	. . . .	50	50
208c†	½g on 8g Black Rhinoceros	. . . . .	1.00	80
202†	½g on $1 African Elephant	. . . . .	50	50
198†	1g on ½g Giraffe	. . . .	1.00	1.00
205†	1g on $3 Lion	. . . .	90	90
200†	2½g on ½g Leopard	. . . .	90	90

1961

517	5c African Ass ('Wild Ass')
518	15c Eland
519	25c African Elephant ('Elephant')
520	35c Giraffe
521	50c Gemsbok ('Beisa')
522	$1 Lion

Set of 6   6.00   2.00

STANLEY GIBBONS
STAMP COLLECTING SERIES

Introductory booklets on *How to Start*, *How to Identify Stamps* and *Collecting by Theme*. A series of well illustrated guides at a low price.
Write for details.

1966

641 5c Black Rhinoceros ('Rhinoceros')
642 10c Leopard
643 20c Eastern Black-and-White Colobus
    ('Geureza')
644 30c Mountain Nyala ('Nyala')
645 60c Ibex ('Walia')

Set of 5   4.00   1.00

1975

926 5c Warthog
927 10c Aardvark
928 20c Simian Jackal ('Semien Wolf')
929 40c Gelada ('Gelada Baboon')
930 80c African Civet ('Civet')

Set of 5   2.00   1.00

1980

1164 10c Grevy's Zebra
1165 15c Dibatag
1166 25c Hunting Dog
1167 60c Hartebeest ('Swayne's Harte Beest')
1168 70c Cheetah

Set of 5   1.60   90

1985

1309 20c Hippopotamus (*Hippopotamus*
     amphibius)
1310 25c Gerenuk (*Litocranius walleri*)
1311 40c Common Duiker (*Sylvicapra grimmia*)
1312 1b Gunther's Dik-Dik (*Rhynchotragus*
     guentheri)

Set of 4   1.50   1.25

FALKLAND ISLANDS
South Atlantic)
1929 12 pence = 1 shilling
20 shillings = 1 pound
1971 100 pence = 1 pound

1929

116 ½d Fin Whale
117 1d Fin Whale
118 2d Fin Whale
119 2½d Fin Whale
120 4d Fin Whale
121 6d Fin Whale
122 1s Fin Whale
123 2s6d Fin Whale
124 5s Fin Whale
125 10s Fin Whale
126 £1 Fin Whale

Set of 11   £550   £700

1933

133† 6d Fin Whale ('Whale') 32.00 42.00

1938

161† 5s Southern Sealion ('Sea Lion') 45.00 35.00

1952

184† 10s Southern Sealion ('Sea Lion'), South
     American Fur Seal ('Clapmatch') 19.00 30.00

1972

289   1p Southern Sealion
290   10p Southern Sealion

Set of 2   1.50   1.10

1974

296† 2p South American Fur Seal ('Fur Seal')   2.00   1.00

1975

320† 16p Southern Sealion ('Sea Lion') 1.75   2.75

1980

371   3p Peale's Dolphin ('Peale's Porpoise')
372   6p Commerson's Dolphin
373   7p Hourglass Dolphin ('Hour-glass
        Dolphin')
374   11p Spectacled Porpoise
375   15p Dusky Dolphin
376   25p Killer Whale

Set of 6   3.00   3.25

1982

424†   25p Falkland Island Wolf ('The Warrah')
         (now extinct)   65   75

1984

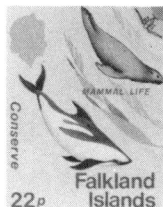

494† 22p Dusky Dolphin, Southern Sealion   . .   40   45

FALKLAND ISLANDS DEPENDENCIES

South Atlantic
100 pence = 1 pound

1982

98   5p Reindeer ("Introduced Reindeer during
       Calving – Spring")
99   13p Reindeer ("Bull at the Rut – Autumn")
100   25p Reindeer ("Reindeer and Mountains –
        Winter")
101   26p Reindeer ("Reindeer Feeding on
        Tussock Grass – Late Winter")

Set of 4   2.75   3.75

COLLECT BIRDS ON STAMPS

The first Stanley Gibbons thematic catalogue – a few
copies still available at £4.95 (p.+p. £1.30) plus FREE
1983–84 Supplement from:
Stanley Gibbons Publications Ltd, 5, Parkside,
Christchurch Road, Ringwood, Hants BH24 3SH.

FEDERATED MALAY STATES

South-east Asia
100 cents = 1 dollar

1900

Nos. 5/8, 10 and 12/14 of Negri Sembilan overprinted
FEDERATED MALAY STATES

1	1c Tiger	
2	2c Tiger	
3	3c Tiger	
4	5c Tiger	
5	10c Tiger	
6	20c Tiger	
7	25c Tiger	
8	50c Tiger	

Set of 8 £150 £200

Nos. 66 and 68 of Perak overprinted
FEDERATED MALAY STATES

9†	5c Tiger	14.00	25.00
10†	10c Tiger	24.00	30.00

15†	1c Tiger (black and green)	25	40
28†	1c Tiger (green)	60	45
52†	1c Tiger (brown)	2.50	2.25
53†	1c Tiger (black)	60	25
55†	2c Tiger (green)	45	15
54†	2c Tiger (brown)	3.75	2.50
16b†	3c Tiger (black and brown)	40	25
58†	3c Tiger (brown)	50	40
34†	3c Tiger (red)	1.75	10
35†	3c Tiger (grey)	1.50	45
57†	3c Tiger (green)	5.50	2.50
36a†	4c Tiger (black and red)	3.00	65
38†	4c Tiger (red)	80	25
60†	4c Tiger (orange)	40	15
39c†	5c Tiger (green and red on yellow)	2.25	1.50
61†	5c Tiger (mauve on yellow)	75	35
62†	5c Tiger (brown)	1.00	15
63†	6c Tiger (orange)	55	45
64†	6c Tiger (red)	65	15
41a†	8c Tiger (black and blue)	6.00	2.75
42†	8c Tiger (blue)	11.00	1.25
43a†	10c Tiger (black and mauve)	3.25	25
65†	10c Tiger (blue)	1.50	2.75
66†	10c Tiger (black and blue)	2.00	1.25
67†	10c Tiger (purple on yellow)	6.50	80
68†	12c Tiger (blue)	1.75	30
45†	20c Tiger (mauve and black)	2.00	45
70†	25c Tiger (purple and mauve)	3.00	1.25
71†	30c Tiger (purple and orange)	4.50	95
72†	35c Tiger (red on yellow)	7.00	9.00
73†	35c Tiger (red and purple)	15.00	15.00
74a†	50c Tiger (black and orange)	12.00	4.50
75†	50c Tiger (black on green)	5.50	2.75
77†	$1 Tiger (black and red on blue)	15.00	3.00
79†	$2 Tiger (green and red on yellow)	32.00	28.00
81†	$5 Tiger (green and red on green)	£110	£120

FERNANDO POO

Off West Africa
100 centavos = 1 peso

1960

233	10c + 5c Sperm Whale		
234	20c + 5c Humpback Whale		
235	30c + 10c Sperm Whale		
236	50c + 20c Humpback Whale		

Set of 4 50 20

1966

292	10c Greater White-nosed Monkey (*Cercopithecus nicticans*)		
293	40c Moustached Monkey (*Cercopithecus cephus*)		
294	1p50 Greater White-nosed Monkey		
295	4p Moustached Monkey		

Set of 4 60 25

1967

300	1p African Linsang (*Poiana richardsoni*)		
301	1p50 Western Needle-clawed Bushbaby (*Euoticus elegantulus*)		
302	3p50 Lord Derby's Flying Squirrel (*Anomalurus fraseri*)		

Set of 3 70 25

STANLEY GIBBONS
STAMP COLLECTING SERIES

Introductory booklets on *How to Start, How to Identify Stamps* and *Collecting by Theme.* A series of well illustrated guides at a low price.

Write for details.

FINLAND
Northern Europe
100 penni = 1 Finnish markka

1953

518	10m + 2m Eurasian Red Squirrel (*Sciurus vulgaris*)	
519	15m + 3m Brown Bear (*Ursus arctos*)	
520	25m + 5m Elk (*Alces alces*)	
	Set of 3	3.00 3.00

1957

575	10m + 2m Wolverine (*Gulo luscus*)	
576	20m + 3m Lynx (*Lynx lynx*)	
577	30m + 5m Reindeer (*Rangifer tarandus*)	
	Set of 3	2.40 2.40

1960

621† 10m + 2m Reindeer 90 90

1961

627	10m + 2m Muskrat (*Ondatra zibethica*)	
628	20m + 3m European Otter (*Lutra lutra*)	
629	30m + 5m Ringed Seal (*Phoca hispida*)	
	Set of 3	2.10 2.10

1962

642	10m + 2m Brown Hare (*Lepus europaeus*)	
643	20m + 3m Pine Marten (*Martes martes*)	
644	30m + 5m Stoat (*Mustela erminea*)	
	Set of 3	2.10 2.10

1982

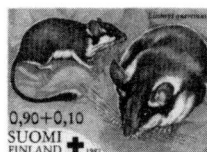

1034	90p + 10p Garden Dormouse (*Eliomys quercinus*)	
1035	1m10 + 15p Siberian Flying Squirrel (*Pteromys volans*)	
1036	1m20 + 20p European Mink (*Mustela lutreola*)	
	Set of 3	1.60 1.50

1037† 90p Red Deer, Red Fox, Arctic Hare .. 25 10

FRANCE
Western Europe
100 centimes =1 franc

1969

1847 45c Mouflon ('Mouflon Mediterranean') .. 30 20

1971

1921   65c Chamois ('Isard') 35   20

1972

1958†   1f Red Deer 50   10

1973

2002†   40c Guadeloupe Racoon ('Raton Laveur
        de la Guadeloupe')   30   15

1974

2046   40c European Bison ('Bison d'Europe')
2047   65c Giant Armadillo ('Tatou Geant de la
       Guyane')
                          Set of 2   60   25

STAMP MONTHLY

– finest and most informative magazine for all collectors.
Obtainable from your newsagent or by postal subscription – details on request

---

FRENCH CONGO
North West Africa
100 centimes = 1 franc

1900

36†	1c Leopard	. . . .	15	15
37†	2c Leopard	. . . .	15	15
38†	4c Leopard	. . . .	20	15
39†	5c Leopard	. . . .	40	15
40†	10c Leopard	. . . .	1.00	45
41†	15c Leopard	. . . .	35	20

FRENCH EQUATORIAL AFRICA
Central Africa
100 centimes = 1 franc

1947

235†	10c Black Rhinoceros	. . . .	10	10
236†	30c Black Rhinoceros	. . . .	10	10
237†	40c Black Rhinoceros	. . . .	10	10

1957

288   1f Giant Eland ('Elan de Derby')
289   2f Lion
290   3f African Elephant ('Elephant')
291   4f Greater Kudu ('Grand Koudou')
                          Set of 4   50   20

FRENCH GUIANA
South America
100 centimes = 1 franc

1904

58†	1c Giant Anteater	10	10
59†	2c Giant Anteater	10	10
60†	4c Giant Anteater	10	10
61†	5c Giant Anteater (green)	15	10
83†	5c Giant Anteater (orange)	10	10
62†	10c Giant Anteater (red)	10	10
84†	10c Giant Anteater (green)	10	10
104†	10c Giant Anteater (orange)	10	10
63†	15c Giant Anteater	25	20

1915
No. 62 surcharged with red cross over 5

81	10c + 5c Giant Anteater	3.50	3.50

No. 62 surcharged and red cross beside 5c

82	10c + 5c Giant Anteater	15	15

1922
No. 63 surcharged

89†	0.01 on 15c Giant Anteater	10	10
90†	0.02 on 15c Giant Anteater	10	10
91†	0.04 on 15c Giant Anteater	10	10
92†	0.05 on 15c Giant Anteater	10	10
95†	25c on 15c Giant Anteater	10	10

FRENCH MOROCCO
North-west Africa
100 centimes = 1 franc

1939

228†	70c Scimitar Oryx	10	10
301†	4f50 Scimitar Oryx	10	10
247†	5f Scimitar Oryx	15	10
248†	10f Scimitar Oryx	20	20
305†	15f Scimitar Oryx	35	30
250†	20f Scimitar Oryx	40	40
307†	25f Scimitar Oryx	50	50

1947
No. 301 surcharged JOURNEE DU TIMBRE 1947 +5F50

316	4f50 + 5f50 Scimitar Oryx	35	35

1948
No. 250 surcharged

352	8f on 20f Scimitar Oryx	20	15

FRENCH SOMALI COAST
East Africa
100 centimes = 1 franc

1958

432†	30c Warthog ('Phacochere')	10	10
433†	40c Cheetah ('Guepard')	15	10
434†	50c Gerenuk ('Gazelle-Chameau')	20	15
447†	100f Bohar Reedbuck ('Gazelles') (air)	1.90	1.10

1962

455†	4f Large-toothed Rock Hyrax ('Daman')	70	35
457†	25f Fennec Fox ('Fennecs')	1.75	1.40
459†	50f Klipspringer ('Oreotraque')	3.25	2.75

FRENCH SOUTHERN AND ANTARCTIC TERRITORIES
Antarctica and nearby islands
100 centimes =1 franc

1956

7†	4f Leopard Seal ('Leopard de Mer')	3.50	3.50
8†	5f Kerguelen Fur Seal	1.00	3.00
9†	8f Kerguelen Fur Seal	7.00	9.00
10†	10f Southern Elephant-Seal	1.50	5.50
12†	15f Southern Elephant-Seal	1.75	5.50
14†	25f Kerguelen Fur Seal ('Otarie de Kerguelen')	30.00	18.00

1963

26†	5f Blue Whale ('Grande Baleine Bleue') ..	5.00	5.00
27†	8f Southern Elephant-Seal ('Combat d'Elephant de Mer')	4.00	3.00
30†	15f Killer Whale ('Orque')	20.00	17.00

1976

100†	90c Kerguelen Fur Seal ('Otarie Femelle')	4.00	3.00
101†	1f Weddell Seal ('Phoque de Weddell') ..	6.50	6.50

1977

113	1f10 Blue Whale ('Rorqual Bleu')		
114	1f50 Commerson's Dolphin ('Dauphin de Commerson')		
	Set of 2	5.00	4.25

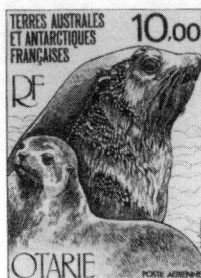

125†	10f Kerguelen Fur Seal ('Otarie')	7.50	7.50

STAMP MONTHLY
– finest and most informative magazine for all collectors. Obtainable from your newsagent or by postal subscription – details on request

1979

131†	4f Kerguelen Fur Seal (as No. 125)	1.60	1.60
132†	10f Southern Elephant-Seal ('Elephant de Mer')	4.00	4.00
	(130/2 Set of 3)	5.75	5.75

1980

152†	1f30 Leopard Seal ('Leopard de Mer') ..	60	50
153†	1f80 Leopard Seal	80	60

1984

184†	60c Crabeater Seal ('Phoque Crabier') ..	40	40
187†	5f90 Crabeater Seal	1.60	1.60

1985

198†	70c Mouflon	12	10

1973

200 1f80 Humpback Whale
201 5f20 Humpback Whale
                              Set of 2   1.25   1.10

587 30f Gemsbok (*Oryx beisa*)
588 50f Salt's Dik-Dik (*Madoqua saltiana*)
590 66f Caracal (*Felis caracal*)
                              Set of 3   3.00   2.10

205 30f Fur Seal sp. 5.25   4.50

FRENCH TERRITORY OF THE AFARS AND THE ISSAS

East Africa
100 centimes = 1 franc

1967

603 20f Olive Baboon (*Papio anubis*)
604 50f Large-spotted Genet (*Genetta tigrina*)
605 66f Abyssinian Hare (*Lepus habessinicus*)
                              Set of 3   2.50   1.75

508† 60f Unstriped Ground Squirrel (*Xerus rutilus*) 4.75   3.25

1975

641 50f White-tailed Mongoose (*Ichneumia albicauda*)
642 60f North African Crested Porcupine (*Hystrix galeata ambigua*)
643 70f Zorilla (*Ictonyx striatus*)
                              Set of 3   3.00   1.90

1971

566† 60f Dugong (*Halicore dugong*) 1.10   80

STANLEY GIBBONS STAMP COLLECTING SERIES

Introductory booklets on *How to Start, How to Identify Stamps* and *Collecting by Theme*. A series of well illustrated guides at a low price.
Write for details.

659   15f Savanna Monkey (*Cercopithecus aethiops*)
660   200f Aardvark (*Orycteropus afer*)
                    Set of 2   2.50   1.90

1976

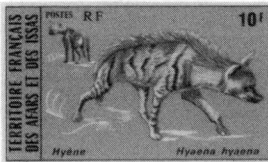

662   10f Striped Hyena (*Hyaena hyaena*)
663   15f African Ass (*Equus asinus somalicus*)
664   30f Beira Antelope (*Dorcatracus megalotis*)
                    Set of 3   80   60

FRENCH WEST AFRICA

West Africa
100 centimes = 1 franc

1947

41†   1f20 Hippopotamus   20   20

1955

82   5f Chimpanzee ('Chimpanze')
83   8f Giant Ground Pangolin ('Pangolin')
                    Set of 2   1.00   50

FUJEIRA

Arabia
1964 100 naye paise = 1 rupee
1967 100 dirhams = 1 riyal

1964

2†	2np Arabian Oryx	10	10
4†	4np Asiatic Wild Ass	10	10
7†	15np Leopard	10	10
8†	20np Dromedary	10	10
11†	50np Arabian Oryx	20	10
13†	1r Asiatic Wild Ass	35	15
16†	3r Leopard	1.00	50
17†	5r Dromedary	1.75	85

1965
Designs as Nos. 2/17, but inscribed "AIR MAIL"

40†	25np Arabian Oryx	10	10
42†	50np Asiatic Wild Ass	20	10
45†	2r Leopard	65	30
46†	3r Dromedary	1.00	45

1967
Various stamps with currency names changed by overprinting to dirhams or riyals

86†	2d on 2np Arabian Oryx (No. 2)	10	10
88†	4d on 4np Asiatic Wild Ass (No. 4)	10	10
91†	15d on 15np Leopard (No. 7)	10	10
92†	20d on 20np Dromedary (No. 8)	10	10
95†	50d on 50np Arabian Oryx (No. 11) . .	20	20
97†	1r on 1r Asiatic Wild Ass (No. 13)	35	35
100†	3r on 3r Cheetah (No. 16)	1.00	1.00
101†	5r on 5r Dromedary (No. 17)	1.75	1.75
124†	25d on 25np Arabian Oryx (No. 40) (air). .	10	10
126†	50d on 50np Asiatic Wild Ass (No. 42) . .	20	20
129†	2r on 2r Leopard (No. 45)	65	65
130†	3r on 3r Dromedary (No. 46)	1.00	1.00

OFFICIAL STAMPS

1965

O49†	40np Arabian Oryx	15	10
O51†	75np Asiatic Wild Ass	35	20
O54†	2r Leopard (air)	90	45
O55†	3r Dromedary	1.40	65

1967
Various stamps with currency names changed by overprinting to dirhams or riyals

O159†	40d on 40np Arabian Oryx (No. O49) . .	15	15
O161†	75d on 75np Asiatic Wild Ass (No. O51)	35	35
O164†	2r on 2r Leopard (No. O54)	90	90
O165†	3r on 3r Dromedary (No. O55)	1.40	1.40

Appendix
The following stamps have either been issued in excess of postal needs, or have not been made available to the public in reasonable quantities at face value. Miniature sheets, imperforate stamps etc., are excluded from this section.

1969

Wild Animals (Zebra, Hyena, Rhinoceros, Leopard, Gorilla, Giraffe, Tiger, Elephant, Lion). Postage 15, 25, 50, 75d, 1r; Air 1r50, 2, 3, 5r.

1971

Wild Animals (Orang-Utan, Kudu, Rhinoceros, Cheetah, Zebra). 20, 40, 60d, 1, 2r.

Monkeys (Various species). 30, 70d, 1, 2, 3r.

Wild Animals (Speke's Gazelle, Sloth Bear, Rhinoceros, Leopard, Koala). 30, 70d, 1, 2, 3r.

GABON

West Africa
100 centimes = 1 franc

1964

212†	60f Gorilla ('Gorille')	70	40
213†	80f African Buffalo ('Buffles')	85	65
	(211/3 *Set of* 3)	2.00	1.25

1967

275†	1f Hippopotamus ('Hippopotames')	10	10
277†	3f Water Chevrotain ('Chevrotain		
	Aquatiques')	10	10
278†	5f Chimpanzee ('Chimpanzes')	15	10
279†	10f African Elephant ('Elephants')	25	15
280†	20f Leopard ('Pantheres')	35	15
	(275/80 *Set of* 6)	1.00	60

STANLEY GIBBONS
STAMP COLLECTING SERIES

Introductory booklets on *How to Start, How to Identify Stamps* and *Collecting by Theme*. A series of well illustrated guides at a low price.

Write for details.

1970

399	5f Bushbuck ('Guib Harnache')		
400	15f Pel's Flying Squirrel ('Ecureuil Volant')		
401	25f White-cheeked Mangabey ('Cercocebe		
	A Joues Grises (Singe)')		
402	40f African Golden Cat ('Chat Dore')		
403	60f Servaline Genet ('Genette Servaline')		
	Set of 5	2.40	1.50

1974

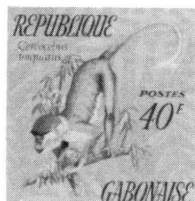

513	40f White-collared Mangabey (*Cercocebus torquatus*)		
514	60f Moustached Monkey (*Cercopithecus cephus*)		
515	80f Mona Monkey (*Cercopithecus mona nigripes*)		
	Set of 3	1.60	80

1978

676†	100f Gorilla	1.00	60

1983

840†	90f African Buffalo ('Buffles')	40	20

849† 90f Water Chevrotain ('Chevrotain
      ' Aquatique')   40   20
851† 225f African Elephant ('Elephant') 1.00   65

GALAPAGOS ISLANDS

Pacific
100 centavos = 1 sucre

1957

1†   20c Californian Sealion ('Lobos Marinos') . .   20   10

GAMBIA

West Africa
1922 12 pence = 1 shilling
20 shillings = 1 pound
1971 100 bututs = 1 dalasy

1922

122 ½d African Elephant
124 1d African Elephant
125 1½d African Elephant
126 2d African Elephant
127 2½d African Elephant
128 3d African Elephant
118 4d African Elephant
130 5d African Elephant
131 6d African Elephant
119 7½d African Elephant
133 10d African Elephant
134 1s African Elephant
135 1s6d African Elephant
136 2s African Elephant
137 2s6d African Elephant
138 3s African Elephant
140 4s African Elephant
141 5s African Elephant
142 10s African Elephant
                         Set of 19   £120   £180

1938

150   ½d African Elephant
151   1d African Elephant
152a 1½d African Elephant (pink and red)
152b 1½d African Elephant (blue and black)
153   2d African Elephant (blue and black)
153a 2d African Elephant (pink and red)
154   3d African Elephant
154a 5d African Elephant
155   6d African Elephant
156   1s African Elephant
156a 1s3d African Elephant
157   2s African Elephant
158   2s6d African Elephant
159   4s African Elephant
160   5s African Elephant
161   10s African Elephant
                      Set of 16   45.00   38.00

1953

As 1938 issue but with portrait of Queen Elizabeth II
185† £1 African Elephant 13.00   16.00

1976

356   10b Serval ('Serval Cat')
357   20b Bushbuck ('Harnessed Antelope')
358   50b Sitatunga
359   1d25 Leopard
                         Set of 4   5.00   2.75

1977

384† 10b Lesser Kudu   15   10

GERMANY
West Germany
100 pfenninge = 1 deutschmark

1958

1206   10p Giraffe, Lion   50   50

1966

1416   10p + 5p Roe Deer ('Rehbock')
1417   20p + 10p Chamois ('Gemse')
1418   30p + 15p Fallow Deer ('Damhirsch')
1419   50p + 25p Red Deer ('Rothirsch')
                                 Set of 4   1.50   1.50

1967

1434   10p + 5p Common Rabbit ('Kaninchen')
1435   20p + 10p Stoat ('Wiesel')
1436   30p + 15p Common Hamster ('Hamster')
1437   50p + 25p Red Fox ('Fuchs')
                                 Set of 4   2.00   2.00

1968

1454   10p + 5p Wild Cat ('Wildkatze')
1455   20p + 10p European Otter ('Fischotter')
1456   30p + 15p Eurasian Badger ('Dachs')
1457   50p + 25p Eurasian Beaver ('Biber')
                                 Set of 4   3.50   4.00

West Berlin
100 pfenninge = 1 deutschmark

1966
As No. 1416/19 of Germany (West Germany), but inscribed
"BERLIN"
B285   10p + 5p Roe Deer ('Rehbock')
B286   20p + 10p Chamois ('Gemse')
B287   30p + 15p Fallow Deer ('Damhirsch')
B288   50p + 25p Red Deer ('Rothirsch')
                                 Set of 4   1.75   1.50

1967
As No. 1434/7 of Germany (West Germany), but inscribed
"BERLIN"
B293   10p + 5p Common Rabbit ('Kaninchen')
B294   20p + 10p Stoat ('Wiesel')
B295   30p + 15p Common Hamster ('Hamster')
B296   50p + 25p Red Fox ('Fuchs')
                                 Set of 4   1.75   1.50

1968
As No. 1454/7 of Germany (West Germany), but inscribed
"BERLIN"
B310   10p + 5p Wild Cat ('Wildkatze')
B311   20p + 10p European Otter ('Fischotter')
B312   30p + 15p Eurasian Badger ('Dachs')
B313   50p + 25p Eurasian Beaver ('Biber')
                                 Set of 4   2.75   2.25

1969

MSB332   10p Orang-Utan; 30p Gaur; 50p
         Common Zebra ('Zebra') 2.10   2.10
The fourth design in this miniature sheet shows Pelicans.

East Germany
100 pfenninge = 1 mark

1953

E145   24p Lion   75   50

STAMP MONTHLY
– finest and most informative magazine for all collectors.
Obtainable from your newsagent or by postal subscription – details on request

1956

E287†	5p Indian Elephant	10	10
E289†	15p Black Rhinoceros	2.50	1.75
E290†	20p Mouflon	15	10
E291†	25p European Bison	20	10
E292†	30p Polar Bear	20	15
	(E287/92 Set of 6)	3.00	2.10

1959

E425†	25p Eurasian Beaver ('Biber')	20	10

E470	5p Eurasian Red Squirrel ('Eichhornchen')	
E471	10p Brown Hare ('Hase')	
E472	20p Roe Deer ('Reh')	
E473	25p Red Deer ('Hirsch')	
E474	40p Lynx ('Luchs')	
	Set of 5	3.00	2.00

1961

E560	10p Common Zebra	
E561	20p Eastern Black-and-White Colobus	
	Set of 2	2.25	1.25

1962

E609†	10p Weasel (Mustela nivalis)	10	10
E610†	20p Eurasian Common Shrew (Soricidae)	15	10
E611†	40p Common Long-eared Bat (Chiroptera)	25	25

1963

E670†	20p Red Fox (Silver Fox race)	15	10

E703†	70p West European Hedghog (Erinaceus europaeus)	25	25

1965

E811†	10p Giraffe	10	10
E813†	30p Black Wildebeest	50	45

1968

E1082†	40p Brown Hare (Lepus europaeus)	1.50	1.00

1970

E1263†	20p Red Fox ('Fuchs')	10	10
E1264†	25p European Mink ('Nerz')	70	70
E1265†	40p Common Hamster ('Hamster')	20	20
	(E1262/5 Set of 4)	1.00	1.00

1978

E1338† 10p Musk Ox (*Ovibos moschatus*) . . 10 10
E1340† 20p Addax (*Addax nasomaculatos*) . . 10 10
E1341† 25p Sun Bear (*Helarctos malayanus*) 80 80
(E1338/41 *Set of* 4) 1.00 1.00

E2037 10p Lion (*Panthera leo*)
E2038 20p Leopard (*Panthera pardus*)
E2039 35p Tiger (*Panthera tigris*)
E2040 50p Snow Leopard (*Uncia uncia*)
Set of 4 1.60 1.60

1980

1975

E1746† 10p Orang-Utan 10 10
E1747† 15p Ibex ('Sibirischer Steinbock') . . 10 10
E1748† 20p Indian Rhinoceros
('Panzernashorn') 15 10
E1749† 25p Pygmy Hippopotamus
('Zwergflusspferd') 15 10
E1750† 30p Grey Seal ('Kegelrobbe') 15 10
E1751† 35p Tiger ('Sibirischer Tiger') 25 15
E1752† 50p Common Zebra ('Bohm-Zebra') . . 1.75 1.75
(E1745/52 *Set of* 8) 2.50 2.40

E2241† 5p Okapi 10 10
E2242† 10p Lesser Panda ('Katzenbaren') . . 10 10
E2243† 15p Maned Wolf ('Mahnenwolf') 10 10
E2244† 20p Arabian Oryx ('Arabische Oryx-
Antilope') 15 10
E2246† 35p Musk Ox ('Moschusochsen') . . 1.25 1.25
(E2241/6 *Set of* 6) 1.50 1.40

1982

1977

E2386 10p Alpine Marmot ('Murmeltier')
E2387 20p Polecat ('Iltis')
E2388 25p European Mink ('Nerz')
E2389 35p Beech Marten ('Steinmarder')
Set of 4 1.25 1.25

E1985† 10p Mouflon 10 10
E1986† 15p Red Deer 2.00 2.00
E1988† 25p Red Fox 25 10
E1989† 35p Roe Deer 15 10
E1990† 70p Wild Boar 25 15
(E1985/90 *Set of* 6) 2.50 2.25

COLLECT BIRDS ON STAMPS

The first Stanley Gibbons thematic catalogue – a few copies still available at £4.95 (p.+p. £1.30) plus FREE 1983–84 Supplement from:
Stanley Gibbons Publications Ltd, 5, Parkside, Christchurch Road, Ringwood, Hants BH24 3SH.

GHANA
West Africa
1959 12 pence = 1 shilling
20 shillings = 1 pound
1965 100 pesewas = 1 cedi
1967 100 new pesewas = 1 new cedi
1972 100 pesewas = 1 cedi

1959

225a† £1 Red-fronted Gazelle 9.00   4.75

1963

306† 2s6d Topi   40   50

1964

357† 1d African Elephant   15   10
364† 2s6d Hippopotamus   .. .. ../ 2.25   4.00

1965
No. 225a surcharged **Ghana New Currency 19th July, 1965**
391† C2.40 on £1 Red-fronted Gazelle 5.50   9.00

1967
No. 225a surcharged
452† 2nc on £1 Red-fronted Gazelle 20.00   26.00

470   20np Bush Hare   20   5

492† 4np Leopard   25   10
495† 50np Waterbuck 3.00   4.25

1968

511† 5np North African Crested Porcupine
('Porcupine')   15   8

1969
No. 470 overprinted **NEW CONSTITUTION 1969**
551† 20np Bush Hare   35   40

1970

587† 12½np Lion ('Lioness')   85   45
589† 40np African Elephant ('Elephant') 2.75   3.00

1972

637† 15p Mona Monkey (*Cercopithecus mona*)   55   65
639† 1c De Winton's Tree Squirrel (*Funisciurus substriatus*) 3.75   5.00

1974

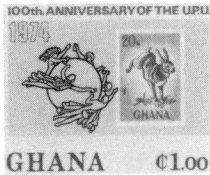

708† 1c Bush Hare (on stamp No. 470) 1.25   1.90
MS709 60p Bush Hare (on stamp No. 470) . . 2.00   2.50

1977

811 8p Olive Colobus
812 20p Temminck's Giant Squirrel ('Ebien Palm Squirrel')
813 30p Hunting Dog ('African Wild Dog')
814 60p African Manatee ('West African Manatee')
         Set of 4   5.75   4.00

1982

979† 20p African Clawless Otter ('Clawless Otter') 15   15
980† 65p Bushbuck 40   40
981† 80p Aardvark 50   50
MS985 5c Chimpanzee 2.50   3.25

994† 3c African Elephant 1.60   1.60

1983

1032 1c Short-finned Pilot Whale ('Short Fin Pilot Whale')
1033 1c40 Risso's Dolphin ('Grey Dolphin (Risso's)')
1034 2c30 False Killer Whale
1035 3c Spinner Dolphin
1036 5c Atlantic Hump-backed Dolphin ('Atlantic Humpback Dolphin')
         Set of 5   45   55
MS1037 6c Atlantic Hump-backed Dolphin . . 25   30

No. 470 surcharged
1031a 1c on 20np Bush Hare 10   5

1044† 3c White-collared Mangabey (*Cercocebus torquatus*) 12   15
1045† 4c Demidoff's Galago (*Galagiodes demidovi*) 15   20

1984

No. 994 surcharged
1071† 30c on 3c African Elephant 1.25   1.40

Nos. 1035/7 surcharged **19th U.P.U. CONGRESS — HAMBURG**
1093 10c on 3c Spinner Dolphin
1094 50c on 5c Atlantic Hump-backed Dolphin
         Set of 2   2.50   2.50
MS1095 60c on 6c Atlantic Hump-backed Dolphin   2.50   2.75

1114 1c Bongo
1115 2c Bongo
1116 3c Bongo
1117 20c Bongo
         Set of 4   95   1.00
MS1118 70c Kob 3.00   3.25

GIBRALTAR
South-west Europe
1960 12 pence = 1 shilling
20 shillings =1 pound
1971 100 pence = 1 pound

1960

169† 1s Barbary Ape ('Rock Ape') 1.25 45

GREAT BRITAIN
Western Europe
1966 12 pence = 1 shilling
20 shillings = 1 pound
1971 100 pence = 1 pound

1961

624† 3d Eurasian Red Squirrel 10 10

1963

638† 4½d Eurasian Badger, Roe Deer (fawn) .. 25 45

COLLECT BIRDS ON STAMPS
The first Stanley Gibbons thematic catalogue – a few
copies still available at £4.95 (p.+p. £1.30) plus FREE
1983–84 Supplement from:
Stanley Gibbons Publications Ltd, 5, Parkside,
Christchurch Road, Ringwood, Hants BH24 3SH.

1977

1039 9p West European Hedgehog
      ('Hedgehog')
1040 9p Brown Hare ('Hare')
1041 9p Eurasian Red Squirrel ('Red Squirrel')
1042 9p European Otter ('Otter')
1043 9p Eurasian Badger ('Badger')
                              Set of 5 1.40 1.40

Jersey

1971

59† 7½p Western Black-and-White Colobus
        ('Ursine Colobus Monkey') 13.00 4.75
60† 9p Ring-tailed Lemur 13.00 4.75

1972

73† 2½p Cheetah 50 15
75† 7½p Spectacled Bear 2.40 2.50

1979

218†	8p Orang-Utan	20	20
220†	13p Gorilla ('Lowland Gorilla')	35	35
221†	15p Rodriguez Flying Fox ('Rodrigues Fruit Bat')	40	40

1981

278†	18p Blue Whale	45	45

1984

324†	9p Golden Lion Tamarin	20	25
325†	12p Snow Leopard	30	30

GREECE
South-east Europe
100 lepta = 1 drachma

1970

1154†	8d Wild Goat (*Capra aegagrus cretensis*)	5.00	2.50

GREENLAND
North Atlantic
100 ore = 1 krone

1938

6†	30ore Polar Bear	10.00	9.00
6a†	40ore Polar Bear	35.00	7.00
7†	1k Polar Bear	12.00	9.00

1945

8†	1ore Harp Seal	35.00	27.00
9†	5ore Harp Seal	35.00	27.00
10†	7ore Harp Seal	35.00	27.00
14†	1k Polar Bear	35.00	27.00

Nos. 8/10 *and* 14 *overprinted* **DANMARK BEFRIET 5 MAJ 1945**

17†	1ore Harp Seal	50.00	35.00
18†	5ore Harp Seal	50.00	35.00
19†	7ore Harp Seal	50.00	35.00
23†	1k Polar Bear	70.00	45.00

1956
Nos. 6a *and* 7 *surcharged*

37	60ore on 40ore Polar Bear		
38	60ore on 1k Polar Bear		
		Set of 2 55.00	8.00

1963

56†	1k Polar Bear	1.00	50
57†	2k Polar Bear	3.00	1.00
58†	5k Polar Bear	3.00	1.00
59†	10k Polar Bear	3.00	1.50

STANLEY GIBBONS
STAMP COLLECTING SERIES

Introductory booklets on *How to Start, How to Identify Stamps* and *Collecting by Theme*. A series of well illustrated guides at a low price.
Write for details.

1969

69 1k Bowhead Whale (tail only)
70 2k Narwhal
71 5k Polar Bear
72 10k Walrus
73 25k Musk Ox

Set of 5 10.00 4.00

1981

130 1k60 + 20ore Wolf 60 60

131 3k50 Reindeer
132 5k Walrus

Set of 2 1.50 1.50

1982

134 2k70 Walrus 50 50

136† 2k Bowhead Whale 40 40

1984

144 3k70 Polar Bear 75 50

145† 2k70 Bowhead Whale 50 50

GRENADA
West Indies
100 cents = 1 dollar

1968

315† 25c Greater Trinidadian Murine Opossum
      (*Marmosa chapmani*) 40 20
316† 35c Nine-banded Armadillo (*Dasypus*) . . 45 20
317† 50c Mona Monkey (*Cercopithecus mona*) 60 25

1972
No. 315 overprinted **VOTE FEB 28 1972**
481 25c Greater Trinidadian Murine Opossum 40 50

Nos. 315/17 overprinted **AIR MAIL**
505† 25c Greater Trinidadian Murine Opossum 30 20
507† 35c Nine-banded Armadillo 35 25
510† 50c Mona Monkey 45 35

1973

549† 35c Brazilian Tapir (*Tapirus terrestris*) . . 80 65
551† 70c Ocelot (*Felis pardalis*) 1.50 1.50

1974
Nos. 315/16 overprinted **INDEPENDENCE 7TH FEB. 1974**
601† 25c Greater Trinidadian Murine Opossum 45 35
602† 35c Nine-banded Armadillo 75 50

1975

713†	½c Eurasian Red Squirrel	10	5

1976

GRENADA

762†	1c Brazilian Agouti ('Orange-rumped Agouti')	10	5
767†	$2 Nine-banded Armadillo ('Antillean Armadillo')	4.00	2.50

1982

1232	15c Killer Whale		
1233	40c Sperm Whale		
1234	70c Blue Whale		
1235	$3 Common Dolphin		
	Set of 4	2.40	2.40
MS1236	$5 Humpback Whale	2.50	2.75

GRENADINES OF GRENADA
West Indies
100 cents = 1 dollar

1974
No. 315 of Grenada overprinted **GRENADINES**

11†	25c Greater Trinidadian Murine Opossum (*Marmosa chapmani*)	20	15

1982

537	10c Short-finned Pilot Whale ('Pilot Whale')		
538	60c Dall's Porpoise ('Dall Porpoise')		
539	$1.10 Humpback Whale		
540	$3 Bowhead Whale ('Bowfin Whale')		
	Set of 4	3.00	3.00
MS541	$5 Spotted Dolphin	2.50	2.75

1983

MS551	$5 Bottle-nosed Dolphin	2.75	3.00

1984
No. MS551 *overprinted* **OPENING OF POINT SALINE INT'L AIRPORT**

MS638	$5 Bottle-nosed Dolphin	3.25	3.50

GRENADINES OF ST. VINCENT
West Indies
100 cents = 1 dollar

1979

150†	40c Common Opossum ('Manicou') . .	20	20

STAMP MONTHLY
– finest and most informative magazine for all collectors. Obtainable from your newsagent or by postal subscription – details on request

1980

163 10c False Killer Whale
164 50c Spinner Dolphin
165 90c Bottle-nosed Dolphin ('Bottled Nosed Dolphin')
166 $2 Short-finned Pilot Whale ('Blackfish')
Set of 4   1.50   1.25

GUATEMALA
Central America
100 centavos = 1 quetzal

1979

1125† 3c White-tailed Deer ('Venado de Cola Blanca')   25   10
1128† 9c Ocelot ('Tigrillo')   55   10

GUINEA
West Africa
1959 100 centimes = 1 franc
1973 100 caury = 1 syli

1959

206† 15f African Elephant   30   15
208† 25f African Elephant   60   20

COLLECT BIRDS ON STAMPS
The first Stanley Gibbons thematic catalogue – a few copies still available at £4.95 (p.+p. £1.30) plus FREE 1983–84 Supplement from:
Stanley Gibbons Publications Ltd, 5, Parkside, Christchurch Road, Ringwood, Hants BH24 3SH.

1961

268 5f Bohar Reedbuck
269 10f Bohar Reedbuck
270 25f Bohar Reedbuck
271 40f Bohar Reedbuck
272 50f Bohar Reedbuck
273 75f Bohar Reedbuck
Set of 6   2.75   1.00

Nos. 268/73 surcharged **POUR LA PROTECTION DE NOS ANIMAUX + 5 FRS**
283 5f + 5f Bohar Reedbuck
284 10f + 5f Bohar Reedbuck
285 25f + 5f Bohar Reedbuck
286 40f + 5f Bohar Reedbuck
287 50f + 5f Bohar Reedbuck
288 75f + 5f Bohar Reedbuck
Set of 6   3.50   2.00

1962

326 10f Hippopotamus ('Hippopotame')
327 25f Lion
328 30f Leopard ('Panthere')
329 50f Hippopotamus
330 75f Lion
331 100f Leopard
Set of 6   4.00   1.75

1964

447 5f Striped Hyena (*Hyaena hyaena*)
448 30f Striped Hyena
449 40f African Buffalo (*Syncerus caffer*)
450 75f African Elephant (*Loxodonta africana*)
451 100f African Elephant
452 300f African Buffalo
Set of 6   5.00   2.75

1967

| 610† | 30f African Elephant | 50 | 50 |
| 612† | 200f African Elephant (air) | 1.50 | 1.00 |

1968

652†	30f African Buffalo	20	10
653†	40f Leopard	30	20
655†	70f Hippopotamus (air)	50	20
656†	300f Lion	2.25	1.10

658†	5f Olive Baboon (*Papio anubis*)	10	8
659†	10f Leopard (*Acinonyx jubatus*) (latin name on stamp erroneous)	15	8
660†	15f Hippopatamus (*Hippopotamus amphibius*)	20	15
662†	30f Warthog (*Phacochoerus aethiopicus*)	40	20
663†	50f Kob (*Kobus kob*)	50	25
664†	75f African Buffalo (*Syncerus caffer*)	70	45
665†	100f Lion (*Felis leo*) (air)	95	40
666†	200f African Elephant (*Loxodonta africana*)	1.90	90
	(658/66 *Set of* 9)	4.75	2.40

1969

689	25f Chimpanzee ("Tarzan")
690	30f Chimpanzee ("Tarzan")
691	75f Chimpanzee ("Tarzan et famille")
692	100f Chimpanzee ("Tarzan")

Set of 4   2.00   1.00

1975

871	1s Chimpanzee (*Pan troglodytes*)
872	2s Impala (*Aepyceros melampus*)
873	3s Warthog (*Phacochoeros aethiopicus*)
874	4s Waterbuck (*Kobus defassa*)
875	5s Leopard (*Panthera pardus*)
876	6s Greater Kudu (*Tragelaphus strepsiceros*)
877	6s50 Common Zebra (*Equus quagga granti*)
878	7s50 African Buffalo (*Syncerus caffer*)
879	8s Hippopotamus (*Hippopotamus amphibius*)
880	10s Lion (*Panthera leo*)
881	12s Black Rhinoceros (*Diceros bicornis*)
882	15s African Elephant (*Loxodonta africana*)

Set of 12   5.00   3.00

884	5s Lion
885	7s African Elephant
886	10s Lion
887	20s African Elephant

Set of 4   3.00   1.50

1977

948 1s Eland (*Taurotragus oryx*) (lying down)
949 1s Eland (*Taurotragus oryx*) (grazing)
950 1s Eland (*Taurotragus oryx*) (facing left)
951 2s Chimpanzee (*Pan troglodytes*) (hanging on one arm)
952 2s Chimpanzee (*Pan troglodytes*) (with arms up)
953 2s Chimpanzee (*Pan troglodytes*) (sitting)
954 2s50 African Elephant (*Loxodonta africana cyclotis*) (facing right)
955 2s50 African Elephant (*Loxodonta africana cyclotis*) (front view)
956 2s50 African Elephant (*Loxodonta africana cyclotis*) (facing left)
957 3s Lion (*Panthera leo*) (standing)
958 3s Lion (*Panthera leo*) (lioness)
959 3s Lion (*Panthera leo*) (lioness at rest)
960 4s Indian Palm Squirrel (*Funambulus palmarum*) (facing right)
961 4s Indian Palm Squirrel (*Funambulus palmarum*) (facing left)
962 4s Indian Palm Squirrel (*Funambulus palmarum*) (at rest)
963 5s Hippopotamus (*Hippopotamus amphibius*) (feeding)
964 5s Hippopotamus (*Hippopotamus amphibius*) (swimming)
965 5s Hippopotamus (*Hippopotamus amphibius*) (head)

966 5s Eland (air)
967 5s Eland
968 5s Eland
969 8s African Elephant
970 8s African Elephant
971 8s African Elephant
972 9s Hippopotamus
973 9s Hippopotamus
974 9s Hippopotamus
975 10s Chimpanzee
976 10s Chimpanzee
977 10s Chimpanzee
978 12s Indian Palm Squirrel
979 12s Indian Palm Squirrel
980 12s Indian Palm Squirrel
981 13s Lion
982 13s Lion
983 13s Lion

Set of 36 18.00 6.00

STAMP MONTHLY

– finest and most informative magazine for all collectors. Obtainable from your newsagent or by postal subscription – details on request

GUINEA–BISSAU
West Africa
100 cents = 1 peso

1983

735 1p Hamadryas Baboon (*Comopithecus hamadryas*)
736 1p50 Gorilla (*Gorilla gorilla*)
737 3p50 Gelada (*Theropithecus gelada*)
738 5p Mandrill (*Mandrillus sphinx*)
739 8p Chimpanzee (*Pan troglodytes*)
740 20p Eastern Black-and-White Colobus (*Colobus abyssinicus*)
741 30p Diana Monkey (*Ceropithecus diana*)
Set of 7 5.00 50

1984

857 3p Tiger (*Panthera tigris*)
858 6p Lion (*Panthera leo*)
859 10p Clouded Leopard (*Neofelis nebulosa*)
860 12p Cheetah (*Acinonyx jubatus*)
861 15p Lynx (*Lynx lynx*)
862 35p Leopard (*Panthera pardus*)
863 40p Snow Leopard (*Uncia uncia*)
Set of 7 3.00 45

882 5p Grey Whale (*Eschrichtius gibbosus*)
883 8p Blue Whale (*Balaenoptera musculus*)
884 15p Bottle-nosed Dolphin (*Tursiops truncatus*)
885 20p Sperm Whale (*Physeter macrocephalus*)
886 24p Killer Whale (*Orcinus orca*)
887 30p Bowhead Whale (*Balaena mysticetus*)
888 35p Sei Whale (*Balaenoptera borealis*)
Set of 7 3.50 50

GUYANA
South America
100 cents = 1 dollar

1968

458†	50c Brazilian Agouti ('Accouri')	70	40
496†	60c White-lipped Peccary ('Peccary') ..	55	55
497†	$1 Paca ('Labba')	85	95
498†	$2 Nine-banded Armadillo ('Armadillo') ..	3.50	4.50
499†	$5 Ocelot	7.50	9.50

1978

685†	8c American Manatee ('Manatee')	15	5

1981

756	30c Brazilian Tree Porcupine ('Tree Porcupine')	
757	30c Red Howler ('Howler Monkey')	
758	30c Common Squirrel-Monkey ('Squirrel Monkey')	
759	30c Two-toed Sloth	
760	30c Brazilian Tapir ('Tapir')	
761	30c Collared Peccary	
762	30c Six-banded Armadillo	
763	30c Tamandua ('Ant Eater')	
764	30c Giant Anteater	
765	30c Murine Opossum ('Mouse Opossum')	
766	30c Brown Four-eyed Opossum ('Four-eyed Opossum')	
767	30c Brazilian Agouti ('Orange-rumped Agouti')	
	Set of 12	2.10	2.10

1983
No. 762 overprinted 1983

1202†	30c Six-banded Armadillo	12	15

1984
Nos. 458 and 496/9 optd **Protecting our Heritage** and some surch also

1246†	60c White-lipped Peccary	25	30
1249†	$2 Nine-banded Armadillo	2.00	1.25
1251†	260c on $1 Paca	95	1.00
1254†	390c on 50c Brazilian Agouti	1.50	1.75
1255†	450c on $5 Ocelot	1.60	1.90

HONDURAS
Central America
100 centavos = 1 lempira

1976

885†	10c White-tailed Deer	15	10
889†	50c White-tailed Deer	80	30
893†	60c White-tailed Deer	70	40

HONG KONG
South-east coast of China
100 cents = 1 dollar

1968

245	10c Rhesus Macaque		
246	$1.30 Rhesus Macaque		
	Set of 2	9.50	4.75

1974

302	10c Tiger		
303	$1.30 Tiger		
	Set of 2	6.50	4.75

1982

411 20c Large Indian Civet ('Five-banded
         Civet')
412 $1 Chinese Pangolin ('Pangolin')
413 $1.30 Chinese Porcupine
414 $5 Indian Muntjac ('Barking Deer')
                        Set of 4   2.00   2.00

HUNGARY

Central Europe
100 filler = 1 forint

1953

1271 20fi Eurasian Red Squirrel ('Mokus')
1272 30fi West European Hedgehog ('Sun')
1273 40fi Brown Hare ('Mezei nyul')
1274 50fi Beech Marten ('Nyest')
1275 60fi European Otter ('Videa')
1276 70fi Red Fox ('Roka')
1277 80fi Fallow Deer ('Damszarvas')
1278 1fo Roe Deer ('Oz')
1279 1fo50 Wild Boar ('Vaddiszno')
1280 2fo Red Deer ('Gimszarvas')
                        Set of 10   8.00   5.00

1961

1716†	20fi Eastern Grey Kangaroo	15	10
1717†	30fi American Bison	20	10
1718†	40fi Brown Bear	30	10
1719†	60fi Indian Elephant	40	10
1720†	80fi Tiger	50	10
1721†	1fo Ibex	80	10
1722†	1fo40 Polar Bear	1.75	15
1723†	2fo Common Zebra	1.75	50
1724†	2fo60 European Bison	2.00	80
	(1716/25 Set of 10)	7.00	2.00

1964

2035†	30fi Wild Boar (*Sus scrofa*)	15	10
2037†	60fi Brown Hare (*Lepus timidus*) (wrong latin name)	25	10
2038†	80fi Fallow Deer (*Dama dama*)	40	15
2039†	1fo Mouflon (*Ovis musimon*)	60	15
2040†	1fo70 Red Deer (*Cervus elaphus*)	1.00	20
2042†	2fo50 Roe Deer (*Capreolus capreolus*)	1.50	30

1965

2128† 2fo + 1fo Red Deer (on stamp No. 1280)   1.40   1.40

1966

2205 20fi Red Fox (*Vulpes vulpes*)
2206 60fi Wild Boar (*Sus scrofa*)
2207 70fi Wild Cat (*Felis silvestris*)
2208 80fi Roe Deer (*Capreolus capreolus*)
2209 1fo50 Red Deer (*Cervus elaphus*)
2210 2fo50 Fallow Deer (*Dama dama*)
2211 3fo Mouflon (*Ovis musimon*)
                        Set of 7   3.50   1.00

COLLECT BIRDS ON STAMPS

The first Stanley Gibbons thematic catalogue – a few
copies still available at £4.95 (p.+p. £1.30) plus FREE
1983–84 Supplement from:
Stanley Gibbons Publications Ltd, 5, Parkside,
Christchurch Road, Ringwood, Hants BH24 3SH.

1971

2583†	40fi European Bison	.. ..	10	10
2584†	60fi Wild Boar	.. ..	10	10
2585†	80fi Red Deer	.. ..	30	10
2587†	1fo20 Red Deer	.. ..	60	25
MS2591	10fo Roe Deer	.. ..	4.50	4.50

1972

| 2659† | 40fi Brown Hare | .. .. | 10 | 10 |

1974

| 2935† | 40fi Red Colobus | .. .. | 10 | 10 |

1976

3014	40fi Wild Boar (Sus scrofa)		
3015	60fi Eurasian Red Squirrel (Sciurus vulgaris)		
3016	80fi Lynx (Lynx lynx)		
3017	1fo20 Wolf (Canis lupus)		
3018	2fo Red Fox (Vulpes vulpes)		
3019	4fo Brown Bear (Ursus arctos)		
3020	6fo Lion (Panthera leo)		
		Set of 7	3.25	75

1977

3155	40fi Lesser Panda (Ailurus fulgens)		
3156	60fi Giant Panda (Ailuropoda melanoleuca)		
3157	1fo Asiatic Black Bear (Selenarctos tibetanus)		
3158	4fo Polar Bear (Thalassarctos maritimus)		
3159	6fo Brown Bear (Ursus arctos)		
		Set of 5	4.50	1.00

1978

| 3195 | 3fo American Beaver (on Canada stamp No. 10) | .. .. | 2.00 | 2.00 |

1979

3274	40fi European Otter (Lutra lutra)		
3275	60fi Wild Cat (Felis silvestris)		
3276	1fo Pine Marten (Martes martes)		
3277	2fo Eurasian Badger (Meles meles)		
3278	4fo Steppe Polecat (Mustela eversmanni)		
3279	6fo Beech Marten (Marten foina)		
		Set of 6	4.50	1.00

STAMP MONTHLY

– finest and most informative magazine for all collectors. Obtainable from your newsagent or by postal subscription – details on request

1981

3359†	40fi Cheetah ('Gepard')	15	10
3360†	60fi Lion ('Oroszlan')	15	10
3361†	1fo Leopard	25	10
3362†	2fo Black Rhinoceros ('Orrszarvu') . .	50	15
3363†	3fo Greater Kudu ('Nagy Kudu')	60	20
3364†	4fo African Elephant ('Afrikai Elefant') . .	90	25
	(3359/65 Set of 7)	4.50	1.75

3367†	2fo Walrus	30	10

3380	2fo Red Deer	30	10

1984

MS3547	4fo Eastern Grey Kangaroo (on stamp No. 1716)	5.00	5.00

ICELAND
North Atlantic
100 aurar = 1 krona

1980

582†	90k Arctic Fox (*Alopex lagopus*)	25	25
585†	190k Common Seal (*Phoca vitulina*) . .	50	50

IFNI
North-west Africa
100 centimos = 1 peseta

1951

74	5c + 5c Fennec Fox
75	10c + 5c Fennec Fox
76	60c + 15c Fennec Fox

		Set of 3	50	20

1953

87	60c Addra Gazelle
88	1p20 Addra Gazelle
89	1p60 Addra Gazelle
90	2p Addra Gazelle
91	4p Addra Gazelle
92	10p Addra Gazelle

Set of 6	10.00	2.00

1955

123   5c + 5c Eurasian Red Squirrel
124   15c + 5c Eurasian Red Squirrel
125   70c Eurasian Red Squirrel
                              Set of 3   50   20

1956

130† 5c + 5c Bohar Reedbuck   10   10

1957

136   10c + 5c Golden Jackal ('Chacal (Canis)')
137   15c + 5c Golden Jackal ('Chacal (Canis)')
138   20c Golden Jackal
139   70c Golden Jackal
                              Set of 4   60   20

1960

157† 10c + 5c Dromedary   10   10
158† 15c + 5c Wild Boar   10   10
160† 80c Dromedary   30   15
                        (157/60 Set of 4)   60   40

1964

201   25c Edmi Gazelle
202   50c Roe Deer
203   1p Edmi Gazelle
                              Set of 3   50   20

INDIA
Southern Asia
1949 12 pies = 1 anna, 16 annas = 1 rupee
1957 100 naye paisa = 1 rupee
1964 100 paisa = 1 rupee

1949

309† 3p Indian Elephant   15   5

1962

449   15np Indian Rhinoceros   12   5

460   15np Indian Rhinoceros ('Rhino')   12   8

1963

472 10np Gaur
473 15np Lesser Panda ('Himalayan Panda')
474 30np Indian Elephant
475 50np Tiger
476 1r Lion ('Indian Lion')

		Set of 5	5.75	1.50

1965

508†	8p Spotted Deer ('Chital')	25	30

1969

603	20p Tiger	15	8

1974

(a) Values expressed with "p"

721†	15p Tiger	30	5
722†	25p Spotted Deer ('Chital')	45	5

(b) Values expressed as numericals only

730†	15p Tiger (as No. 721)	10	5

STANLEY GIBBONS
STAMP COLLECTING SERIES

Introductory booklets on *How to Start, How to Identify Stamps* and *Collecting by Theme*. A series of well illustrated guides at a low price.
Write for details.

1976

799	25p Tiger	25	10

825 25p Swamp Deer
826 50p Lion
827 1r Leopard
828 2r Caracal

		Set of 4	2.50	2.75

1982

1052	2r85 Red Deer ('Kashmir Stag')	30	35

1983

1086	1r Swamp Deer	12	15

अन्तर्राष्ट्रीय आयोग
लाओस

No. 309 of India overprinted as above, for use in Laos
N6† 3p Indian Elephant 12   45

1096 1r Golden Langur
1097 2r Liontail Macaque ('Lion Tailed
      Macaque')
                        Set of 2   35   45

अन्तर्राष्ट्रीय आयोग
कम्बोज

No. 309 of India overprinted as above, for use in Vietnam
N11† 3p Indian Elephant 12   45

1105 2r Tiger ("Project Tiger") 25   30

INDONESIA
South-east Asia
100 sen = 1 rupiah

1955

INDIAN CUSTODIAN FORCES IN KOREA
East Asia
12 pies = 1 anna, 16 annas = 1 rupee

1953

689† 75s + 25s Sika Deer 10   10

भारतीय
संरक्षा कटक
कोरिया

1956

No. 309 of India overprinted as above
K1† 3p Indian Elephant 20   55

713 5s Lesser Malay Chevrotain ('Kantjil')
714 10s Lesser Malay Chevrotain

INDIAN FORCES IN INDO–CHINA
South-east Asia
12 pies = 1 anna, 16 annas = 1 rupee

715 15s Lesser Malay Chevrotain
716 20s Hairy-nosed Otter ('Lingsang')
717 25s Hairy-nosed Otter
718 30s Hairy-nosed Otter

1954

719 35s Malayan Pangolin (Trenggiling')
720 40s Malayan Pangolin
721 45s Malayan Pangolin

अन्तर्राष्ट्रीय आयोग
वियत नाम

722 50s Banteng
723 60s Banteng
724 70s Banteng
725 75s Sumatran Rhinoceros ('Badak')
726 80s Sumatran Rhinoceros

No. 309 of India overprinted as above, for use in Cambodia
N1† 3p Indian Elephant 12   45

727 90s Sumatran Rhinoceros
                        Set of 15   1.50   75

1959

798†	10s Babirusa	10	10
799†	15s Anoa	10	10
800†	20s Orang-Utan ('Orangutan')	10	10
801†	50s Javan Rhinoceros ('Badak')	10	10
803†	1r Malayan Tapir ('Tapir')	15	10
	(798/803 *Set of* 6)	60	50

1977

1489	20r Proboscis Monkey (*Nasalis larvatus*)		
1490	40r Indian Elephant (*Elaphas indicus*)		
1491	100r Tiger (*Panthera tigris*)		
	Set of 3	1.60	1.25

1978

1515	40r Long-nosed Echidna (*Zaglosus bruijni*)		
1516	75r Sambar (*Cervus unicolor*)		
1517	100r Clouded Leopard (*Neofelis nebulosa*)		
	Set of 3	1.60	1.25

1979

1558†	60r Bottle-nosed Dolphin (*Tursiops aduncus*)	40	15
1559†	125r Irrawaddy Dolphin (*Orcaella brevirostris*)	60	25
	(1558/60 *Set of* 3)	1.50	75

IRAN

Western Asia
100 dinars = 1 rial

1974

1853†	1r Asiatic Wild Ass	15	15
1855†	6r Fallow Deer	25	20

IRAQ

Western Asia
1000 fils = 1 dinar

1969

829†	2f Striped Hyena (*Hyaena hyaena*)	15	15
830†	3f Leopard (*Panthera pardus*)	15	15
831†	5f Mountain Gazelle (*Gazella gazella*)	15	15

OFFICIAL STAMPS

1971
Nos. 829/30 *surcharged* **Official**

O985†	15f on 3f Leopard	1.25	80
O986†	25f on 2f Striped Hyena	1.25	80

STANLEY GIBBONS
STAMP COLLECTING SERIES

Introductory booklets on *How to Start, How to Identify Stamps* and *Collecting by Theme*. A series of well illustrated guides at a low price.
Write for details.

IRELAND
Western Europe
100 pence = 1 pound

1980

461   12p Stoat (*Mustela erminea hibernica*)
462   15p Arctic Hare (*Lepus timidus hibernicus*)
463   16p Red Fox (*Vulpes vulpes*)
464   25p Red Deer (*Cervus elaphus*)
                                    Set of 4   1.50   1.25

1983

564†   22p Bearded Seal   30   35

1967

374   12a Ibex (*Capra ibex*)
375   18a Caracal (*Felis caracal*)
376   60a Dorcas Gazelle (*Gazella dorcas*)
                                    Set of 3   50   40

1971

471   2a Fallow Deer (*Dama mesopotamica*)
472   3a Asiatic Wild Ass (*Equus hemionus*)
473   5a Arabian Oryx (*Oryx leucoryx*)
474   78a Cheetah (*Acinonyx jubatus*)
                                    Set of 4   50   40

ISRAEL
Western Asia
1950 1000 prutot = 1 pound
1960 1000 agorot = 1 pound
1980 1000 agorot = 1 shekel

1950

53   500p Dromedary 9.00   7.00

STAMP MONTHLY
– finest and most informative magazine for all collectors.
Obtainable from your newsagent or by postal subscription – details on request

ITALIAN EAST AFRICA
East Africa
100 centisimi = 1 lira

1938

1†   2c Grant's Gazelle   10   10
8†   30c Grant's Gazelle   10   10
17†   3li70 Grant's Gazelle 2.00   2.50

ITALY
Southern Europe
100 centisimi = 1 lira

IVORY COAST
West Africa
100 centimes =1 franc

1967

1177   20li Ibex
1178   40li Brown Bear
1179   90li Red Deer
1180   170li Fallow Deer

Set of 4   1.00   40

1978

1548†   170li Mediterranean Monk Seal
(Monachus monachus)   50   10

1984

1834†   450li Eurasian Badger, Wild Boar,
Eurasian Red Squirrel   65   45
1836†   450li Common Rabbit   65   45

COLLECT BIRDS ON STAMPS
The first Stanley Gibbons thematic catalogue – a few copies still available at £4.95 (p.+p. £1.30) plus FREE 1983–84 Supplement from:
Stanley Gibbons Publications Ltd, 5, Parkside, Christchurch Road, Ringwood, Hants BH24 3SH.

1959

†80   10f African Elephant ('Elephant')
181   25f African Elephant
182   30f African Elephant

Set of 3   1.00   50

1963

227   1f Yellow-backed Duiker (Cephalophus
sylvicultor)
228   2f Potto (Perodicticus potto)
229   4f Beecroft's Hyrax (Dendrohyrax dorsalis)
230   5f Water Chevrotain (Hyemoschus
aquaticus)
247   5f African Manatee ('Lamantin')
231   10f Hartebeest (Alcelaphus major)
248   10f Pygmy Hippopotamus ('Hippopotame
Nain')
232   15f Giant Forest Hog ('Hylochere')
249   15f Royal Antelope ('Antelope Royal')
233   20f Warthog (Phacochoerus aethiopicus)
234   25f Bongo (Boocercus euryceros)
235   45f Hunting Dog (Lycaon pictus)
236   50f Western Black-and-White Colobus
(Colobus polycomos)

Set of 13   6.00   2.50

1968

311   30f Impala   60   30

1970

340   30f Impala, Lion   60   35

613   40f Jentink's Duiker (*Cephalophus jentinki*)
614   60f Olive Colobus (*Colobus verus*)
615   75f African Manatee (*Trichechus senegalensis*)
616   100f Temminck's Giant Squirrel (*Epixerus ebii*)
617   150f Pygmy Hippopotamus (*Choeropsis liberiensis*)
618   300f Chimpanzee (*Pan troglodytes*)
                                    Set of 6   6.00   2.00

1983

348†   300f African Elephant (silver foil) 4.50
349†   1200f African Elephant (gold foil) 16.00

1978

755   35f Long-tailed Pangolin (*Manis*)
756   90f Bush Pig (*Potamochoerus porcus*)
757   100f Eastern Black-and-White Colobus (*Colobus guereza*)
758   125f African Buffalo (*Syncerus caffer*)
                                    Set of 4   1.50   1.25

560†   100f African Elephant 1.00   80

1979

780†   100f Impala, Greater Kudu   50   50
781†   125f African Elephant (and others)   60   60

574   5f Sable Antelope ('Hippotragues')
575   20f Yellow-backed Duiker ('Cephalophe')
576   50f Pygmy Hippopotamus ('Hippopotame Nain')
577   60f Aardvark ('Orycterope')
                                    Set of 4   1.10   50

STANLEY GIBBONS
STAMP COLLECTING SERIES

Introductory booklets on *How to Start, How to Identify Stamps* and *Collecting by Theme.* A series of well illustrated guides at a low price.

Write for details.

JAMAICA
West Indies
100 cents = 1 dollar

1973

365	8c Small Indian Mongoose ('Mongoose')			
366	40c Small Indian Mongoose ('Mongoose')			
367	60c Small Indian Mongoose ('Mongoose')			
	Set of 3	1.60	3.00

1981

512	20c Brown's Hutia ('Jamaican Hutia')		
513	20c Brown's Hutia ('Jamaican Hutia')		
514	20c Brown's Hutia ('Jamaican Hutia') (eating)		
515	20c Brown's Hutia ('Jamaican Hutia') (family)		
	Set of 4	70	70

1982

543† 60c American Manatee ('Sea Cow') .. 55 55

JAPAN
East Asia
100 sen = 1 yen

1922

293	4s Sika Deer (green)	2.25	25
266	4s Sika Deer (orange)	7.00	20
211	8s Sika Deer (red)	15.00	5.00
267	8s Sika Deer (olive)	12.00	20
305	20s Sika Deer (blue)	9.00	30
268	20s Sika Deer (purple)	40.00	25

1952

658† 8y Japanese Serow 15 10

1968

1150 15y Siberian Chipmunk 30 10

1971

1228† 10y Sika Deer 10 10

1973

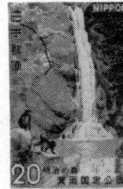

1315† 20y Japanese Macaque 15 10

1974

1348 20y Iriomote Cat (*Mayailurus iriomotensis*) 15 10

1356 20y European Otter (*Lutra lutra whiteleyi*) 15 10

1361 20y Ryukyu Rabbit (*Pentalagus furnessi*) 15 10

1372 20y Bonin Islands Flying Fox (*Pteropus pselaphon*) 15 10

1982

1660	60y Gorilla	
1661	60y Lion	
1662	60y Giant Panda, Indian Elephant	
1663	60y Giraffe, Common Zebra	
	Set of 4	2.50 2.00

JAPANESE OCCUPATION OF NORTH BORNEO
South-east Asia
100 cents = 1 dollar

1942

北日本来軍政府

Nos. 306 and 309 of North Borneo overprinted as above

J4†	4c Proboscis Monkey	. . . .	32.00 55.00
J7†	10c Orang-Utan	. . . .	48.00 70.00

STAMP MONTHLY
– finest and most informative magazine for all collectors. Obtainable from your newsagent or by postal subscription – details on request

1944

オ ネ ル ボ 北

Nos. 306 and 309 of North Borneo overprinted as above

J23†	4c Proboscis Monkey	. . . .	1.50 2.00
J26†	10c Orang-Utan	. . . .	1.75 3.00

No. J7 overprinted as Nos. J23/6

J32a	10c Orang-Utan	. . . .	£100

JERSEY
See under Great Britain

JOHORE
South-east Asia
100 cents = 1 dollar

1960

160†	10c Tiger	. . . .	15 5

JORDAN
Middle East
1000 fils =1 dinar

1967

808†	1f Dromedary	. . . .	10 10
811†	4f Striped Hyena	. . . .	10 10
813†	60f Goitred Gazelle	. . . .	70 35

1968

825†	30f Mountain Gazelle ('Gazelle')	50	20
826†	40f Arabian Oryx ('Oryx')	60	25
828†	60f Ibex . . . . •	80	40

1972

980† 30f Dromedary 35 20

JUNAGADH

See under Soruth

KAMPUCHEA

South-east Asia
100 cents = 1 riel

1984

535 10c Coyote (*Canis latrans*)
536 40c Dingo (*Canis dingo*)
537 80c Hunting Dog (*Lycaon pictus*)
538 1r Golden Jackal (*Canis aureus*)
539 1r20 Red Fox (*Vulpes vulpes*)
540 2r Maned Wolf (*Chrysocyon brachyurus*)
541 2r50 Wolf (*Canis lupus*)

Set of 7 4.75 2.00

571 10c Gazelle sp (*Gazelle sp*)
572 40c Roe Deer (*Capreolus capreolus*)
573 80c Hare sp (*Lepus sp*)
574 1r Red Deer (*Cervus elaphus*)
575 1r20 Indian Elephant (*Elephas maximus*)
576 2r Genet sp (*Genetta sp*)
577 2r50 Kouprey (*Bibos sauveli*)

Set of 7 3.50 1.40

KATANGA

Central Africa
100 centimes = 1 franc

1960

Nos. 339/50 of Belgian Congo overprinted **KATANGA**
23 10c Roan Antelope
24 20c White Rhinoceros
25 40c Giraffe
26 50c Demidoff's Galago
27 1f Gorilla
28 1f50 African Buffalo
29 2f Eastern Black-and-White Colobus
30 3f African Elephant
31 5f Okapi
32 6f50 Impala
33 8f Giant Ground Pangolin
34 10f Eland, Common Zebra

Set of 12 20.00 12.00

KEDAH

South-east Asia
100 cents = 1 dollar

1957

97† 10c Tiger 15 5

1959

109†	10c Tiger (sepia)	15	5
109a†	10c Tiger (purple)	25	5

KELANTAN
South-east Asia
100 cents = 1 dollar

1957

88†	10c Tiger (sepia)	15	5
89†	10c Tiger (purple)	1.00	1.25

1961

101†	10c Tiger	15	5

KENYA
East Africa
100 cents = 1 shilling

1963

10†	1s30 African Elephant	80	5

1964

17†	50c Lion	45	20

1966

20†	5c Thomson's Gazelle	10	5
21†	10c Sable Antelope	10	5
22†	15c Aardvark ('Ant Bear')	10	5
23†	20c Lesser Bushbaby ('Bush-Baby')	10	5
24†	30c Warthog	10	5
25†	40c Common Zebra ('Zebra')	15	8
26†	50c African Buffalo ('Buffalo')	15	5
27†	65c Black Rhinoceros ('Rhino')	1.75	1.50
29†	1s Greater Kudu	30	5
30†	1s30 African Elephant ('Elephant')	1.50	12
31†	1s50 Bat-eared Fox	2.00	1.75
32†	2s50 Cheetah	2.25	90
33†	5s Savanna Monkey ('Velvet Monkey') ..	1.50	60
34†	10s Giant Ground Pangolin ('Pangolin') ..	5.00	2.25
35†	20s Lion	12.00	6.50
	(20/35 Set of 16)	26.00	13.50

1977

79†	3s Hippopotamus	1.40	1.40

84†	5s African Elephant	1.90	1.60

92† 5s Black Rhinoceros, African Elephant,
Waterbuck   75   75

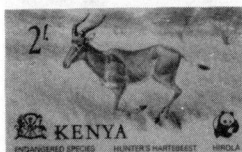

98†   2s Hunter's Hartebeest 1.25   95
99†   3s Red Colobus 1.75   1.50
100† 5s Dugong 2.50   2.25

105   5s African Elephant, African Buffalo 2.75   2.00

1981

212   50c Giraffe ('Reticulated Giraffe')
213   2s Bongo
214   5s Roan Antelope
215   10s Agile Mangabey ('Mangabey')
                                    Set of 4   2.75   2.40

KENYA, UGANDA AND TANGANYIKA
East-central Africa
100 cents = 1 shilling

1935

112†   10c Lion 1.75   20
123†   £1 Lion £130   £120

1938

150ab†   £1 Lion 12.00   8.00

1941
No. 120 of South Africa surcharged **KENYA TANGANYIKA
UGANDA**
154†   70c on 1s Black Wildebeest, Blue
        Wildebeest 1.25   2.00

1954

168†   10c Giraffe   10   5
169†   15c African Elephant   35   12
170†   20c Lion   15   5
172†   40c Lion   85   20
173†   50c Giraffe   20   5
175†   1s Lion   30   5
176†   1s30 African Elephant 1.50   5
178†   5s African Elephant 5.50   40

1960

186†	20c Blue Wildebeest	10	5
188†	30c Thomson's Gazelle	12	5
190†	50c Common Zebra	15	5
191†	65c Cheetah	40	60
193†	1s30 Hippopotamus	30	5
194†	2s Giraffe	45	15
195†	2s50 Black Rhinoceros ('Rhinoceros')	70	70
197†	10s African Buffalo ('Buffalo')	4.25	1.75

1966

223†	30c African Elephant ("Game Park Lodge")	10	5
224†	50c Hippopotamus ("Murchison Falls Uganda)	15	5

1972

319†	40c Kob ('Uganda Kob')	15	5

1975

367†	40c Lion, Black Rhinoceros	15	5
369†	1s50 African Elephant	60	60

STAMP MONTHLY

– finest and most informative magazine for all collectors.
Obtainable from your newsagent or by postal subscription – details on request

379	50c African Elephant	
380	1s African Buffalo ('Albino Buffalo')	
381	2s African Elephant	
382	3s Abbott's Duiker	
	Set of 4	3.50	3.75

386†	3s Hippopotamus	1.40	1.75

OFFICIAL STAMPS

1959
Nos. 168/78 overprinted **OFFICIAL**

O2†	10c Giraffe	10	5
O3†	15c African Elephant	10	5
O4†	20c Lion	10	5
O6†	50c Giraffe	12	5
O7†	1s Lion	20	5
O8†	1s30 African Elephant	45	20
O10†	5s African Elephant	1.75	1:25

1960
. *Nos. 186, 188 and 190 overprinted* **OFFICIAL**

O16†	20c Blue Wildebeest	10	5
O17†	30c Thomson's Gazelle	10	8
O18†	50c Common Zebra	12	10

KHMER REPUBLIC
South-east Asia
100 cents = 1 riel

1972

339	3r Javan Rhinoceros (*Rhinoceros sondaicus*)	
340	4r Mainland Serow (*Capricornis sumatrensis*)	
341	6r Thamin (*Cervus eldi*)	
342	7r Banteng (*Bibos banteng*)	
343	8r Water Buffalo (*Bubalus bubalis*)	
344	10r Gaur (*Bibos gaurus*)	
	Set of 6	3.50	1.00

KOREA

South Korea
East Asia
1953 100 weun = 1 hwan
1962 100 chun = 1 won

1953

280†	30h Tiger	1.00	25
250†	100h Sika Deer	4.25	15
285†	200h Sika Deer	2.00	25
319†	500h Sika Deer	20.00	1.25
320†	1000h Sika Deer	28.00	2.25

1962

551†	50w Sika Deer	2.10	25

1966
As No. 511, but inscribed "Republic of Korea"

711†	50w Sika Deer	1.75	10

676	3w Eurasian Badger
677	5w Asiatic Black Bear
678	7w Tiger

	Set of 3	4.00	2.25

1970

887†	30w Tiger	1.10	30

1973

1064†	5w Siberian Chipmunk	15	15

1979

1391†	20w Common Goral	20	10

1980

1424†	60w Tiger	60	30

North Korea
East Asia
100 chon = 1 won

1959

N201†	5c Chinese Water Deer	75	20
N202†	5c Siberian Weasel	50	10
N203†	5c Steppe Polecat	50	10
N204†	5c European Otter	1.10	35
N205†	10c Sika Deer	2.00	50
	(N201/6 *Set of* 6)	4.50	1.50

1961

N298†	5c Common Dolphin	50	10
N299†	10c Whale sp	75	20

1962

N369	2c Tiger
N370	2c Racoon-Dog
N371	5c Chinese Ferret-Badger
N372	10c Asiatic Black Bear

Set of 4   1.75   35

N435	4c European Mink
N436	5c Chinese Hare
N437	10c Eurasian Red Squirrel
N438	10c Common Goral
N439	20c Siberian Chipmunk

Set of 5   2.00   50

1964

N554	2c Lynx
N555	5c Leopard Cat
N556	10c Leopard
N557	10c Yellow-throated Marten

Set of 4   2.00   30

1966

N754	2c Red Deer
N755	5c Sika Deer
N756	10c Indian Muntjac
N757	10c Reindeer
N758	70c Fallow Deer

Set of 5   4.00   1.25

1974

N1251	2c Leopard Cat
N1252	5c Lynx
N1253	10c Red Fox
N1254	10c Wild Boar
N1255	20c Dhole
N1256	40c Brown Bear
N1257	60c Leopard
N1258	70c Tiger
N1259	90c Lion

Set of 9   3.75   2.10

1975

N1352	10c Common Zebra
N1353	10c African Buffalo
N1354	20c Giant Panda
N1355	25c Bactrian Camel
N1356	30c Indian Elephant

Set of 5   1.75   45

1976

N1560†	10c Roe Deer	10	10
N1563†	40c Tiger	50	20
MSN1564	50c Tiger	1.00	35

1979

N1834	20c Walrus	40	10

N1895	5c Sika Deer
N1896	10c Sika Deer
N1897	15c Sika Deer
N1898	20c Sika Deer
N1899	30c Sika Deer
N1900	50c Sika Deer

Set of 6   1.90   90

N1921†	50c Northern Sealion (*Eumetopias jubatus*)	75	30

1982

N2195	20c Tiger
N2196	30c Tiger (vert)
N2197	30c Tiger (horiz)
N2198	40c Tiger
N2199	Tiger

Set of 5   6.50   3.00

1983

N2310	20c Giant Panda	65	30

KUWAIT

Arabian Peninsula
1000 fils =1 dinar

1982

937	30f Lion (and stylised whale)
938	80f Lion

Set of 2   1.40   1.00

LABUAN

Off north coast of Borneo
100 cents = 1 dollar

1894

No. 69 of North Borneo in different colours overprinted **LABUAN**
63†   2c Sambar 1.10   1.10

1896

No. 63 overprinted **1846 JUBILEE 1896**
84†   2c Sambar 4.00   5.00

1897

No. 94a of North Borneo in different colours overprinted **LABUAN**
90†   2c Sambar 3.00   1.60

1900

Nos. 95, 98/9 and 104 of North Borneo in different colours
overprinted **LABUAN**
111†	2c Sambar	. . . .	1.75	3.00
112†	4c Orang-Utan (black and brown)	. . . .	2.75	6.00
113†	4c Orang-Utan (black and red)	. . . . . .	2.40	1.50
115†	10c Sun Bear	. . . .	8.00	

POSTAGE DUE STAMPS

1901

Nos. 111 and 113 overprinted **POSTAGE DUE**
D1†	2c Sambar	. . . .	5.00	2.00
D3†	4c Orang-Utan	. . . .	5.50	

LAOS

South-east Asia
100 cents = 1 kip

1965

166   25k Leopard Cat (*Felis bengalensis*)
167   55k Phayre's Flying Squirrel (*Hylopetes*)
168   75k Javan Mongoose (*Herpestes*
    javanicus)
169   100k Chinese Porcupine (*Hystrix*
    hodgsoni)
170   200k Binturong (*Arctictis binturong*)
    Set of 5   5.00   3.00

1969

270   15k Chinese Pangolin (*Panis auritas*)
271   30k Chinese Pangolin
272   70k Sun Bear (*Ursus malaynus*)
273   120k Common Gibbon (*Hylobates*)
274   150k Tiger (*Felis regalis*)
    Set of 5   4.00   2.00

1970

300   20k Wild Boar (*Sus vittadus*)
301   60k Wild Boar
302   210k Leopard (*Panthera pardus delacouri*)
303   500k Gaur (*Bisos gaurus*)
    Set of 4   6.00   3.00

1971

331   25k Common Palm Civet (*Paradoxurus*
    hermaphroditus)
332   40k Common Palm Civet
333   50k Lesser Malay Chevrotain (*Tragulus*
    kanchil)
334   85k Sambar (*Cervus unicolor*)
335   300k Javan Rhinoceros (*Rhinoceros*
    sondaicus)
    Set of 5   3.50   2.50

STAMP MONTHLY

– finest and most informative magazine for all collectors.
Obtainable from your newsagent or by postal subscription – details on request

1981

MS502   10k Giant Panda 2.50   2.50

1983

627†   4k Wild Horse ('Chevaux') 1.00   60

1984

704   25c Tiger (*Panthera tigris*)
705   25c Tiger (*Panthera tigris*) (two tigers)
706   3k Tiger (*Panthera tigris*)
707   4k Tiger (*Panthera tigris*)
                                    Set of 4   2.50   2.00

512   10c Wild Cat (*Felis silvestris ornata*)
513   20c Fishing Cat (*Felis viverrinus*)
514   30c Caracal (*Felis caracal*)
515   40c Clouded Leopard (*Neofelis nebulosa*)
516   50c Flat-headed Cat (*Felis planiceps*)
517   9k Jungle Cat (*Felis chaus*)
                                    Set of 6   4.50   4.50

778   50c Greater Glider (*Schoinobates volans*)
779   1k Platypus (*Ornithorhynchus anatinus*)
780   2k Southern Hairy-nosed Wombat
             (*Lasiorhinus latifrons*)
781   2k Tasmanian Devil (*Sarcophilus harrisii*)
782   3k Thylacine (*Thylacinus cynocephalus*)
783   4k Tiger Cat (*Dasyurops maculatus*)
784   8k Wallaby sp (*Wallabia isabelinus*)
                                    Set of 7   3.50   1.25
MS785   10k Red Kangaroo (*Macropus rufus*) ..   1.90   85

1982

521†   1k Indian Elephant   25   10
524†   4k Indian Elephant   90   45
525†   5k Indian Elephant 1.25   45
526†   5k50 Indian Elephant 1.40   60
                              (521/6 Set of 6)   4.50   4.50
Two additional stamps depict domesticated elephants

STANLEY GIBBONS
STAMP COLLECTING SERIES

Introductory booklets on *How to Start, How to Identify
Stamps* and *Collecting by Theme*. A series of well illustrated guides at a low price.

Write for details.

LEBANON

Middle East
100 centimes = 1 piastre

1967

995† 5p Dromedary   10   10

1984

611 15s Eland ('Cape Eland Calf') ·
612 20s Chacma Baboon ('Young Chacma
      Baboons')
613 30s Oribi ('Oribi Calf')
614 75s Natal Red Hare ('Young Red Rock
      Hares)'
615 1m Black-backed Jackal ('Black-backed
      Jackal Pups')
                                Set of 5   1.90   2.10

LESOTHO

Southern Africa
1968 100 cents = 1 rand
1979 100 lisente = 1 maloti

1977

329 4c Large-toothed Rock Hyrax ('Rock
      Rabbit')
330 5c Cape Porcupine ('Porcupine')
331 10c Zorilla ('Striped Polecat')
332 15c Klipspringer
333 25c Chacma Baboon ('Baboon')
                                Set of 5   3.25   3.00

1981

468 6s Wild Cat ('African Wild Cat')
469 20s Chacma Baboon
470 25s Eland ('Cape Eland')
471 40s Cape Porcupine ('Porcupine')
472 50s Oribi
                                Set of 5   2.40   2.25
MS473 1m50 Black-backed Jackal 2.40   2.75

LIBERIA

West Africa
100 cents = 1 dollar

1892

77† 4c African Elephant 2.50   2.25
84† $1 Hippopotamus 6.00   8.00

1897

146† 2c Hippopotamus (black and bistre)   ..   2.50   1.75
147† 2c Hippopotamus (black and red) 2.50   2.00
148† 5c African Elephant (black and lake)   ..   3.50   3.00
149† 5c African Elephant (black and blue)   ..   2.00   1.75

1901

Nos. O96, O127 and O159/62 overprinted **ORDINARY**

178†	2c Hippopotamus (black and brown)	..	£100	45.00
179†	2c Hippopotamus (black and red)	.. ..	25.00	30.00
181†	5c African Elephant (black and red)	..	£100	£100
182†	5c African Elephant (black and blue)	..	20.00	25.00
172†	$1 Hippopotamus		£900	
193†	$1 Hippopotamus		£150	£250

1902

No. 84 surcharged **75c** and bar

206	75c on $1 Hippopotamus	.. ..	7.50	10.00

1904

No. O89 surcharged **TWO**

220†	2c on 4c African Elephant		3.50	4.50

1906

224†	1c African Elephant	.. ..	1.00	50
226†	5c Chimpanzee	.. ..	2.75	50
233†	75c Pygmy Hippopotamus		6.00	1.60

1916

No. 224 surcharged **L F F 1 C**

333†	1c on 1c African Elephant		£250	£250

1918

349†	1c Bongo		1.00	25
350†	2c African Palm Civet		1.00	25

Nos. 349/50 surcharged **TWO CENTS** and red cross

375†	1c + 2c Bongo		75	75
376†	2c + 2c African Palm Civet	.. .. ..	75	75

1920

Nos. 349/50 surcharged **1920** and value

393†	3c on 1c Bongo	.. ..	1.50	2.25
394†	4c on 2c African Palm Civet	.. .. ..	1.50	2.50

STAMP MONTHLY

– finest and most informative magazine for all collectors.
Obtainable from your newsagent or by postal subscription – details on request

1921

407†	25c Leopard	.. ..	2.75	50
411†	$1 Bongo		18.00	1.00
413†	$5 African Elephant	.. ..	18.00	1.50

Nos. 407, 411 and 413 overprinted **1921**

421†	25c Leopard	.. ..	7.50	1.00
425†	$1 Bongo		20.00	1.50
427†	$5 African Elephant	.. ..	18.00	3.00

1923

476†	15c Hippopotamus	.. ..	13.00	50
477†	20c Kob	.. ..	10.00	50
478†	25c African Buffalo	.. ..	30.00	50

1926

No. 349 surcharged **Two Cents**

504	2c on 1c Bongo	.. ..	2.50	4.00

1936

No. 350 surcharged **1936** and new value in figure

536†	1c on 2c African Palm Civet	.. .. ..	30	50

No. O363 surcharged with **1936** and new value

547†	1c on 2c African Palm Civet	.. .. ..	30	50

1937

560†	2c Bushbuck	.. ..	1.00	30
561†	3c African Buffalo		1.00	35
562†	4c Hippopotamus		1.50	60

1942

622 1c Royal Antelope
623 2c Water Chevrotain
624 3c Jentink's Duiker ('White-shouldered
        Duiker')
625 4c Bushbuck ('Harnessed Antelope')
626 5c Banded Duiker ('Zebra Antelope')
627 10c Diana Monkey ('Bay-thighed Diana
        Monkey')

		Set of 6	9.00	3.00

1944

Nos. 560/2 surcharged

634†	1c on 4c Hippopotamus	45.00	38.00
635†	2c on 3c African Buffalo	45.00	38.00
638†	6c on 2c Bushbuck	12.00	15.00

1956

784†	4c Eastern Grey Kangaroo	10	15

1966

951†	2c Giraffe	10	5
952†	3c Lion	20	15
954†	10c Chimpanzee	40	20
955†	15c Leopard	50	25
956†	20c Black Rhinoceros	60	40
957†	25c African Elephant	70	50
	(951/7 Set of 7)	2.00	1.00

1971

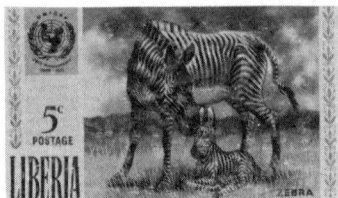

1083 5c Common Zebra ('Zebra')
1084 7c Koala ('Koala Bear')
1085 8c Guanaco ('Llamas')
1086 10c Red Fox ('Fox')
1087 20c Savanna Monkey ('Monkey')
1088 25c Brown Bear

		Set of 6	2.50	1.00
MS1089	50c Tiger ('Bengal Tiger')		1.50	1.50

1090†	2c Sika Deer (Cervus nippon yesoensis)	10	10
1092†	5c Brown Bear (Ursus arctos yesoensis)	15	10
1094†	15c Northern Pika (Ochotna hyperborea yesoensis)	30	20

1975

1240 1c Yellow Baboon
1241 3c African Elephant
1242 5c African Buffalo
1243 6c Kob
1244 25c Lion
1245 50c Common Zebra

		Set of 6	2.50	1.00

1976

1290 2c Black Rhinoceros (*Diceros bicornis*)
1291 3c Bongo (*Boocereus euryceros*)
1292 5c Chimpanzee (*Pan troglodytes*)
1293 15c Pygmy Hippopotamus (*Choeropsis liberiensis*)
1294 25c Leopard (*Panthera pardus*)
1295 $1 Gorilla (*Gorilla gorilla*)

Set of 6	3.75	1.60
MS1296 50c African Elephant (*Loxodonta africana*)	1.25	1.25

1979

1377†	35c African Elephant, Giraffee, Common Zebra, Dibatag, Lion, Cheetah	50	50

1984

1591 6c Pygmy Hippopotamus
1592 10c Pygmy Hippopotamus
1593 20c Pygmy Hippopotamus
1594 31c Pygmy Hippopotamus

Set of 4	2.00	1.00

OFFICIAL STAMPS

1892
Nos. 77 and 84 overprinted **OFFICIAL**

O89†	4c African Elephant	2.50	4.00
O96†	$1 Hippopotamus	15.00	18.00

1894
Nos. 77 and 84 overprinted **OS**

O121†	4c African Elephant	2.75	3.00
O127†	$1 Hippopotamus	20.00	22.00

1898
Nos. 146/9 *overprinted* **OS**

O159†	2c Hippopotamus (black and brown) ..	1.50	2.00
O160†	2c Hippopotamus (black and red)	2.00	2.50
O161†	5c African Elephant (black and lake) ..	2.25	1.75
O162†	5c African Elephant (black and blue) ..	2.50	2.50

1906
Nos. 224, 226 *and* 233 *in different colours overprinted* **OS**

O237†	1c African Elephant	50	50
O239†	5c Chimpanzee	2.00	35
O246†	75c Pygmy Hippopotamus	3.00	75

1914
No. 233 *surcharged* **CENTS 20 OFFICIAL**

O287	20c on 75c Pygmy Hippopotamus	11.00	4.50

1915
No. O237 *overprinted* **L F F 1c**

O336†	1c on 1c African Elephant	£200	£200

1918
Nos. 349/50 *overprinted* **OS**

O362†	1c Bongo	50	15
O363†	2c African Palm Civet	50	15

1920
Nos. O362/3 *surcharged* **1920** *and value*

O400 3c on 1c Bongo
O401 4c on 2c African Palm Civet

Set of 2	3.50	4.50

1921
Nos. 407, 411 *and* 413 *in different colours overprinted* **O S** *or* **OFFICIAL**

O435†	25c Leopard	3.50	50
O439†	$1 Bongo	12.00	1.50
O441†	$5 African Elephant	12.00	1.50

Nos. O435, O439 *and* O441 *overprinted* **1921**

O449†	25c Leopard	3.50	70
O453†	$1 Bongo	10.00	1.50
O455†	$5 African Elephant	10.00	2.50

1923
Nos. 476/8 *in different colours overprinted* **O S**

O490†	15c Hippopotamus	4.50	40
O491†	20c Kob	4.50	40
O492†	25c African Buffalo	8.00	40

1926
No. O362 *surcharged* **Two Cents**

O506	2c on 1c Bongo	3.00	3.50

STANLEY GIBBONS
STAMP COLLECTING SERIES

Introductory booklets on *How to Start, How to Identify Stamps* and *Collecting by Theme.* A series of well illustrated guides at a low price.
Write for details.

LIBYA

North Africa
1966 1000 milliemes = 1 pound
1972 1000 dirhams = 1 dinar

1976

| 696† | 15dh Fin Whale | ● 15 | 10 |
| 700† | 115dh Barbary Sheep | 75 | 40 |

1979

873	5dh Dorcas Gazelle		
874	20dh Dorcas Gazelle		
875	50dh Dorcas Gazelle		
	Set of 3	75	40

877†	10dh Addax (*Addax nasomaculata*)	8	5
878†	15dh Algerian Hedgehog (*Erinaceus algirus*)	20	10
879†	20dh North African Crested Porcupine (*Hystrix galeata*)	20	10
880†	30dh Dromedary (*Camelus dromedarius*)	30	12
881†	35dh Wild Cat (*Felis lybica*)	40	15
882†	45dh Dorcas Gazelle (*Gazella dorcas*)	50	25
883†	115dh Cheetah (*Acinonyx jubatus*)	1.10	40
	(876/83 *Set of* 8)	2.50	1.00

COLLECT BIRDS ON STAMPS

The first Stanley Gibbons thematic catalogue – a few copies still available at £4.95 (p.+p. £1.30) plus FREE 1983–84 Supplement from:
Stanley Gibbons Publications Ltd, 5, Parkside, Christchurch Road, Ringwood, Hants BH24 3SH.

LIECHTENSTEIN

Central Europe
100 rappen = 1 franc

1946

252†	20r Red Deer	2.00	1.25
255†	20r Chamois	2.50	2.25
283†	20r Roe Deer	6.50	3.75
253†	30r Arctic Hare	2.00	1.50
256†	30r Alpine Marmot	3.00	2.50
285†	80r Eurasian Badger	30.00	28.00

1976

| 628† | 40r Mouflon | 50 | 50 |

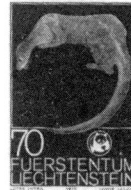

| 632† | 70r European Otter | 60 | 60 |

LUXEMBOURG

Western Europe
100 centimes = 1 franc

1970

| 853† | 6f West European Hedgehog | 50 | 50 |

MADAGASCAR AND DEPENDENCIES
Indian Ocean off East Africa
100 centimes =1 franc

1952

327† 200f Ring-tailed Lemur (*Lemur catta*) .. 4.00 1.00

MALACCA
South-east Asia
100 cents =1 dollar

1957

44† 10c Tiger 15 5

1960

55† 10c Tiger 15 5

STANLEY GIBBONS
STAMP COLLECTING SERIES

Introductory booklets on *How to Start, How to Identify Stamps* and *Collecting by Theme.* A series of well illustrated guides at a low price.
Write for details.

MALAGASY REPUBLIC
Indian Ocean off East Africa
100 centimes = 1 franc

1961

29 2f Grey Gentle Lemur (*Hapalemur griseus*)
30 4f Ruffed Lemur (*Lemur varius*)
31 12f Mongoose-Lemur (*Lemur mongoz*)
32 65f Diadem Sifaka (*Propithecus diadema*)
33 85f Indri (*Indri brevicaudatus*)
34 250f Verreaux's Sifaka (*Propithecus verreauxi coquereli*)
Set of 6 6.50 3.50

1968
No. 33 surcharged
143† 20f on 85f Indri 50 30

1970

187 20f Aye-Aye 35 30

1973

261 5f Greater Dwarf Lemur (*Cheirogaleus major*)
262 25f Weasel-Lemur (*Lepilemur mustelinus*)
263 150f Weasel-Lemur (air)
264 200f Greater Dwarf Lemur
Set of 4 2.75 1.50

1975

| 321† | 40f Ryukyu Rabbit (*Pentalagus furnessi*) | 25 | 15 |
| 324† | 125f Sika Deer (*Gervus var kerama*) (air) | 70 | 40 |

1979

409†	25f Ring-tailed Lemur (*Lemur catta*)		25	15
410†	125f Black Lemur (*Lemur macaco*)		1.10	80
411†	1000f Malagasy Civet (*Cryptoprocta ferox*)		8.00	3.00
413†	95f Black Lemur (*Lemur macaco*) (air)		80	60
	(409/13 *Set of* 5)		9.00	4.00

1983

489	30f Ruffed Lemur (*Lemur variegatus*)			
490	30f Verreaux's Sifaka (*Propithecus verreauxi verreauxi*)			
491	30f Lesser Mouse-Lemur (*Microcebus murinus*)			
492	30f Aye-Aye (*Daubentonia madagascariensis*)			
493	200f Indri (*Indri indri*)			
		Set of 5	2.00	1.75
MS494	500f Potto (*Perodicticus potto*)	.. ..	3.00	3.00

MALAWI

Central Africa
1964 12 pence = 1 shilling, 20 shillings = 1 pound
1970 100 tambalas = 1 kwacha

1964

MALAWI

| 227 | £1 Nyala | .. .. | 9.50 | 7.00 |

1971

375	1t Greater Kudu		
376	2t Nyala		
377	3t Mountain Reedbuck ('Reed Buck')		
378	5t Puku		
379	8t Impala		
380	10t Eland		
381	15t Klipspringer		
382	20t Suni ('Livingstone's Suni')		
383	30t Roan Antelope		
384	50t Waterbuck		
385	1k Bushbuck		
386	2k Red Forest Duiker ('Red Duiker')		
387	4k Common Duiker ('Grey Duiker')		
		Set of 13	29.00	24.00

1975

496	3t Thick-tailed Bushbaby ('Bush Baby')		
497	10t Leopard		
498	20t Roan Antelope		
499	40t Common Zebra ('Burchell's Zebra')		
		Set of 4	1.50	1.60

1978

567 4t Nyala
568 10t Lion
569 20t Common Zebra ('Burchell's Zebra')
570 40t Mountain Reedbuck ('Reedbuck')
                              Set of 4   1.75   1.25

1980

629† 5t African Elephant   10   5

1981

633 7t Suni ('Livingstone's Suni')
634 10t Blue Duiker
635 20t African Buffalo
636 1k Lichtenstein's Hartebeest
                              Set of 4   1.75   1.75

1982

650† 7t Impala   15   10
651† 10t Lion   20   12
652† 20t Greater Kudu   35   25
                         (650/4 Set of 4) 2.00 1.75

1984

703 7t Smith's Red Hare ('Nyika Red Hare')
704 20t Gambian Sun Squirrel ('Sun Squirrel')
705 30t South African Hedgehog ('Hedgehog')
706 1k Large-spotted Genet (*Genetta tigrina*)
                              Set of 4   1.50   1.75

MALAYSIA
South-east Asia
100 cents = 1 dollar

1979

190† 30c Tiger (*Panthera tigris*)   20   5
191† 40c Malayan Flying Lemur
        (*Cynocephalus variegatus*)   25   5
192† 50c Lesser Malay Chevrotain (*Tragulus
        javanicus*)   30   5
193† 75c Malayan Pangolin (*Manis javanicus*)   45   5
195† $2 Malayan Tapir (*Tapirus indicus*) 1.25   10
196† $5 Gaur (*Bos gaurus*) 3.00   60
197† $10 Orang-Utan (*Pongo pygmaeus*)   ..   6.00 3.00
                         (190/7 Set of 8)   10.50 3.50

MALDIVE ISLANDS
Indian Ocean
100 larees = 1 rupee

1973

459† 2la Indian Flying Fox (*Pteropus*)   10   5
464† 3r Indian Flying Fox 2.75 2.75

1978

781†	1r Indian Rhinoceros ('Rhinoceros') ..	30	30	
782†	1r80 Brown Hard ('Hare')	50	50	

209†	90f Dromedary ('Dromadaire')	65	50

1983

1004 30la Rough-toothed Dolphin ('Roughtooth
Dolphin')
1005 40la Indo-Pacific Hump-backed Dolphin
('Indopacific Humpback Dolphin')
1006 4r Finless Porpoise
1007 6r Pygmy Sperm Whale

Set of 4	1.90	2.00
MS1008 5r Striped Dolphin	95	1.10

1978

655†	110f Common Zebra	50	30

1979

678†	200f Dromedary	2.00	1.00

685 100f African Manatee (Trichechus
senegalensis)
686 120f Chimpanzee (Pan satyrus)
687 130f Topi (Damaliscus korrigum)
688 180f Gemsbok (Oryx algazella)
689 200f Giant Eland (Taurautragus derbianus)

Set of 5	3.00	1.50

MALI
West Africa
100 centimes = 1 franc

1965

98   1f Waterbuck (Kobus defassa)
99   5f African Buffalo (Syncerus caffer)
100 10f Scimitar Oryx (Aegoryx algazel)
101 30f Leopard (Panthera pardus)
102 90f Giraffe (Giraffa camelopardalis)

Set of 5	2.00	1.50

STAMP MONTHLY
– finest and most informative magazine for all collectors.
Obtainable from your newsagent or by postal subscription – details on request

1980

741 90f African Ass (*Equus asinus*)
742 120f Addax (*Addax nasomaculatus*)
743 130f Cheetah (*Acinonyx jubatus*)
744 140f Barbary Sheep (*Ammotragus lervia*)
745 180f African Buffalo (*Syncerus caffer caffer*)

Set of 5   3.00   1.50

1981

857 110f Dorcas Gazelle
858 160f Patas Monkey
859 300f Cheetah

Set of 3   2.75   2.75

1982

931† 200f Dromedary (on stamp No. 678)   ..   1.00   1.00

1983

967† 700f Lion 2.00   2.00

MANAMA
Arabian Peninsula
100 dirhams = 1 riyal

1966
No. 12 of Ajman surcharged **Manama** *and new value*
2† 70d on 70np Dromedary   25   25

Appendix
The following stamps have either been issued in excess of postal needs, or have not been made available to the public in reasonable quantities at face value. Miniature sheets, imperforate stamps etc., are excluded from this section.

1969
Wild Animals (Dromedary, African Elephant, Zebra, Rhinoceros, Black Bear, Lion). 1r × 6.

1971
Wild Life Conservation (Potto, Zebra, Rhinoceros, Waterbuck, Hunting Dog, Thomson's Gazelle, Bat-eared Fox, Eland, Duiker, African Buffalo, Hippopotamus, Cheetah, Giraffe, African Elephant, Lion, Gnu). Postage 1, 2, 3, 7, 12, 15, 25, 30, 40, 50, 65, 80d; Air 1r, 1r25, 1r50, 2r.
Other values show birds or reptiles.

MARSHALL ISLANDS
North Pacific
100 cents = 1 dollar

1984

25 20c Common Dolphin
26 20c Risso's Dolphin
27 20c Spotted Dolphin
28 20c Bottle-nosed Dolphin ('Bottlenose Dolphin')

Set of 4   1.50   1.25

STANLEY GIBBONS
STAMP COLLECTING SERIES
Introductory booklets on *How to Start, How to Identify Stamps* and *Collecting by Theme*. A series of well illustrated guides at a low price.
Write for details.

MAURITANIA
West Africa
1960 100 centimes = 1 franc
1973 100 cents =1 ouguiya (um)

1960

135†	3f Barbary Sheep ('Mouflon a Manchettes')	10	10
136†	4f Fennec Fox ('Fennecs')	10	10
145†	85f Scimitar Oryx ('Oryx Blanc')	1.50	75

1963

165†	50c Striped Hyena ('Hyene Rayee') ..	5	5
166†	1f Spotted Hyena ('Hyene Tachetee') ..	5	5
167†	1f50 Cheetah ('Guepard')	8	5
168†	2f Guinea Baboon ('Babouins')	12	5
169†	5f Dromedary ('Dromadaire')	20	12
170†	10f Leopard	30	15
171†	15f Bongo	35	15
172†	20f Aardvark ('Orycterope')	35	20
173†	25f Patas Monkey ('Patas')	50	25
174†	30f North African Crested Porcupine ('Porc-Epic')	75	30
175†	50f Dorcas Gazelle ('Gazelle Dorcas') ..	1.25	60
	(165/76 Set of 12)	4.75	2.50

1968

318†	15f Dromedary ('Chamelle')	15	10

STAMP MONTHLY
– finest and most informative magazine for all collectors.
Obtainable from your newsagent or by postal subscription – details on request

1973

418	40f Mediterranean Monk Seal (*Monachus monachus*)		
419	135f Mediterranean Monk Seal (*Monachus monachus*) (air)		
	Set of 2	2.40	1.40

420	100f Lion		
421	250f Lion, Giant Forest Hog		
	Set of 2	3.50	1.75

1974
Nos. 418/21 surcharged with value in new currency

440†	8u on 40f Mediterranean Monk Seal ..	30	20
444†	27u on 135f Mediterranean Monk Seal ..	90	60
445†	20u on 100f Lion	65	45
446†	50u on 250f Lion, Giant Forest Hog ..	1.90	1.25

1977

536	5u Bush Hare ('Lapin')		
537	10u Golden Jackal ('Chacal')		
538	12u Warthog ('Phacochere')		
539	14u Lion		
540	15u African Elephant ('Elephant')		
	Set of 5	2.25	1.25

543†	14u Lion	50	30

1978

573†	5u Scimitar Oryx		25	12
574†	12u Addra Gazelle		65	25
575†	14u African Manatee		75	35
576†	55u Barbary Sheep		3.00	1.00
577†	60u African Elephant		3.25	1.25
		(573/8 Set of 6)	8.50	4.00

592†   20u Spotted Hyena   1.25   75

1984
No. 537 surcharged **Aide au Sahel 84** and new value
815   18u on 10u Golden Jackel

MAURITIUS
Indian Ocean
100 cents =1 rupee

1950

287†   1r Timor Deer ('Mauritius Deer')   1.00   70

1953

303†   1r Timor Deer   50   10

1978

559†   1r50 Greater Mascarene Flying Fox
('Flying Fox')   50   35

MEXICO
Central America
100 centavos = 1 peso

1978

1453   1p60 Mule Deer (*Odocoileus hemionus*)
1454   1p60 Ocelot (*Felis pardalis*)
Set of 2   40   20

1982

1639†   4p Grey Whale ('Ballena Gris')   50   30

MIDDLE CONGO
Central Africa
100 centimes = 1 franc

1907

1†	1c Leopard	10	10
2†	2c Leopard	10	10
3†	4c Leopard	10	10
4†	5c Leopard (green and blue)	10	10
21†	5c Leopard (yellow and blue)	20	20
5†	10c Leopard (red and blue)	15	10
22†	10c Leopard (green)	50	50
6†	15c Leopard	40	25
7†	20c Leopard	75	60

1916
*No. 5 surcharged **5c** and large red cross*

18	10c + 5c Leopard	25	20

*No. 5 surcharged **5c** and small red cross*

20	10c + 5c Leopard	15	15

1924
Stamps of 1907, some in different colours, overprinted
AFRIQUE EQUATORIALE FRANCAISE

36†	1c Leopard	10	10
37†	2c Leopard	10	10
38†	4c Leopard	10	10
39†	5c Leopard	10	10
40†	10c Leopard (green and turquoise)	10	10
41†	10c Leopard (red and grey)	10	10
42†	15c Leopard	10	10
43†	20c Leopard (brown and blue)	10	10
44†	20c Leopard (green)	10	10
45†	20c Leopard (brown and purple)	15	15

1970

970	40c Common Seal ("Protection des Bebes Phoques")	30	25

979†	50c Common Seal ('Veau Marin')	30	20
980†	80c Chamois ('Isard')	40	25
982†	1f15 European Otter ('Loutre')	75	40

1983

1599	3f30 Blue Whale (*Balaenoptera musculus*)	70	60

MONACO
Southern Europe
100 centimes = 1 franc

1955

534†	8f Puma	35	35

MONGOLIA
Central Asia
100 mung = 1 tugrik

1932

58†	10t Wild Horse	6.00	5.00

1958

130†	30m Ibex (green)	2.50	1.50
131†	30m Ibex (turquoise)	2.50	1.00
132†	60m Yak (bistre) (with calf)	3.00	1.75
133†	60m Yak (orange)	3.00	1.00
134†	1t Yak (blue) (facing right)	4.00	1.50
135†	1t Yak (light blue)	3.50	1.00
136†	1t Bactrian Camel (rose)	4.00	2.50
137†	1t Bactrian Camel (red)	3.50	1.75

142†	25m Bactrian Camel	35	10
147†	1t Bactrian Camel	1.50	50

1959

171†	5m Sable	12	5
173†	15m Muskrat	45	10
174†	20m European Otter	45	12
175†	30m Argali	50	15
176†	50m Saiga	1.10	30
177†	1t Siberian Musk Deer	1.75	40
	(171/7 Set of 7)	4.50	1.10

1965

358†	60m Polar Bear	50	20

1966

388†	5m Sable (Martes zibellina)	15	5
389†	10m Red Fox (Vulpes vulpes)	15	5
390†	15m European Otter (Lutra lutra)	25	5
391†	20m Cheetah (Acinonyx jubatus)	25	5
392†	30m Pallas's Cat (Felis manul)	35	10
393†	60m Beech Marten (Martes foina)	55	25
394†	80m Stoat (Mustela ermina)	85	40
	(388/95 Set of 8)	4.00	1.25

1968

458†	5m Bactrian Camel	10	10
464†	80m Roe Deer	40	30
465†	1t Reindeer	65	40

1970

554†	5m Wolf (Canis lupus)	20	5
555†	10m Brown Bear (Ursus arctos)	20	5
556†	15m Lynx (Felis lunh)	40	5
557†	20m Wild Boar (Sus scrofa)	45	8
558†	30m Elk (Alces alces)	55	15
559†	60m Bobak Marmot (Marmota sibirica) . .	60	15
560†	80m Argali (Ovis ammon)	70	30
	(554/61 Set of 8)	3.25	1.25

STAMP MONTHLY

– finest and most informative magazine for all collectors. Obtainable from your newsagent or by postal subscription – details on request

1971

| 635† | 20m Yak | 20 | 10 |
| 636† | 30m Bactrian Camel | 20 | 10 |

1972

MS668 4t Wild Horse ('Hulan') 5.50 5.50

1973

771	5m Siberian Weasel (Mustela sibirica)		
772	10m Siberian Chipmunk (Tamias sibiricus)		
773	15m Siberian Flying Squirrel (Pteromys volans)		
774	20m Eurasian Badger (Meles meles)		
775	30m Eurasian Red Squirrel (Sciurus vulgaris)		
776	60m Wolverine (Gulo gulo)		
777	80m American Mink (Mustela vison)		
778	1t Arctic Hare (Lepus timidus)		
	Set of 8	3.00	1.10

STANLEY GIBBONS
STAMP COLLECTING SERIES

Introductory booklets on *How to Start, How to Identify Stamps* and *Collecting by Theme.* A series of well illustrated guides at a low price.
Write for details.

1974

843† 80m Wild Horse 50 25

845	10m Brown Bear (Ursus horribilis)		
846	20m Giant Panda (Ailurus fulgens) (Latin name wrong!)		
847	30m Giant Panda (Ailuropoda melanoleucus)		
848	40m Brown Bear (Ursus arctos)		
849	60m Sloth Bear (Melursus ursinus)		
850	80m Asiatic Black Bear (Selanarctos tibetanus)		
851	1t Brown Bear (Ursus arctos bruinosus)		
	Set of 7	3.25	1.40

852†	10m Red Deer	12	5
853†	20m Eurasian Beaver	25	8
854†	30m Leopard	30	10
856†	60m Roe Deer	65	25
857†	80m Argali	70	30
858†	1t Siberian Musk Deer	1.00	45
	(852/8 Set of 7)	3.25	1.40

880† 80m Sable 65 40

1975

925 1t50 Argali 90 35

926† 10m Red Fox 35 10
927† 20m Lynx 35 10
928† 30m Bobak Marmot 40 10
930† 50m Wild Boar 50 20
931† 60m Wolf 65 35
932† 1t Brown Bear 90 40
(926/32 Set of 7) 3.25 1.25

COLLECT BIRDS ON STAMPS

The first Stanley Gibbons thematic catalogue – a few copies still available at £4.95 (p.+p. £1.30) plus FREE 1983–84 Supplement from:
Stanley Gibbons Publications Ltd, 5, Parkside, Christchurch Road, Ringwood, Hants BH24 3SH.

1977

1091 10m Giant Panda (*Ailuropus melanoleucus*)
1092 20m Giant Panda (*Ailuropus melanoleucus*)
1093 30m Giant Panda (*Ailuropus melanoleucus*)
1094 40m Giant Panda (*Ailuropus melanoleucus*)
1095 60m Giant Panda (*Ailuropus melanoleucus*)
1096 80m Giant Panda (*Ailuropus melanoleucus*)
1097 1t Giant Panda (*Ailuropus melanoleucus*)
Set of 7 3.50 1.25

1978

1138† 20m Eurasian Beaver, American Beaver
(on stamp of Canada No. 473) 20 10
1141† 50m Argali, American Bighorn (on stamp
of Canada No. 449) 70 35
1142† 60m Brown Bear, Polar Bear (on stamp
of Canada No. 447) 80 40
1143† 80m Elk 90 45

1166† 20m Bactrian Camel 20 10
1167† 30m Bactrian Camel 25 10
1168† 40m Bactrian Camel 35 15
1170† 60m Bactrian Camel 60 25

1979

1226 10m Pallas's Cat (*Otocolobus manul*)
1227 30m Lynx (*Lynx lynx*)
1228 50m Tiger (*Panthera tigris*)
1229 60m Snow Leopard (*Uncia uncia*)
1230 70m Leopard (*Panthera pardus*)
1231 80m Cheetah (*Acinonyx jubatus*)
1232 1t Lion (*Panthera leo*)

Set of 7	3.25	1.25

1980

1316†	30m Blue Whale (*Balaenoptera musculus*)	50	15
1318†	50m Weddell Seal (*Leptonychotes weddelli*)	75	25
1321†	80m Killer Whale (*Orcinus orca*) . ..	1.10	40

1981

1392†	30m Arctic Fox	30	15
1393†	40m Walrus	40	20
1394†	50m Polar Bear	45	25
1395†	60m Polar Bear (on Russia No. 585) ..	60	30
1396†	80m Polar Bear (on Russia No. 586) ..	75	40
1397†	1t20 Northern Sealion, Polar Bear (on Russia No. 587)	1.25	55
	(1391/7 *Set of 7*)	3.50	1.75

1982

1454†	40m Roe Deer	35	20
1455†	50m Bactrian Camel	45	25
1458†	1t20 Wild Boar	95	55

1480†	40m Eurasian Beaver	35	20
1482†	60m Goitred Gazelle	50	30
1484†	1t20 Bactrian Camel	95	55

1983

1524†	40m Roe Deer	35	15
1525†	50m Argali	45	20

1563 20m Pallas's Pika (*Ochotona pallasii*)
1564 30m Long-eared Jerboa (*Euchoreutes naso*)
1565 40m Eurasian Red Squirrel (*Sciurus vulgaris*)
1566 50m Daurian Hedgehog (*Erinaceus dauricus*)
1567 60m Harvest Mouse (*Micromys minutus*)
1568 80m Eurasian Water Shrew (*Neomys fodiens*)
1569 1t20 Siberian Chipmunk (*Tamias sibiricus*)

          Set of 7   3.25   1.40

MOROCCO
North-west Africa
100 francs = 1 dirhams

1972

335 25f Sand Gazelle ('Gazelle de Cuvier')
336 40f Barbary Sheep ('Mouflon a Manchettes')

          Set of 2   1.10   50

1973

377† 25f Striped Hyena ('Hyene de Berberie')   40   15

STAMP MONTHLY
– finest and most informative magazine for all collectors. Obtainable from your newsagent or by postal subscription – details on request

1974

405† 70f Leopard ('Panthere')   60   40

1975

427† 1d Caracal (*Lynx caracal*)   60   40

1979

532† 40f European Otter (*Lutra*)   25   15

1984

657 80f Fennec Fox ('Fennec')
658 2d Lesser Egyptian Jerboa ('Gerboise')

          Set of 2   90   60

MOZAMBIQUE

South-east Africa
1977 100 centavos = 1 escudo
1980 100 centavos = 1 metical

1976

MOÇAMBIQUE

675	50c Thick-tailed Bushbaby (*Galago (Otolemur) crassicaudatus*)		
676	1e Ratel (*Mellivora capensis*)		
677	1e50 Temminck's Ground Pangolin (*Manis (Smutsia) temmincki*)		
678	2e Steenbok (*Raphicerus campestris*)		
679	2e50 Diademed Monkey (*Cercopithecus mitis*)		
680	3e Hunting Dog (*Lycaon pictus*)		
681	4e Cheetah (*Acinonyx jubatus*)		
682	5e Spotted Hyena (*Crocuta crocuta*)		
683	7e50 Warthog (*Phacochoerus aethiopicus*)		
684	8e Hippopotamus (*Hippopotamus amphibius*)		
685	10e White Rhinoceros (*Diceros (Ceratotherium) simus*)		
686	15e Sable Antelope (*Hippotragus niger*)		
	Set of 12	5.00	2.00

1978

698†	10e Nyala (*Tragelaphus angasi*)	.. ..	50	15

1980

797†	50c African Elephant	.. ..	8	5
798†	1e50 Black Rhinoceros	.. ..	25	10
799†	2e50 Giraffe	.. ..	35	15
800†	3e Eland	.. ..	45	15
802†	7e50 African Buffalo	.. ..	75	25
	(797/802 Set of 6)		2.00	75

1981

856†	50c Giraffe (*Giraffa camelopardalis*)	..	10	10
857†	1m50 Topi (*Damaliscus lunatus*)	.. ..	10	10
858†	2m50 Aardvark (*Orycteropus afer*)	.. ..	10	10

876†	2m African Buffalo	.. ..	10	10
878†	6m Topi	.. ..	30	30
880†	12m50 African Elephant ('Elefantes')	..	60	60

1983

MOÇAMBIQUE

1005	1m Four-toed Elephant-Shrew (*Petrodromus t. tetradactylus*)		
1006	2m Four-striped Grass Mouse (*Rhabdomys pumilio*)		
1007	4m Vincent's Bush Squirrel (*Paraxerus vincenti*)		
1008	8m Hottentot Mole-Rat (*Cryptomys hottettotus*)		
1009	12m Natal Red Hare (*Pronolagus crassicaudatus*)		
1010	16m Straw-coloured Fruit Bat (*Eidolon helvum*)		
	Set of 6	2.40	1.75

MOZAMBIQUE COMPANY

South-east Africa
100 centavos = 1 escudo

1937

286†	1c Giraffe	10	10
290†	20c Common Zebra	15	10
292†	40c White Rhinoceros	15	10
293†	45c Lion	15	10
295†	60c Leopard	15	10
297†	80c Hippopotamus	15	10
301†	2e Greater Kudu	75	15

1939

Nos. 292/3 and 301 overprinted **28-VII-1939 Visita Presidencial**

306†	40c White Rhinoceros	1.00	50
307†	45c Lion	1.00	50
311†	2e Greater Kudu	1.00	50

NEGRI SEMBILAN

South-east Asia
100 cents =1 dollar

1891

2	1c Tiger
3	2c Tiger
4	5c Tiger

Set of 3   18.00   20.00

STANLEY GIBBONS
STAMP COLLECTING SERIES

Introductory booklets on *How to Start, How to Identify Stamps* and *Collecting by Theme.* A series of well illustrated guides at a low price.
Write for details.

1896

5	1c Tiger
6	2c Tiger
7	3c Tiger
8	5c Tiger
9	8c Tiger
10	10c Tiger
11	15c Tiger
12	20c Tiger
13	25c Tiger
14	50c Tiger

Set of 10   £150   £160

1898

Nos. 2, 4, 7, 9 and 11 surcharged

15	1c on 15c Tiger
16	4c on 1c Tiger
17	4c on 3c Tiger
18	4c on 5c Tiger
19	4c on 8c Tiger

Set of 5   65.00   90.00

1957

73†	10c Tiger (sepia)	15	5
74†	10c Tiger (purple)	25	5

NEPAL

Central Asia
100 paisa = 1 rupee

1959

124†	8p Siberian Musk Deer	20	10
125†	12p Indian Rhinoceros	20	10

1973

293† 3r25 Yak 1.50 1.50

1975

321 2p Tiger (*Panthera tigris*)
322 5p Swamp Deer (*Cervus duvauceli*)
323 1r Lesser Panda (*Ailurus fulgens*)
                Set of 3 1.10 1.00

1984

449† 25p Snow Leopard (*Panthera uncia*) .. 25 25
450† 50p Blackbuck (*Antilope cervicapra*) .. 35 35
          (448/50 Set of 3) 75 75

NETHERLANDS
North-west Europe
100 cents = 1 gulden

1964

971† 8c + 5c Red Deer 25 20
973† 30c + 9c European Bison 55 45

1976

1241† 40c + 20c West European Hedgehog .. 75 55

1984

1447 70c Giant Panda 40 10

NEW CALEDONIA
South Pacific
100 centimes = 1 franc

1978

600 20f New Caledonian Flying Fox (*Pteropus macmilliani*) 50 40

1982

676 150f House Rat 2.50 2.50

STAMP MONTHLY
– finest and most informative magazine for all collectors. Obtainable from your newsagent or by postal subscription – details on request

POSTAGE DUE STAMPS

1928

D179 2c Sambar
D180 4c Sambar
D181 5c Sambar
D182 10c Sambar
D183 15c Sambar
D184 20c Sambar
D185 25c Sambar
D186 30c Sambar
D187 50c Sambar
D188 60c Sambar
D189 1f Sambar
D190 2f Sambar
D191 3f Sambar

Set of 13   4.00   4.00

1983

D703 1f New Caledonian Flying Fox
D704 2f New Caledonian Flying Fox
D705 3f New Caledonian Flying Fox
D706 4f New Caledonian Flying Fox
D707 5f New Caledonian Flying Fox
D708 10f New Caledonian Flying Fox
D709 20f New Caledonian Flying Fox
D710 40f New Caledonian Flying Fox
D711 50f New Caledonian Flying Fox

Set of 9   5.00   4.50

NEWFOUNDLAND

North Atlantic
100 cents = 1 dollar

1866

26† 5c Common Seal (brown) £500   £190

1868

As No. 26, but colour changed

38† 5c Common Seal (black) £190   £100
43† 5c Common Seal (blue) £170   11.00

1880

59a† 5c Common Seal 23.00   6.00

1897

69† 4c Reindeer ('Caribou Hunting') 4.00   3.50
75† 15c Grey Seal 12.00   7.00

1919

130 1c Reindeer ('Trail of the Caribou')
131 2c Reindeer
132a 3c Reindeer
133 4c Reindeer
134 5c Reindeer
135 6c Reindeer
136 8c Reindeer
137 10c Reindeer
138 12c Reindeer
139 15c Reindeer
140 24c Reindeer
141 36c Reindeer

Set of 12   75.00   £120

No. 132a *overprinted* **FIRST TRANS-ATLANTIC AIR POST**
April, 1919
142 3c Reindeer £12000 £8000

No. 75 *surcharged* **Trans-Atlantic AIR POST 1919**
ONE DOLLAR
143 $1 on 15c Grey Seal 90.00   48.00

1923

156†	9c Reindeer	12.00	22.00

1930

No. 141 *surcharged* **Trans Atlantic AIR MAIL By B. M.** "**Colum-bia**" **September 1930 Fifty Cents**

191	50c on 36c Reindeer	£4000	£3500

1932

213†	5c Reindeer ('Caribou') (purple)	3.50	1.00
225c†	5c Reindeer (violet)	70	10
217†	15c Harp Seal ('Northern Seal, Baby Whitecoat')	2.50	2.50

1937

259†	7c Reindeer ('Caribou')	1.25	1.00
263†	15c Harp Seal ('Northern Seal')	4.50	4.00

NEW HEBRIDES

South Pacific
100 centimes =1 franc

"F" No. is inscribed in French; the other in English

1974

187†	1f15 Grey-headed Flying Fox ('Flying Fox')	3.25	2.50
F202†	1f15 Grey-headed Flying Fox ('Rousette') (as No. 187)	4.00	4.00

NEW SOUTH WALES

Australia
12 pence = 1 shilling, 20 shillings = 1 pound

1888

270†	1s Eastern Grey Kangaroo	10.00	90

OFFICIAL STAMPS

1888

No. 270 *overprinted* **O.S.**

O46†	1s Eastern Grey Kangaroo	8.00	1.25

NEW ZEALAND

Australasia
1956 12 pence =1 shilling, 20 shillings =1 pound
1967 100 cents =1 dollar

1956

752†	2d Sperm Whale ('The Whalers of Foveaux Strait')	20	15

1970

931†	30c Chamois	2.50	65

1978

1177† 23c Humpback Whale, Bottle-nosed
Dolphin 60 50

1984

1328† 40c Crabeater Seal 30 35

NICARAGUA

Central America
100 centavos = 1 cordoba

1947

1108† 6c Baird's Tapir ('Danta de las
Montanas de Nicaragua') 10 10

1974

1947 1c Tamandua (*Tamandua tetradactyla*)
1948 2c Puma (*Felis concolor*)
1949 3c Common Racoon (*Procyon lotor*)
1950 4c Ocelot (*Felis pardalis*)
1951 5c Kinkajou (*Potos flavus*)
1952 10c Coypu (*Myocastor coypus*)
1953 15c Collared Peccary (*Tayassu tajacu*)
1954 20c Baird's Tapir (*Tapirus bairdi*)

1955 3cor Red Brocket (*Mazama americana*)
(air)
1956 5cor Jaguar (*Leo onca*)

Set of 10 4.00 3.50

1978

2168† 4c African Elephant 10 10

1981

MS2295 10cor Giant Panda 2.75 2.75

1983

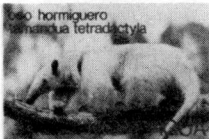

MS2486 15cor Ibex 4.00 3.00

MS2503 15cor Jaguar 4.00 3.00

STAMP MONTHLY

– finest and most informative magazine for all collectors.
Obtainable from your newsagent or by postal subscription – details on request

OFFICIAL STAMPS

1947

O1123† 20c Baird's Tapir 20 10

NIGER REPUBLIC
West Africa
100 centimes = 1 franc

1959

99†	50c African Manatee ('Lamantin')	10	10
104†	10f African Manatee	20	10
105†	15f Barbary Sheep ('Mouflons')	20	10
106†	20f Barbary Sheep	25	10
107†	25f Giraffe ('Girafes')	35	10
108†	30f Giraffe	40	20
111†	85f Lion	1.60	60
112†	100f Lion	2.00	70
114†	500f Topi, Roan Antelope, African Buffalo, African Elephant (air)	6.00	4.00

1960
Nos. 112 surcharged 200F and Independance 3–8–60
117 200f on 100f Lion 6.00 6.00

1969

310 50f Giraffe 70 65

No. 114 overprinted **L'HOMME SUR LA LUNE JUILLET 1969 APOLLO 11** and moon module
324 500f Topi, Roan Antelope, African Buffalo, African Elephant 6.00 6.00

1970

346 25f Giraffe (on stamp No. 107) 1.00 60

1972

453 25f Red Fox ('Le Renard')
454 50f Lion, Brown Rat ('Le Rat')
455 75f Leopard, Chimpanzee ('Le Singe')
Set of 3 1.60 80

1973

482 150f Lion ('Lionne')
483 200f Tiger ('Tigre')
Set of 2 3.50 1.75

485† 35f African Elephant ('Elephant') 40 20
486† 40f Hippopotamus ('Hippopotame') 45 20
487† 80f Warthog ('Phacochere') 65 35
(484/7 Set of 4) 1.60 80

1974

537 250f Javan Rhinoceros 2.75 1.60

1977

674† 90f Bushbuck (*Tragelaphus scriptus*) .. 70 45

1978

734† 100f Giraffe 90 65

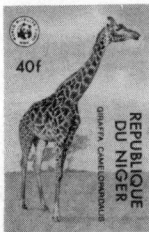

735†	40f Giraffe (*Giraffa camelopardalis*)	..	40	25
737†	70f Cheetah (*Acinonyx jubatus*)	.. ..	65	35
738†	150f Scimitar Oryx (*Oryx dammah*) ..	..	1.25	75

739†	200f Addax (*Addax nasomaculatus*)	..	1.75	95
740†	300f Hartebeest (*Alcalaphus buselaphus*			
	major)		2.50	1.25
	(735/40 *Set of* 6)		6.00	3.50

1981

839†	20f Scimitar Oryx ('Oryx')		15	10
840†	25f Addra Gazelle ('Gazelle Dama')	..	20	15
842†	60f Giraffe ('Girafe')		40	15
843†	150f Addax		1.00	45

NIGERIA

West Africa
1965 12 pence =1 shilling, 20 shillings =1 pound
1973 100 kobo = 1 naira

1965

172†	½d Lion	15	15
173†	1d African Elephant ('Elephants')	20	5
176†	3d Cheetah	50	5
177a†	4d Leopard	20	5
182†	2s6d Kob	1.00	30
183†	5s Giraffe	2.25	70
184†	10s Hippopotamus	6.00	3.00
185†	£1 African Buffalo ('Buffalos')	17.00	8.50

1969

As Nos. 172/83 but inscribed "N.S.P. & Co. Ltd" at foot

220†	1d African Elephant ('Elephants')	40	5
223†	3d Cheetah	60	10
224†	4d Leopard	1.25	5
229†	2s6d Kob	2.50	3.25
230†	5s Giraffe	2.50	3.00

STAMP MONTHLY

– finest and most informative magazine for all collectors.
Obtainable from your newsagent or by postal subscription – details on request

1973

| 344† | 10k Cheetah | . . . . | 15 | 12 |

1984

469	10k Waterbuck
470	25k Hartebeest
471	30k African Buffalo ('Buffalo')
472	45k Diademed Monkey ('African Golden Monkey')

| | | Set of 4 | 1.90 | 2.00 |

NIUE
South Pacific
100 cents = 1 dollar

1983

487	12c Black Right Whale ('Right Whale')
488	25c Fin Whale
489	35c Sei Whale
490	40c Blue Whale
491	58c Bowhead Whale
492	70c Sperm Whale
493	83c Humpback Whale
494	$1.05 Minke Whale ('Lesser Rorqual')
495	$2.50 Grey Whale ('Gray Whale')

| | | Set of 9 | 5.50 | 6.00 |

1984

552	25c Koala
553	35c Koala
554	40c Koala
555	58c Koala
556	70c Koala
557	83c Red Kangaroo (air)
558	$1.05 Red Kangaroo
559	$2.50 Red Kangaroo

| | | Set of 8 | 4.75 | 5.50 |
| MS560 | $1.75 Koala; $1.75 Wallaby sp | . . . . | 3.00 | 3.25 |

NIUAFO'OU
South Pacific
100 seniti = 1 pa'anga

1984

| 43† | 32s Insular Flying Fox ('Fruit Bat') | . . . . | 40 | 45 |
| 44† | 47s Humpback Whale | . . . . | 60 | 65 |

| 48† | 32s Eastern Grey Kangaroo (on Australia No. 138) | . . . . | 35 | 40 |

STANLEY GIBBONS
STAMP COLLECTING SERIES

Introductory booklets on *How to Start, How to Identify Stamps* and *Collecting by Theme*. A series of well illustrated guides at a low price.

Write for details.

NORFOLK ISLAND

Australasia
100 cents = 1 dollar

1982

284	24c Sperm Whale			
285	55c Black Right Whale ('Southern Right Whale')			
286	80c Humpback Whale			
		Set of 3	1.90	1.90

NORTH BORNEO

South-east Asia
100 cents = 1 dollar

1894

69†	2c Sambar		3.25	4.50

1897

Designs as No. 69 but with Malay inscription inserted

94a†	2c Sambar (black and red)	.. .. ..	5.00	2.75
95†	2c Sambar (black and green)	.. .. ..	7.00	3.25
98†	4c Orang-Utan (black and green)	.. ..	4.75	15.00
99†	4c Orang-Utan (black and red) ..	.. ..	5.50	4.75
104†	10c Sun Bear		18.00	16.00

1901

Nos. 95, 99 and 104 overprinted **BRITISH PROTECTORATE**

128a†	2c Sambar	.. ..	1.90	2.25
130a†	4c Orang-Utan	.. ..	3.25	2.00
134†	10c Sun Bear	.. ..	10.00	5.00

1909

159†	1c Malayan Tapir	3.00	90	
281†	5c Indian Elephant	.. .. ..	2.50	1.75
282†	6c Sumatran Rhinoceros	.. ..	2.25	90
284†	10c Wild Boar..	2.25	95	
175†	18c Banteng	38.00	45.00	1.60

No. 175 surcharged **20 CENTS**

287†	20c on 18c Banteng	.. ..	4.50	4.25

1916

No. 282 surcharged

187†	4c on 6c Sumatran Rhinoceros	.. ..	5.50	6.00

Nos. 159, 281/2 and 284 overprinted with a cross

189†	1c Malayan Tapir	7.50	16.00
193†	5c Indian Elephant	.. ..	18.00	30.00
206†	6c Sumatran Rhinoceros	.. .. ..	18.00	35.00
208†	10c Wild Boar	.. ..	20.00	42.00

1918

Nos. 159, 281/2 and 284 surcharged **RED CROSS TWO CENTS**

214†	1c + 2c Malayan Tapir	.. ..	1.60	6.50
219†	5c + 2c Indian Elephant	.. .. ..	3.75	9.00
221†	6c + 2c Sumatran Rhinoceros ..	.. ..	3.75	17.00
223†	10c + 2c Wild Boar	.. ..	3.50	12.00

Nos. 159, 281/2 and 284 surcharged +**FOUR CENTS**

235†	1c + 4c Malayan Tapir	.. ..	75	3.50
239†	5c + 4c Indian Elephant	.. .. ..	1.75	5.50
240†	6c + 4c Sumatran Rhinoceros ..	.. ..	1.60	7.50
242†	10c + 4c Wild Boar	.. ..	2.75	14.00

1922

Nos. 159, 281/2 and 284 overprinted **MALAYA–BORNEO EXHIBITION 1922**

253†	1c Malayan Tapir	3.75	12.00
258†	5c Indian Elephant	.. ..	4.00	13.00
260†	6c Sumatran Rhinoceros	.. .. ..	3.00	13.00
263†	10c Wild Boar	.. ..	4.50	20.00

1931

| 296† | 6c Orang-Utan | 14.00 | 4.50 |
| 299† | 25c Clouded Leopard | 25.00 | 25.00 |

1939

| 306† | 4c Proboscis Monkey | 80 | 80 |
| 309† | 10c Orang-Utan | 8.00 | 3.75 |

1945
Nos. 306 *and* 309 *overprinted* **BMA**

| 323† | 4c Proboscis Monkey | 6.00 | 4.50 |
| 326† | 10c Orang-Utan | 1.50 | 1.25 |

1947
Nos. 306 *and* 309 *overprinted with GR cypher and bars obliterating* "The State of" *and* "British Protectorate"

| 338† | 4c Proboscis Monkey | 20 | 15 |
| 341† | 10c Orang-Utan | 40 | 20 |

1961

391†	1c Sambar ('Payau')	10	5
392†	4c Sun Bear ('Honey Bear')	15	25
393†	5c Clouded Leopard	15	5
396†	12c Banteng ('Tembadau')	15	10
398†	25c Sumatran Rhinoceros ('Rhinoceros')	30	20
403†	$1 Orang-Utan	2.00	35

POSTAGE DUE STAMPS

Overprinted **POSTAGE DUE**

1895
| D2† | 2c Sambar (on No. 69) | 4.25 | 6.00 |

1897
| D12† | 2c Sambar (on No. 94a) | 3.00 | 5.00 |
| D15† | 2c Sambar (on No. 95) | 4.00 | 5.50 |

1902
D36†	2c Sambar (on No. 128a)	1.25	75
D38†	4c Orang-Utan (on No. 130a)	3.50	2.50
D42†	10c Sun Bear (on No. 134)	13.00	7.50

1930
D52†	5c Indian Elephant (on No. 281)	2.00	2.25
D53†	6c Sumatran Rhinoceros (on No. 282)	3.75	5.50
D55†	10c Wild Boar (on No. 284)	4.25	7.00

NORTH KOREA
See under Korea

NORTH VIETNAM
See under Vietnam

NORTHERN RHODESIA
Central Africa
12 pence = 1 shilling

1925

1	½d Giraffe, African Elephant
2	1d Giraffe, African Elephant
3	1½d Giraffe, African Elephant
4	2d Giraffe, African Elephant
5	3d Giraffe, African Elephant
6	4d Giraffe, African Elephant
7	6d Giraffe, African Elephant
8	8d Giraffe, African Elephant
9	10d Giraffe, African Elephant
10	1s Giraffe, African Elephant
11	2s Giraffe, African Elephant
12	2s6d Giraffe, African Elephant
13	3s Giraffe, African Elephant
14	5s Giraffe, African Elephant
15	7s6d Giraffe, African Elephant
16	10s Giraffe, African Elephant
17	20s Giraffe, African Elephant

Set of 17   £350   £375

1938

As 1925 issue, but with portrait of King George VI

25 ½d Giraffe, African Elephant (green)
26 ½d Giraffe, African Elephant (brown)
27 1d Giraffe, African Elephant (brown)
28 1d Giraffe, African Elephant (green)
29 1½d Giraffe, African Elephant (red)
30 1½d Giraffe, African Elephant (orange)
31 2d Giraffe, African Elephant (orange)
32 2d Giraffe, African Elephant (red)
33 2d Giraffe, African Elephant (purple)
34 3d Giraffe, African Elephant (blue)
35 3d Giraffe, African Elephant (red)
36 4d Giraffe, African Elephant
37 4½d Giraffe, African Elephant
38 6d Giraffe, African Elephant
39 9d Giraffe, African Elephant
40 1s Giraffe, African Elephant
41 2s6d Giraffe, African Elephant
42 3s Giraffe, African Elephant
43 5s Giraffe, African Elephant
44 10s Giraffe, African Elephant
45 20s Giraffe, African Elephant

Set of 21 £110 60.00

1953

As 1925 issue but with portrait of Queen Elizabeth II

61 ½d Giraffe, African Elephant
62 1d Giraffe, African Elephant
63 1½d Giraffe, African Elephant
64 2d Giraffe, African Elephant
65 3d Giraffe, African Elephant
66 4d Giraffe, African Elephant
67 4½d Giraffe, African Elephant
68 6d Giraffe, African Elephant
69 9d Giraffe, African Elephant
70 1s Giraffe, African Elephant
71 2s6d Giraffe, African Elephant
72 5s Giraffe, African Elephant
73 10s Giraffe, African Elephant
74 20s Giraffe, African Elephant

Set of 14 38.00 65.00

NORWAY

Northern Europe
100 ore = 1 krone

1925

167 2 ore Polar Bear
168 3 ore Polar Bear
169 5 ore Polar Bear
170 10 ore Polar Bear
171 15 ore Polar Bear
172 20 ore Polar Bear
173 25 ore Polar Bear

Set of 7 50.00 50.00

1938

262† 15 ore Reindeer 1.00 60

1970

644† 40 ore Wolf (*Canis lupus*) 1.25 50

1975

745† 1k40 Polar Bear 1.40 1.40

1978

819† 1k25 Polar Bear (on stamp No. 170) .. 1.00 1.00
820† 1k25 Polar Bear (on stamp No. 171) .. 1.00 1.00
823† 1k25 Polar Bear (on stamp No. 172) .. 1.00 1.00
824† 1k25 Polar Bear (on stamp No. 173) .. 1.00 1.00

NYASALAND PROTECTORATE

Central Africa
12 pence = 1 shilling, 20 shillings = 1 pound

1934

114	½d Leopard
115	1d Leopard
116	1½d Leopard
117	2d Leopard
118	3d Leopard
119	4d Leopard
120	6d Leopard
121	9d Leopard
122	1s Leopard

Set of 9   15.00   24.00

1938

As 1934 issue but with portrait of King George VI

130	½d Leopard (green)
130a	½d Leopard (brown)
131	1d Leopard (brown)
131a	1d Leopard (green)
132	1½d Leopard (red)
132a	1½d Leopard (grey)
133	2d Leopard (grey)
133a	2d Leopard (red)
134	3d Leopard
135	4d Leopard
136	6d Leopard
137	9d Leopard
138	1s Leopard

Set of 13   5.50   5.50

1945

160†   1d Leopard   20   10

1953

As No. 160, but with portrait of Queen Elizabeth II
174†   1d Leopard (as No. 160)   15   5

STAMP MONTHLY

– finest and most informative magazine for all collectors.
Obtainable from your newsagent or by postal subscription – details on request

1964

210†   £1 Nyala 8.50   9.50

NYASSA COMPANY

South-east Africa
1901 1000 reis = 1 milreis
1912 100 centavos = 1 escudo

1901

27	2½r Giraffe
28	5r Giraffe
29	10r Giraffe
30	15r Giraffe
31	20r Giraffe
32	25r Giraffe
33	50r Giraffe
34	75r Dromedary
35	80r Dromedary
36	100r Dromedary
37	150r Dromedary
38	200r Dromedary
39	300r Dromedary

Set of 13   10.00   6.00

1903

Nos. 35, 37 and 39 surcharged in figures and words

40	65r on 80r Dromedary
41	115r on 150r Dromedary
42	130r on 300r Dromedary

Set of 3   2.00   1.50

Nos. 30 and 32 overprinted **PROVISORIO**

43	15r Giraffe
44	25r Giraffe

Set of 2   1.50   1.00

1910

Nos. 27 and 36 overprinted **PROVISORIO** *and surcharged in figures and words*

50   5r on 2½r Giraffe
51   50r on 100r Dromedary

Set of 2   1.50   1.00

1911

96†	½c Giraffe		60	50
97†	½c Giraffe		60	50
98†	1c Giraffe		60	50
99†	1½c Giraffe		60	50
110†	30c Common Zebra		1.00	60
111†	40c Common Zebra		1.00	60
112†	50c Common Zebra		1.00	60
113†	1e Common Zebra		1.25	60

Unissued stamps overprinted **REPUBLICA**

53†	2½r Dromedary	80	50
54†	5r Dromedary	80	50
55†	10r Dromedary	80	50
56†	20r Common Zebra	80	50
57†	25r Common Zebra	80	50
58†	50r Common Zebra	80	50
59†	75r Giraffe	1.00	75
60†	100r Giraffe	1.00	75
61†	200r Giraffe	1.25	1.00

POSTAGE DUE STAMPS

1924

1918

Nos. 27/39 surcharged **REPUBLICA** *and value*

65   ½c on 2½r Giraffe
66   ½c on 5r Giraffe
67   1c on 10r Giraffe
68   1½c on 15r Giraffe
69   2c on 20r Giraffe
70   3½c on 25r Giraffe
71   5c on 50r Giraffe
72   7½c on 75r Dromedary
73   8c on 80r Dromedary
74   10c on 100r Dromedary
75   15c on 150r Dromedary
76   20c on 200r Dromedary
77   30c on 300r Dromedary

Set of 13   75.00   50.00

D132†	½c Giraffe	1.60	1.10
D133†	1c Giraffe	1.60	1.10
D134†	2c Common Zebra	1.60	1.10
D135†	3c Common Zebra	1.60	1.10

1919

Nos. 40/4 surcharged **REPUBLICA** *and value*

78   1½c on 15r Giraffe
79   3½c on 25r Giraffe
80   40c on 65r on 80r Dromedary
81   50c on 115r on 150r Dromedary
82   1e on 130r on 300r Dromedary

Set of 5   10.00   9.00

OMAN

Arabian Peninsula
1000 baizas = 1 rial saidi

1982

1921

Nos. 53/61 surcharged

83†	½c on 2½r Dromedary	1.00	1.00
85†	½c on 5r Dromedary	1.00	1.00
86†	1c on 10r Dromedary	1.00	1.00
88†	2c on 20r Common Zebra	1.00	1.00
89†	2½c on 25r Common Zebra	1.00	1.00
91†	5c on 50r Common Zebra	1.00	1.00
92†	7½c on 75r Giraffe	1.00	1.00
93†	10c on 100r Giraffe	1.00	1.00
95†	20c on 200r Giraffe	1.25	1.25

269†	½r Arabian Tahr (*Hemitragus jayakari*)	2.50	2.50
270†	1r Arabian Oryx (*Oryx leucoryx*)	5.00	5.00

ORANGE FREE STATE
Southern Africa
12 pence = 1 shilling

1903

139	½d Springbok, Black Wildebeest	
140	1d Springbok, Black Wildebeest	
141	2d Springbok, Black Wildebeest	
142	2½d Springbok, Black Wildebeest	
143	3d Springbok, Black Wildebeest	
144	4d Springbok, Black Wildebeest	
145	6d Springbok, Black Wildebeest	
146	1s Springbok, Black Wildebeest	
147	5s Springbok, Black Wildebeest	

Set of 9   70.00   32.00

PAHANG
South-east Asia
100 cents = 1 dollar

1891

11	1c Tiger	
12	2c Tiger	
13	5c Tiger	

Set of 3   7.00   9.50

1895

14	3c Tiger	
15	4c Tiger	
16	5c Tiger	

Set of 3   13.00   9.50

STAMP MONTHLY
– finest and most informative magazine for all collectors.
Obtainable from your newsagent or by postal subscription – details on request

1897
No. 13 divided, and each half surcharged

17	2c on half of 5c Tiger		
18	3c on half of 5c Tiger		

Set of 2   £1000   £500

1898
Nos. 68/71 of Perak overprinted **Pahang**

19†	10c Tiger	12.00	18.00
20†	25c Tiger	26.00	32.00
21†	50c Tiger (green and black)	50.00	50.00
22†	50c Tiger (purple and black)	75.00	75.00

1898
No. 67 of Perak surcharged **Pahang Four cents**

25	4c on 8c Tiger	3.00	4.75

1899
No. 15 surcharged **Four cents**

28	4c on 5c Tiger	8.00	13.00

1957

80†	10c Tiger (sepia)	15	5
81†	10c Tiger (purple)	25	5

PAKISTAN
Indian Sub-continent
100 paisa = 1 rupee

1975

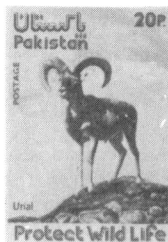

400	20p Urial		
401	3r Urial		

Set of 2   2.25   2.10

1976

417 20p Ibex
418 3r Ibex
                        Set of 2 2.00 2.25

1982

581 40p Indus Dolphin
582 1r Indus Dolphin
                        Set of 2   20   15

1983

600 1r Goitred Gazelle ('Chinkara') (latin name
       on stamp erroneous)   10   12

1984

621 40p Snow Leopard
622 1r60 Snow Leopard
                        Set of 2   25   30

PALAU
North Pacific
100 cents =1 dollar

1983

20† $2 Dugong 3.00 1.50

25 20c Humpback Whale
26 20c Blue Whale
27 20c Fin Whale
28 20c Sperm Whale ('Great Sperm Whale')
                        Set of 4 1.75 1.40

PANAMA
Central America
100 centesimos = 1 balboa

1967

955† 13c Brown Hare   30   20

COLLECT BIRDS ON STAMPS
The first Stanley Gibbons thematic catalogue – a few
copies still available at £4.95 (p.+p. £1.30) plus FREE
1983–84 Supplement from:
Stanley Gibbons Publications Ltd, 5, Parkside,
Christchurch Road, Ringwood, Hants BH24 3SH.

1984

1384 3c American Manatee (*Trichechus manatus*)
1385 30c Tayra (*Eira barbara*) (air)
1386 44c Jaguarundi (*Felis yagouaroundi*)
1387 50c White-lipped Peccary (*Tayassu pecari*)

Set of 4	3.50	3.00

MS1388 1b Brown-throated Sloth (*Bradypus griseus*) 3.00 3.00

Appendix
The following have either been issued in excess of postal needs, or have not been made available to the public in reasonable quantities at face value. Miniature sheets, imperforate stamps etc., are excluded from this section.

1968
Hunting Paintings (Lion, Red Deer, Hippopotamus). Postage 1, 3c; Air 13, 30c.

PAPUA NEW GUINEA
Australasia
1952 12 pence = 1 shilling
20 shillings =1 pound
1966 100 cents =1 Australian dollar
1975 100 toea = 1 kina

1952

1† ½d Matschie's Tree Kangaroo 30 10

1957
No. 1 surcharged
25† 5d on ½d Matschie's Tree Kangaroo 30 5

1963

43† 6d Common Phalanger 1.00 1.25

1971

195 5c Spotted Phalanger (*Phalanger maculatus*)
196 10c Long-fingered Possum (*Dactylonax palpator*)
197 15c Feather-tailed Possum (*Distoechurus pennatus*)
198 25c Long-nosed Echidna (*Zaglossus bruijni*)
199 30c Ornate Tree Kangaroo (*Dendrolagus goodfellowi*)

Set of 5	6.00	5.50

1980

397 7t Dugong ('Bonon')
398 30t New Guinea Marsupial Cat ('Native Spotted Cat')
399 35t Tube-nosed Bat sp. ('Tube-nosed Bat')
400 45t Rufescent Bandicoot ('Mumut')

Set of 4	1.60	1.60

POSTAGE DUE STAMPS

1960
No. 1 surcharged **POSTAL CHARGES** *and value*
D3† 3d on ½d Matschie's Tree Kangaroo 15.00 7.00

PARAGUAY
South America
100 centimos = 1 guarani

1961

930 75c Puma
931 1g50 Puma
932 4g50 Puma
933 10g Puma

934   12g45 Brazilian Tapir ('Tapir')
935   18g15 Brazilian Tapir ('Tapir')
936   34g80 Brazilian Tapir ('Tapir')

Set of 7   6.00   5.00

Appendix

The following stamps have either been issued in excess of postal needs, or have not been made available to the public in reasonable quantities at face value. Miniature sheets, imperforate stamps etc., are excluded from this section.

1971
Hunting Paintings (Red Deer). 50c.

1972
Wildlife Paintings (Tiger, Monkey, Deer). 15, 30, 50c.

South American Fauna (Tamandua, Coati, Armadillo, Marsh Deer, Ocelot, Night Monkey, Vampire Bat, Grey Fox). Postage 10, 15, 20, 25, 30, 50c; Air 12g45, 18g15.
A further value shows a bird.

1975
South American Fauna (Golden Lion Tamarin, Mara, Marmoset, Peccary). 25, 35, 40, 50c.
Other values show fish or reptiles.

PENANG
South-east Asia
100 cents = 1 dollar

1957

49†   10c Tiger (brown)   15   5

1960

60†   10c Tiger (purple)   15   5

PENRHYN ISLAND
South Pacific
100 cents = 1 dollar

1983

290   8c Sperm Whale
291   15c Whale sp. (being harpooned)
292   35c Whale sp. (tail only)
293   60c Whale sp. (harpooned)
294   $1· Blue Whale

Set of 5   2.00   2.25

PERAK
South-east Asia
100 cents = 1 dollar

1892

57   1c Tiger
58   2c Tiger (red)
59   2c Tiger (orange)
60   5c Tiger (blue)

Set of 4   3.00   6.00

1895
No. 60 in different colour surcharged 3 CENTS
61   3c on 5c Tiger (red)   55   1.00

62†	1c Tiger	. . . .	55	70
63†	2c Tiger	. . . .	75	65
64†	3c Tiger	·.	1.50	30
65†	4c Tiger	. . . .	2.50	3.75
66†	5c Tiger	. . . .	2.25	90
67†	8c Tiger	. . . .·.	10.00	1.00
68†	10c Tiger	. . . .	5.50	1.00
69†	25c Tiger	. . . .	38.00	10.00
70†	50c Tiger (purple and black)	. . . . . .	19.00	14.00
71†	50c Tiger (green and black)	. . . . . .	45.00	45.00

1900
Nos. 63, 65/7 and 71 surcharged in words

77†	1c on 2c Tiger	35	65
78†	1c on 4c Tiger	35	90
79†	1c on 5c Tiger	40	2.00
80†	3c on 8c Tiger	2.00	2.75
81†	3c on 50c Tiger	80	2.00

1957

151†	10c Tiger (sepia)	15	5
152†	10c Tiger (purple)	25	5

PERLIS
South-east Asia
100 cents = 1 dollar

1957

34†	10c Tiger (brown)	15	15
35†	10c Tiger (purple)	30	12

PERU
South America
1866 100 centavos = 1 peso
1874 100 centavos = 1 sol

1866

17†	5c Vicuna (green)	6.00	1.00

1886
As No. 17, but colour changed

316†	5c Vicuna (lake)	1.25	60

1952

Inscribed "THOMAS DE LA RUE & CO. LTD" at foot

778†	20c Vicuna ('Vicuña') (brown)	50	15

1960
As No. 778, but inscribed "JOH. ENSCHEDE EN ZONEN–HOLLAND" at foot

829†	20c Vicuna ('Vicuña') (brown)	25	10

1962
As No. 778, but colour changed and inscribed "THOMAS DE LA RUE & CO. LTD" at foot

867†	20c Vicuna ('Vicuña') (purple)	25	10

1966
As No. 778, but inscribed "INA" at foot

921	20c Vicuna ('Vicuña') (red)	10	10

1973

1186†	3s50 Giant Otter (Pteronura brasiliensis)	40	10
1188†	5s Vicuna (Vicugna vicugna)	50	15
1190†	8s Spectacled Bear (Tremarctos ornatus)	60	20
1191†	8s50 Bush Dog (Speothus venaticus)	60	20
1192†	10s Short-tailed Chinchilla (Eriomys chinchilla)	75	25

STANLEY GIBBONS
STAMP COLLECTING SERIES
Introductory booklets on How to Start, How to Identify Stamps and Collecting by Theme. A series of well illustrated guides at a low price.
Write for details.

1974

1245 8s Red Uakari (*Cacajao rubicundus*)
1246 20s Red Uakari
                         Set of 2   2.00   75

1984

1588 1000s Hendee's Woolly Monkey
       (*Lagothrix flavicauda*)   50   40

OFFICIAL STAMPS

1890
No. 17 overprinted **GOBIERNO** *in frame*
O326† 5c Vicuna 4.50   4.50

1979

1515 30s Malay Civet (*Viverra tangalunga*)
1516 1p20 Crab-eating Macaque (*Macaca philippinensis philippinensis*)
1517 2p20 Javan Pig (*Sas celebensis philippensis*)
1518 2p30 Leopard Cat (*Felis minuta*)
1519 5p Oriental Small-clawed Otter (*Amblovx cinerea cinerea*)
1520 5p Malayan Pangolin (*Paramanis culionensis*)
                       Set of 6   6.25   3.25

1984

1843 3p Koala, Eastern Grey Kangaroo (on Australia No. 138)
1844 3p60 Koala, Eastern Grey Kangaroo
                       Set of 2   1.25   1.00
MS1845 20p × 3 Koala, Eastern Grey Kangaroo   7.50   7.50

PHILIPPINES
South-east Asia
100 sentimos = 1 piso

1969

1088 2s Philippine Tarsier ('Tarsier')
1089 10s Tamarau ('Tamaraw')
1090 20s Water Buffalo ('Carabao')
1091 75s Greater Malay Chevrotain ('Mouse Deer')
                       Set of 4   1.25   1.00

POLAND
Eastern Europe
100 groszy = 1 zloty

1954

900 45g European Bison
901 60g Elk
902 1z90 Chamois
903 3z Eurasian Beaver
                       Set of 4   3.00   75

1963

1434† 30g Wild Horse ('Tarpany') 12 5

1965

1613 20g Wolf
1614 30g Lynx
1615 40g Red Fox
1616 50g Eurasian Badger
1617 60g Brown Bear
1618 1z50 Wild Boar
1619 2z50 Red Deer
1620 5z60 European Bison
1621 7z10 Elk

Set of 9 6.50 2.00

1972

2147†	20g Cheetah (Acinonyx jubatus)	10	10
2148†	40g Giraffe (Giraffe camelopardis) ..	10	10
2150†	1z35 Chimpanzee (Pan troglodytes) ..	20	10
2151†	1z65 Common Gibbon (Hylobates lar) ..	40	10
2153†	4z Red Kangaroo (Macropus rufus) ..	1.00	15
2154†	4z50 Tiger (Panthera tigris sumatrac) ..	3.25	1.50
2155†	7z Mountain Zebra (Equus zebra)	4.00	2.00

1973

2232†	50g Wolf (Canis lupus)	5	5
2233†	1z Mouflon (Ovis ammon musimon) ..	10	5
2234†	1z50 Elk (Alces alces)	15	5
2236†	3z Roe Deer (Capreolus capreolus) ..	30	5
2237†	4z50 Lynx (Lynx lynx)	70	20
2238†	4z90 Red Deer (Cervus elaphus)	2.50	60
2239†	5z Wild Boar (Sus scrofa)	2.75	75
	(2232/9 Set of 8)	6.00	1.60

2256† 5z Red Fox 2.00 45

2266†	1z Red Kangaroo	15	10
2269†	1z50 Sable	20	10

1976

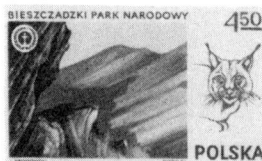

2435†	4z50 Lynx	50	20
2436†	5z Bat sp.	50	20
2437†	6z Elk	60	20

STAMP MONTHLY
– finest and most informative magazine for all collectors.
Obtainable from your newsagent or by postal subscription – details on request

1977

2491†	1z Wolf (*Canis lupus*)	12	10
2494†	6z European Otter (*Lutra lutra*)	60	20

1978

2578 50g Wild Horse (*Eguus przewalskii*)
2579 1z Polar Bear (*Thalarctos maritimus*)
2580 1z50 Indian Elephant (*Elaphas maximus*)
2581 2z Jaguar (*Panthera onca*)
2582 4z20 Grey Seal (*Halichoerus grypus*)
2583 4z50 Hartebeest (*Alcelaphus caama*)
2584 6z Mandrill (*Mandrillus sphinx*)

	Set of 7 2.00	60

1980

2673†	2z Kerguelen Fur Seal	25	10

1981

2752†	2z Wild Boar (*Sus scrofa*)	25	10
2753†	2z Elk (*Alces alces*)	25	10
2754†	2z50 Red Fox (*Vulpes vulpes*)	30	10
2755†	2z50 Roe Deer (*Capreolus capreolus*) ..	30	10

2758 6z50 European Bison (*Bison bonasus*)
2759 6z50 European Bison (*Bison bonasus*)
　　　(two bisons, one grazing)
2760 6z50 European Bison (*Bison bonasus*)
　　　(bison with calf)
2761 6z50 European Bison (*Bison bonasus*)
　　　(calf feeding)
2762 6z50 European Bison (*Bison bonasus*)
　　　(two bisons looking towards right)

	Set of 5 4.00	1.50

1983

2867†	31z Roe Deer, European Bison	1.40	50

1984

2962 4z Weasel (*Mustela nivalis*)
2963 5z Stoat (*Mustela erminea*)
2964 5z Beech Marten (*Martes foina*)
2965 10z Eurasian Beaver (*Castor fiber*)
2966 10z European Otter (*Lutra lutra*)
2967 65z Alpine Marmot (*Marmota marmota*)

	Set of 6 5.00	1.50

COLLECT BIRDS ON STAMPS

The first Stanley Gibbons thematic catalogue – a few copies still available at £4.95 (p.+p. £1.30) plus FREE 1983–84 Supplement from:
Stanley Gibbons Publications Ltd, 5, Parkside, Christchurch Road, Ringwood, Hants BH24 3SH.

PORTUGAL

South-west Europe
100 centavos = 1 escudo

1976

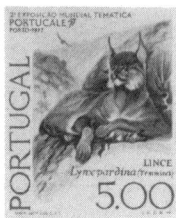

1619† 5e Lynx (*Lynx pardina*) 1.00 30

1980

1797† 16e Red Fox (*Vulpes vulpes*) 70 30
1798† 19e50 Wolf (*Canis lupus signatus*) .. 1.10 40

1983

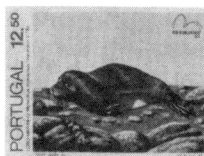

1928 12e50 Mediterranean Monk Seal
(*Monachus monachus*)
1929 30e Common Dolphin (*Delphinus delphis*)
1930 37e50 Killer Whale (*Orcinus orca*)
1931 80e Humpback Whale (*Megaptera novaeangliae*)
Set of 4 2.50 1.80

STANLEY GIBBONS
STAMP COLLECTING SERIES

Introductory booklets on *How to Start, How to Identify Stamps* and *Collecting by Theme*. A series of well illustrated guides at a low price.
Write for details.

1984

1944 16e Tiger (*Panthera tigris altaica*)
1945 16e Cheetah (*Acinonyx jubatus*), Thomson's Gazelle
1946 16e Blesbok (*Albifrons*)
1947 16e White Rhinoceros (*Cerototherium simum*)
Set of 4 1.25 80

PORTUGUESE GUINEA

West Africa
100 centavos = 1 escudo

1948

312† 1e75 Bushbuck 6.50 3.50

QATAR

Arabian Peninsula
100 dirhams = 1 riyal

1971

352† 60d Arabian Oryx 70 50
353† 1r25 Mountain Gazelle 1.25 80
354† 2r Dromedary 1.90 1.10

1974

534† 75d Arabian Oryx 60 35

1970

446† 12½c Hippopotamus 70 25

1974

489 1c Greater Kudu ('Kudu')
490 2½c Eland
491 3c Roan Antelope
492 4c Reedbuck
493 5c Bushbuck
Set of 5   1.25   20

RHODESIA

Central Africa
1966 12 pence = 1 shilling, 20 shillings = 1 pound
1969 100 cents = 1 dollar

1966
Nos. 93 and 95 of Southern Rhodesia overprinted
INDEPENDENCE 11th November 1965
360† 1d African Buffalo ('Buffalo') 10 5
362† 3d Greater Kudu ('Kudu') 12 5

374† 1d African Buffalo ('Buffalo') .. .. .. ' 10 5
376† 3d Greater Kudu ('Kudu') 10 5

1967

408† 2½c and 3d Greater Kudu 60 25

419† 4d White Rhinoceros ('White Rhino') .. 55 70
420† 4d African Elephant ('Elephant') 55 70

1976

529 4c Roan Antelope
530 6c Brown Hyena
531 8c Hunting Dog ('Wild Dog')
532 16c Cheetah
Set of 4   2.00   2.00

1978

560† 9c White Rhinoceros ('Rhinoceros') .. 20 5
561† 11c Lion 20 12
562† 13c Warthog 20 12
563† 15c Giraffe 20 15
564† 17c Common Zebra ('Zebra') 25 5

STAMP MONTHLY
– finest and most informative magazine for all collectors.
Obtainable from your newsagent or by postal subscription – details on request

RIAU–LINGGA ARCHIPELAGO

South-east Asia
100 sen = 1 rupiah

1957

Nos. 714, 717 and 723 of Indonesia overprinted **RIAU**

23	10s Lesser Malay Chevrotain ('Kantjil')	
24	25s Hairy-nosed Otter ('Lingsang')	
25	50s Banteng	

Set of 3   16.50   22.00

1958

Nos. 713/18 and 722 of Indonesia overprinted **RIAU** *in double-lined letters*

26	5s Lesser Malay Chevrotain ('Kantjil')
27	10s Lesser Malay Chevrotain
28	15s Lesser Malay Chevrotain
29	20s Hairy-nosed Otter ('Lingsang')
30	25s Hairy-nosed Otter
31	30s Hairy-nosed Otter
32	50s Banteng

Set of 7   2.50   3.50

RIO MUNI

West Africa
100 centimos = 1 peseta

1961

18	10c + 5c Mandrill		
19	25c + 10c African Elephant		
20	80c + 20c Mandrill		

Set of 3   50   40

21†	25c African Elephant	30	10

1962

32	15c African Buffalo		
33	35c Gorilla		
34	1p African Buffalo		

Set of 3   50   40

1964

45†	25c Giant Ground Pangolin	10	10
47†	1p Giant Ground Pangolin	20	10

49†	25c Leopard	10	10
50†	50c Black Rhinoceros	10	10
52†	1p Leopard	40	10
53†	1p50 Black Rhinoceros	40	10
55†	5p Leopard	1.60	40
56†	10p Black Rhinoceros	5.00	85

1965

67†	1p Leopard	30	10

1966

69	50c African Elephant		
70	1p African Elephant		
71	1p50 Lion		

Set of 3   80   30

72	10c Water Chevrotain (*Hyemoschus aquaticus*)		
73	40c Giant Ground Pangolin (*Smutsia gigantea*)		
74	1p50 Water Chevrotain		
75	4p Giant Ground Pangolin		

Set of 4   50   30

1967

80 1p Bush Pig (*Potamocherus porcus*)
81 1p50 Potto (*Perodicticus potto*)
82 3p50 African Golden Cat (*Profelis aurata*)

		Set of 3	50	30

RUANDA–URUNDI
Central Africa
100 centimes = 1 franc

1916
No. 76 of Belgian Congo overprinted **EST AFRICIAN ALLEMAND OCCUPATION BELGE DUITSCH OOST AFRIKA BELGISCHE BEZETTING**

21†	1f African Elephant	50	40

1918
No. 84 of Belgian Congo overprinted **A.O.**

29†	1f + 1f African Elephant	1.00	1.00

1924
No. 140 of Belgian Congo overprinted **RUANDA URUNDI**

54†	10f African Elephant	13.00	8.00

1931

89†	50c African Buffalo	25	15

1941
No. 89 surcharged

110†	60c on 50c African Buffalo	1.75	1.75

1942

131†	1f75 Leopard	60	35
132†	2f Leopard	60	25
133†	2f50 Leopard	60	15
139†	20f Common Zebra	1.75	85

1944
No. 131 surcharged **Au profit de la Croix Rouge + 100 fr.**
Ten voordeele van het Roode Kruis

149†	1f75 + 100f Leopard	1.10	1.25

1959

203 10c Gorilla
204 20c African Buffalo (*Bubalus*)
205 40c Eastern Black-and-White Colobus
      (*Colobus*)
206 50c Impala
207 1f Gorilla
208 1f50 African Buffalo
209 2f Eastern Black-and-White Colobus
210 3f African Elephant (*Loxodonta africana*)
211 5f Eland (*Taurotragus oryx*), Common
      Zebra (*Hippotigris*)
212 6f50 Impala
213 8f African Elephant
214 10f Eland, Common Zebra

		Set of 12	2.50	1.10

1960
No. 210 surcharged

228	3f50 on 3f African Elephant	25	10

1961

229 20f Leopard (*Panthera pardus*)
230 50f Lion (*Felis leo*)

		Set of 2	2.75	1.50

STANLEY GIBBONS
STAMP COLLECTING SERIES

Introductory booklets on *How to Start, How to Identify Stamps* and *Collecting by Theme*. A series of well illustrated guides at a low price.
Write for details.

RUMANIA

South-east Europe
100 bani = 1 leu

1954

| 2322† | 20b Red Deer | | 3.00 | 20 |

1955

| 2355† | 35b Wild Boar | | 1.25 | 20 |

1956

2423†	20b Brown Hare ('Lepure') (black and green)		2.00	2.00
2426†	50b Wild Boar ('Mistret') (brown and blue)		2.00	2.00
2428†	55b Brown Bear ('Urs') (brown and turquoise)		2.50	2.00
2429†	1le Lynx ('Ris') (lake and green)		4.00	4.00
2430†	1le55 Eurasian Red Squirrel ('Veverita') (lake and blue)		4.50	4.50
2432†	2le Chamois ('Capra Neagra') (brown and blue)		20.00	20.00
2434†	4le25 Red Deer ('Cerb') (brown and salmon)		20.00	20.00

Imperforated. As No. 2423/34, but colours changed

2474†	20b Brown Hare (brown and green)		5.00	5.00
2477†	50b Wild Boar (black and brown)		5.00	5.00
2479†	55b Brown Bear (brown and bistre)		5.00	5.00
2480†	1le Lynx (brown and blue)		5.00	5.00
2481†	1le55 Eurasian Red Squirrel (brown and bistre)		5.00	5.00
2483†	2le Chamois (black and blue)		5.00	5.00
2485†	4le25 Red Deer (brown and violet)		5.00	5.00

1957

| 2556† | 55b Stoat ('Hermina') | | 1.00 | 20 |

1961

2852	10b Roe Deer
2853	20b Lynx
2854	35b Wild Boar
2855	40b Brown Bear
2856	55b Red Deer
2857	75b Red Fox
2858	1le Chamois
2859	1le55 Brown Hare
2860	1le75 Eurasian Badger
2861	2le Roe Deer

Set of 10 12.00 2.50

1964

3201†	55b Tiger (*Panthera tigris*)		75	15
3202†	1le Lion (*Panthera leo*)		1.10	20
3203†	1le55 Grevy's Zebra (*Dolichohippus grevyi*)		1.60	20
3204†	2le Bactrian Camel (*Camelus bactrianus*)		2.40	30

1965

3332	55b Chamois
3333	1le Brown Bear
3334	1le60 Red Deer
3335	1le75 Wild Boar
3336	3le20 Red Deer

Set of 5 7.50 1.50

1968

3604† 1le35 Chamois (*Rupicapra rupicapra*) .. 80 25
3605† 1le60 European Bison (*Bison bonasus*) 1.00 40

1972

1977

4284† 55b Red Deer (*Cervus elaphus*) 20 10
4287† 2le15 European Bison (*Bison bonasus*) 60 10

1980

3885 20b Lynx (*Lynx lynx*)
3886 35b Red Fox (*Vulpes vulpes*)
3887 55b Roe Deer (*Capreolus capreolus*)
3888 1le Wild Boar (*Sus scrofa*)
3889 1le50 Wolf (*Canis lupus*)
3890 2le40 Brown Bear (*Ursus arctos*)
Set of 6 4.00 1.50

1976

4234 20b Red Deer (*Cervus elaphus*)
4235 40b Brown Bear (*Ursus arctos*)
4236 55b Chamois (*Rupicapra rupicapra*)
4237 1le75 Wild Boar (*Sus scrofa*)
4238 2le75 Red Fox (*Canis vulpes*)
4239 3le60 Lynx (*Felis linx*)
Set of 6 3.00 80

4569† 2le15 Red Deer (*Cervus elaphus*) 45 15
4570† 3le40 Roe Deer (*Capreolus capreolus juv*) 70 20
4571† 4le80 European Bison (*Bison bonasus*) 1.10 30

1982

STANLEY GIBBONS
STAMP COLLECTING SERIES

Introductory booklets on *How to Start, How to Identify Stamps* and *Collecting by Theme*. A series of well illustrated guides at a low price.
Write for details.

4738† 1le Brown Bear 25 10

1983

4816†	1le Eurasian Red Squirrel (*Scirurus vulgaris*)	40	25
4819†	1le Lynx (*Lynx lynx*)	40	25

1984

4849†	2le Red Deer	50	20

RUSSIA

Eastern Europe and Northern Asia
100 kopecks = 1 rouble

1931

584 30k Polar Bear
585 35k Polar Bear
586 1r Polar Bear
587 2r Polar Bear

Set of 4 85.00 40.00

1935

687†	50k Polar Bear	35.00	9.00

1939

865†	1r Arctic Fox (pelts and small animals) ..	4.75	1.25

1947

1239†	60k Wild Horse (olive)	1.90	60
1240†	60k Wild Horse (brown)	1.90	60

1956

2043†	40k Tiger	80	25

1957

2058a†	15k Polar Bear	40	15
2059†	20k Sika Deer	65	15
2059a†	20k Brown Hare	40	25
2059b†	25k Tiger	55	25
2059c†	25k Wild Horse	55	25
2061†	30k European Bison	70	20
2062†	40k Elk	1.25	25
2063†	40k Sable	1.25	25
2063a†	40k Eurasian Red Squirrel	65	25
2063b†	40k Yellow-throated Marten	65	25

1959

2350b† 25k Northern Fur Seal 40 10

1961

2534 1k Brown Bear
2535 6k Eurasian Beaver
2536 10k Roe Deer

Set of 3 2.25 80

1964

3000† 1k Indian Elephant 10 10
3001† 2k Giant Panda 10 10
3002† 4k Polar Bear 25 10
3003† 6k Elk 40 10
3005† 12k Tiger 75 20

1966

3308 4k Sable
3309 6k Brown Bear

Set of 2 80 20

1967

3375† 12k Northern Fur Seal 75 25

3452 2k Arctic Fox
3453 4k Red Fox (Silver Fox race)
3454 6k Red Fox
3455 10k Muskrat
3456 12k Stoat
3457 16k Sable
3458 20k European Mink

Set of 7 3.00 1.25

3465 10k Snow Leopard 60 30

1968

3608† 4k American Bison, Common Zebra .. 20 10
3612† 10k Eland, Guanaco 45 20

COLLECT BIRDS ON STAMPS

The first Stanley Gibbons thematic catalogue – a few copies still available at £4.95 (p.+p. £1.30) plus FREE 1983–84 Supplement from:
Stanley Gibbons Publications Ltd, 5, Parkside, Christchurch Road, Ringwood, Hants BH24 3SH.

1969

3730†	6k Red Deer		40	15
3731†	10k European Bison		55	20
3732†	12k Lynx		60	20
3733†	16k Wild Boar		75	25
		(3729/33 Set of 5)	2.40	75

1970

3851†	6k Yellow-throated Marten		45	15
3852†	10k Asiatic Black Bear		50	15
3853†	16k Red Deer		70	20
3854†	20k Tiger		75	25
		(3850/4 Set of 5)	2.50	80

3874† 10k Sika Deer

1971

3967	4k Atlantic White-sided Dolphin
3968	6k Sea Otter
3969	10k Narwhal
3970	12k Walrus
3971	14k Ribbon Seal
	Set of 5	1.75	80

1973

4182†	1k European Bison		5	5
4183†	3k Ibex		10	5
4185†	6k Eurasian Beaver		35	8
4186†	10k Red Deer		50	10
		(4182/6 Set of 5)	90	30

1974

| 4277† | 20k Red Deer (fawn) | | 65 | 30 |

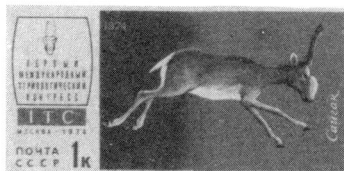

4281	1k Saiga
4282	3k Asiatic Wild Ass
4283	4k Russian Desman
4284	6k Northern Fur Seal
4285	10k Bowhead Whale
	Set of 5	90	40

1975

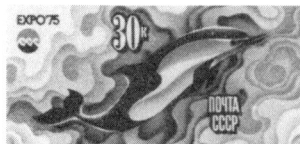

| MS4421 | 30k × 2 Common Dolphin | | 2.10 | 75 |

4434†	4k Siberian Musk Deer	25	10
4435†	6k Sable	30	10
4437†	16k Eurasian Badger	50	15

1977

4725†	16k Polar Bear	40	20
4726†	20k Walrus	50	20
4727†	30k Tiger	75	35

1978

| 4788† | 10k Southern Elephant-Seal | 40 | 15 |

1980

5008	2k Red Fox (Silver Fox race)
5009	4k Arctic Fox
5010	6k European Mink
5011	10k Coypu
5012	15k Sable
	Set of 5	1.00	40

1984

5395†	2k Mandrill	10	10
5396†	3k Blesbok	10	10
5397†	4k Snow Leopard	15	10

| 5466† | 35k Sable | 80 | 60 |

RWANDA

Central Africa
100 centimes = 1 franc

1964

No. 204/14 and 228/30 of Ruanda–Urundi overprinted
REPUBLIQUE RWANDAISE or surcharged also

55	10c on 20c African Buffalo
56	20c African Buffalo
57	30c on 1f50 African Buffalo
58	40c Eastern Black-and-White Colobus
59	50c Impala
60	1f Gorilla
61	2f Eastern Black-and-White Colobus
62	3f African Elephant
63	4f on 3f50 on 3f African Elephant
64	5f Eland, Common Zebra
65	7f50 on 6f50 Impala
66	8f African Elephant
67	10f Eland, Common Zebra
68	20f Leopard
69	50f Lion
	Set of 15	8.50	4.00

COLLECT BIRDS ON STAMPS

The first Stanley Gibbons thematic catalogue – a few
copies still available at £4.95 (p.+p. £1.30) plus FREE
1983–84 Supplement from:
Stanley Gibbons Publications Ltd, 5, Parkside,
Christchurch Road, Ringwood, Hants BH24 3SH.

1965

99†	20c Common Zebra ('Zebre')				10	10
100†	30c Impala				10	10
101†	40c Hippopotamus				25	10
102†	1f African Buffalo ('Buffle')				10	10
103†	3f Hunting Dog ('Lycaon')				10	10
104†	5f Yellow Baboon ('Cynocephale')				3.50	1.10
105†	10f African Elephant				25	15
107†	100f Lion				2.00	25

233	20c Common Zebra
234	80c Common Zebra
235	1f Common Zebra
236	8f Common Zebra
237	10f Common Zebra
238	50f Common Zebra

Set of 6   1.40   1.00

1966

1970

185†	30c Giraffe, Common Zebra			10	10
189†	10f Giraffe, Common Zebra			20	20

1967

369	20c Gorilla ('Gorilles de Montagne')
370	40c Gorilla ('Gorille de Montagne')
371	60c Gorilla ('Gorille de Montagne')
372	80c Gorilla ('Gorille de Montagne')
373	1f Gorilla ('Gorilles de Montagne')
374	2f Gorilla ('Gorille de Montagne')
375	15f Gorilla ('Gorilles de Montagne')
376	100f Gorilla ('Gorilles de Montagne')

Set of 8   2.75   2.25

1972

216†	20c Common Zebra				10	10
217†	40c African Elephant				10	10
218†	60c African Buffalo				10	10
219†	80c Impala				10	10

COLLECT BIRDS ON STAMPS

The first Stanley Gibbons thematic catalogue – a few copies still available at £4.95 (p.+p. £1.30) plus FREE 1983–84 Supplement from:
Stanley Gibbons Publications Ltd, 5, Parkside, Christchurch Road, Ringwood, Hants BH24 3SH.

456†	20c Savanna Monkey ('Cercopitheque'),				
	Impala ('Antilopes')				5	5
457†	30c African Buffalo ('Buffles')			5	5
458†	50c Common Zebra ('Zebres')			5	5
459†	1f White Rhinoceros ('Rhinoceros')			5	5
460†	2f Warthog ('Phacocheres')			5	5
461†	6f Hippopotamus ('Hippopotames')			10	10
462†	18f Spotted Hyena ('Hyenes')			35	35
464†	60f Waterbuck ('Antilopes')			1.50	1.10
465†	80f Lion ('Lions')			2.00	1.50

(456/65 Set of 10)   4.50   3.50

1975

863 10f Mona Monkey ('Cercopitheque Mone')
864 26f Potto
865 60f Savanna Monkey ('Cercopitheque
     Grivet')
866 150f Olive Baboon ('Babouin')

                              Set of 8   5.00   5.00

631 20c Kob ('Cob de l'Ouganda')
632 30c Bongo ('Antilope Bongo')
633 50c Roan Antelope ('Antilope Rouanne'),
     Sable Antelope ('Hippotraque Noir')
634 1f Sitatunga ('Jeunes Situtunga')
635 4f Greater Kudu ('Grand Koudou')
636 10f Impala ('Antilope Impala')
637 34f Waterbuck
638 100f Giant Eland ('Eland de Derby')

                              Set of 8   3.50   3.50

MS639 Two sheets 40f Impala ('Antilope
     Impala'); 60f Greater Kudu ('Grand
     Koudou') 2.25   2.25

899† 30f Greater Kudu   80   60

1979

949† 30c African Elephant (on Belgian Congo
      stamp No. 76)   10   10
952† 10f African Buffalo (on Ruanda-Urundi
      stamp No. 89)   25   25
953† 26f Common Zebra (on Ruanda-Urundi
      stamp No. 139)   60   60

1981

689† 30c Common Zebra   10   10

1977

No. 689 *overprinted* **CONFERENCE MONDIALE DE L'EAU**
806† 30c Common Zebra   10   10

1978

1049 20c Serval ('Imondo')
1050 30c Black-backed Jackal ('Imbwebwe')
1051 2f Servaline Genet ('Urutoni')
1052 2f50 Banded Mongoose ('Isiha')
1053 10f Zorilla ('Agasamunyiga')
1054 15f Zaire Clawless Otter ('Inzibyi')
1055 70f African Golden Cat ('Umubaka')
1056 200f Hunting Dog ('Isega')

                              Set of 8   6.50   6.50

859 20c Chimpanzee ('Chimpanzes')
860 30c Gorilla ('Gorille')
861 50c Eastern Black-and-White Colobus
     ('Colobe Guereza')
862 3f Eastern Needle-clawed Bushbaby
     ('Galago')

STAMP MONTHLY

– finest and most informative magazine for all collectors.
Obtainable from your newsagent or by postal subscription – details on request

1984

1082† 20c Kob   10   10

1210	20c Common Zebra
1211	30c African Buffalo
1212	50c Common Zebra
1213	9f Common Zebra
1214	10f African Buffalo
1215	80f Common Zebra
1216	100f Common Zebra
1217	200f African Buffalo

Set of 8   6.50   6.00

1123† 20c African Elephant   10   10
1124† 30c Lion, Impala   10   10
1126† 4f African Buffalo   10   10
1127† 5f Impala   15   15
1129† 20f Common Zebra   40   40

RYUKYU ISLANDS
Northern Pacific
100 cents = 1 dollar

1966

1133† 20c Kob   10   10

1983

176† 3c Sika Deer   50   45
177† 3c Dugong   50   45
                    (175/7 Set of 3)   1.40   1.25

1169 20c Gorilla ('Gorilles de Montagne')
1170 30c Gorilla ('Gorilles de Montagne')
1171 9f50 Gorilla ('Gorilles de Montagne')
1172 10f Gorilla ('Gorilles de Montagne')
1173 20f Gorilla ('Gorilles de Montagne')
1174 30f Gorilla ('Gorilles de Montagne')
1175 60f Gorilla ('Gorille de Montagne')
1176 70f Gorilla ('Gorille de Montagne')
                    Set of 8   3.25   3.00

SABAH
South-east Asia
100 cents = 1 dollar

1964

Nos. 391/3, 396, 398 and 403 of North Borneo overprinted **SABAH**

408† 1c Sambar   10   5
409† 4c Sun Bear   12   10
410† 5c Clouded Leopard   12   5
413† 12c Banteng   12   5
415† 25c Sumatran Rhinoceros   35   60
420† $1 Orang-Utan 2.50   50

ST. KITTS–NEVIS
West Indies
100 cents = 1 dollar

1978

385   4c Savanna Monkey ('The Green Monkey')
386   5c Savanna Monkey ('The Green Monkey')
387   55c Savanna Monkey
388   $1.50 Savanna Monkey
                        Set of 4   1.50   1.25

ST. LUCIA
West Indies
100 cents = 1 dollar

1980

571†   10c Brazilian Agouti ('The Agouti')   10   10

ST. PIERRE ET MIQUELON
North Atlantic
100 centimes = 1 franc

1947

376†   8f Red Fox (Silver Fox race)   50   50
379†   17f Red Fox   70   70

1955

408†   25f American Mink ('Visons') 1.00   90

1964

431†   3f Common Rabbit (*Cuniculus*)   30   25
432†   4f Red Fox (*Vulpes*)   30   25
433†   5f Roe Deer (*Capreolus*)   35   30
                        (431/4 *Set of* 4)   1.75   1.40

1969

470   1f Ringed Seal ('Phoques')
471   3f Sperm Whale ('Cachalots')
472   4f Long-finned Pilot Whale
            ('Globicephales')
473   6f Common Dolphin ('Dauphins')
                        Set of 4   2.25   1.40

1975

541†   20c Blue Whale   20   20

STANLEY GIBBONS
STAMP COLLECTING SERIES

Introductory booklets on *How to Start, How to Identify Stamps* and *Collecting by Theme.* A series of well illustrated guides at a low price.
Write for details.

ST. VINCENT
West Indies
100 cents = 1 dollar

1975

St.VINCENT 10ᶜ

SPERM WHALE

429†	10c Sperm Whale	30	10
430†	12c Humpback Whale	40	20

1977
No. 429 overprinted **CARNIVAL 1977 JUNE 25th–JULY 5th**

532†	10c Sperm Whale	25	15

1979
Nos. 429/30 overprinted **INDEPENDENCE 1979**

611†	10c Sperm Whale	15	15
612†	12c Humpback Whale	15	15

1980

25c

ST VINCENT

648†	25c Brazilian Agouti ('Agouti')	12	12
650†	$2 Small Indian Mongoose ('Mongoose')	95	1.00
	(648/50 *Set of 3*)	1.25	1.25

SAN MARINO
Southern Europe
100 centisimi = 1 lira

1961

626†	1li Roe Deer	10	10
628†	3li Wild Boar	10	10
630†	5li Red Deer	10	10

1962

682†	4li Roe Deer	10	10
687†	100li Wild Boar	50	50

1966

806†	3li Common Dolphin ('Delfino')	10	10

1979

1120†	5li Red Deer	25	10
1122†	35li Common Racoon	25	10
1123†	50li Tiger	25	10
1125†	90li Yellow-throated Marten	15	15
1126†	100li Koala	15	15
1127†	120li Dromedary	20	15
1128†	150li American Beaver	20	20
1129†	170li African Elephant	25	20

SARAWAK
South-east Asia
100 cents = 1 dollar

1950

172†	2c Western Tarsier ('The Tarsius')	35	40
177†	10c Malayan Pangolin ('The Scaly Ant Eater')	90	1.60

1955

189† 2c Orang-Utan ('A young Orang-Utan') .. 20 10

SAURASHTRA
See under Soruth

SEIYUN
See under Aden Protectorate States

SELANGOR
South-east Asia
100 cents = 1 dollar

1891

49 1c Tiger
50 2c Tiger (red)
51 2c Tiger (orange)
52 5c Tiger (blue)
                              Set of 4   6.00   3.00

1894
No. 52 in different colour surcharged **3 CENTS**
53 3c on 5c Tiger (red)   55   40

1895

54†	2c Tiger	2.75	25
55†	5c Tiger	50	30
56†	8c Tiger	27.00	7.00
57†	10c Tiger	4.50	30
58†	25c Tiger	28.00	20.00
59†	50c Tiger (green and black)	90.00	35.00
60†	50c Tiger (purple and black)	15.00	9.00

1900
Nos. 55 and 59 surcharged in words
66a 1c on 5c Tiger
66b 1c on 50c Tiger
67 3c on 50c Tiger
                              Set of 3   22.00   30.00

1957

121† 10c Tiger (sepia) 15 5
122† 10c Tiger (purple) 25 5

1961

134† 10c Tiger 10 5

SENEGAL
West Africa
100 centimes = 1 franc

1960

228 5f Roan Antelope ('Hippotrague')
229 10f African Buffalo ('Buffle de Savane')
230 15f Warthog ('Phacochere')
231 20f Giant Eland ('Eland de Derby')
232 25f Bushbuck ('Guib')
233 85f Waterbuck ('Cobe Onctueux')
                              Set of 6   3.50   2.00

1967

362† 100f Hippopotamus 1.50 75

1969

417† 35f African Elephant ('Troupeau
d'Elephants') 50 30

1970

420 50f Bottle-nosed Dolphin (*Tursiops
truncatus*) 80 60

1972

493† 40f Lion 45 30

513† 65f Killer Whale (*Orcinus orca*) 60 40
515† 125f Fin Whale (*Balaenoptera physalus*) 1.75 1.00

1974

551 150f Tiger
552 200f Tiger
Set of 2 4.00 2.00

1975

573 125f Lion (on stamp No. D339) 1.00 75

1976

584† 2f Serval 10 10
586† 4f Bush Pig ('Potamochere') 10 10
588† 250f Sitatunga (males) 2.00 1.50
589† 250f Sitatunga (females) 2.00 1.50

STANLEY GIBBONS
STAMP COLLECTING SERIES

Introductory booklets on *How to Start, How to Identify
Stamps* and *Collecting by Theme*. A series of well illus-
trated guides at a low price.
Write for details.

1978

660†	15f Warthog ('Phacochere')	15	15
663†	150f Warthog ('Phacochere')	90	65

682†	100f Lion	1.10	1.00

1980

710†	40f Chimpanzee ('Chimpanze')	25	10
711†	60f African Elephant ('Elephant')	35	20
712†	65f Giant Eland ('Eland de Derby')	35	20
713†	100f Spotted Hyena ('Hyena Tachetee')..	55	30
714†	200f African Elephant, Giant Eland	1.00	70
	(710/15 Set of 6)	3.00	2.00
MS716	125f × 4 Chimpanzee, African Elephant, Giant Eland, Spotted Hyena (designs as Nos. 710/3)	2.75	2.75

COLLECT BIRDS ON STAMPS

The first Stanley Gibbons thematic catalogue – a few copies still available at £4.95 (p.+p. £1.30) plus FREE 1983–84 Supplement from:
Stanley Gibbons Publications Ltd, 5, Parkside, Christchurch Road, Ringwood, Hants BH24 3SH.

POSTAGE DUE STAMPS

1966

D339	1f Lion
D340	2f Lion
D341	5f Lion
D342	10f Lion
D343	20f Lion
D344	30f Lion
D345	60f Lion
D346	90f Lion

Set of 8	3.00	3.00

SEYCHELLES
Indian Ocean
100 cents = 1 rupee

1954

175a†	5c Seychelles Flying Fox ('Flying Fox')	15	20

1962

236†	60c Seychelles Flying Fox ('Flying Fox')	1.00	1.00

1977

Face value shown as "Rs"

414†	1r50 Seychelles Flying Fox ('Flying Fox, Rousette') 50	20	60	50

1981
As No. 414, *but face value shown as* "R"
490† 1r50 Seychelles Flying Fox   30   35

518 40c Seychelles Flying Fox ('Flying Fox,
     Rousette')
519 2r25 Seychelles Flying Fox ('Flying Fox,
     Rousette')
520 3r Seychelles Flying Fox ('Flying Fox,
     Rousette')
521 5r Seychelles Flying Fox ('Flying Fox,
     Rousette')
                              Set of 4   2.00   2.25

1984

601 50c Humpback Whale
602 2r Sperm Whale
603 3r Black Right Whale ('Right Whale')
604 10r Blue Whale
                              Set of 4   3.50   3.75

SHARJAH
Arabia
100 dirhams = 1 riyal

Appendix
The following stamps have either been issued in excess of
postal needs, or have not been made available to the public in
reasonable quantities at face value. Miniature sheets, imperforate
stamps etc., are excluded from this section.

1972
Monkeys (Various species). Postage 20, 25d; Air 75d, 1, 2r.

SIERRA LEONE
West Africa
1933 12 pence = 1 shilling, 20 shillings = 1 pound
1964 100 cents = 1 leone

1933

178† 5s African Elephant £150   £225

1980

655† 1le African Elephant ('Forest Elephant')   95   95

1981

656 6c Serval
657 6c Serval (cubs)
658 31c African Golden Cat
659 31c African Golden Cat (cubs)
660 50c Leopard
661 50c Leopard (cubs)
662 1le Lion
663 1le Lion (cubs)
                              Set of 8   2.75   2.75

STANLEY GIBBONS
STAMP COLLECTING SERIES

Introductory booklets on *How to Start, How to Identify
Stamps* and *Collecting by Theme*. A series of well illus-
trated guides at a low price.
Write for details.

1983

745 6c Chimpanzee
746 10c Chimpanzee
747 31c Chimpanzee
748 60c Chimpanzee

		Set of 4	70	85
MS749	3le African Elephant		1.10	1.25

1984

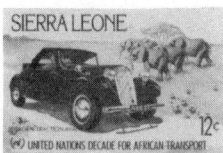

799†	12c African Elephant	10	5
801†	90c Leopard	30	35
802†	1le Monkey sp. (small)	30	35
804†	2le Hippopotamus	60	65
MS805†	6le Bushbuck	1.75	1.90

SINGAPORE
South-east Asia
100 cents = 1 dollar

1972

177†	$1 Common Gibbon	3.75	4.75

STAMP MONTHLY
– finest and most informative magazine for all collectors. Obtainable from your newsagent or by postal subscription – details on request

1973

225 5c Tiger, Orang-Utan
226 10c Leopard, Waterbuck
227 35c Leopard, Thamin
228 75c Lion

	Set of 4	4.75	4.75

SIRMOOR
Indian subcontinent
12 pies =1 anna; 100 annas = 1 rupee

1895

22	3p Indian Elephant
23	6p Indian Elephant
24	1a Indian Elephant
25	2a Indian Elephant
26	3a Indian Elephant
27	4a Indian Elephant
28	8a Indian Elephant
29	1r Indian Elephant

	Set of 8	20.00	30.00

SLOVAKIA
Central Europe
10 haleru = 1 koruna

1939

43†	25h Chamois ('Kamzik') (brown)	40	15
127†	25h Chamois (purple)	15	20

SOMALIA

East Africa

1903 4 besa = 1 anna, 16 annas = 1 rupee
1905 100 centesimi = 1 lira
1922 100 besa = 1 rupia
1926 100 centesimi = 1 lira
1950 100 centesimi = 1 somalo
1961 100 cents =1 Somali shilling

37	6b on 5c on 2b African Elephant
38	18b on 10c on 1a Lion
39	20b on 15c on 2a Lion
40	25b on 15c on 2a Lion
41	30b on 25c on 2½a Lion
42	60b on 1li on 10a Lion
43	1r on 1li on 10a Lion

Set of 11 15.00 16.00

1903

1	1b African Elephant
2	2b African Elephant
3	1a Lion
4	2a Lion
5	2½a Lion
6	5a Lion
7	10a Lion

Set of 7 35.00 22.00

1905

Nos. 1/7 surcharged, without bars at top

8	15c on 5a Lion
9	40c on 10a Lion
10	2c on 1b African Elephant
11	5c on 2b African Elephant
12	10c on 1a Lion
13	15c on 2a Lion
13a	20c on 2a Lion
14	25c on 2½a Lion
15	50c on 5a Lion
16	1li on 10a Lion

Set of 9 £700 £100

For stamps with bars at top, see Nos. 68/75.

1916

Nos. 15/16 further surcharged with bars cancelling original surcharge

17	5c on 50c on 5a Lion
18	20c on 1li on 10a Lion

Set of 2 6.00 6.00

1922

Nos. 11/16, further surcharged at top

23	3b on 5c on 2b African Elephant
24	6b on 10c on 1a Lion
25	9b on 15c on 2a Lion
26	15b on 25c on 2½a Lion
27	30b on 50c on 5a Lion
28	60b on 1li on 10a Lion

Set of 6 10.00 12.00

1923

Nos. 10/16 further surcharged with new values and bars

33	2c on 1b African Elephant (overprinted with bars only at bottom)
34	2b on 2c on 1b African Elephant
35	3b on 2c on 1b African Elephant
36	5b on 50c on 5a Lion

1926

Nos. 10/16 overprinted with bars at top

68	2c on 1b African Elephant
69	5c on 2b African Elephant
70	10c on 1a Lion
71	15c on 2a Lion
72	20c on 2a Lion
73	25c on 2½a Lion
74	50c on 5a Lion
75	1li on 10a Lion

Set of 8 15.00 17.00

1932

176†	10li Hippopotamus	.. ..	4.50	2.00
177†	20li Lesser Kudu	.. ..	18.00	9.00
178†	25li Lion	.. ..	30.00	30.00

1934

Nos. 176/8, colours changed, overprinted **ONORANZE AL DUCA DEGLI ABRUZZI**

184†	10li Hippopotamus	.. ..	1.25	1.50
185†	20li Lesser Kudu	.. ..	1.25	1.50
186†	25li Lion	.. ..	1.25	1.50

196†	80c Cheetah	.. ..	1.10	1.50
197†	1li Cheetah	.. ..	1.10	1.50
198†	2li Cheetah	.. ..	1.10	1.50

1953

270 25c African Elephant, Lion (on stamps
Nos. 1 and 3)
271 35c African Elephant, Lion
272 60c African Elephant, Lion

273 60c African Elephant, Lion (air)
274 1s African Elephant, Lion
Set of 5   2.50   2.75

1955

291 35c Oribi (*Ourebia haggardi*)
292 45c Salt's Dik-Dik (*Madoqua phillipsi*)
293 50c Speke's Gazelle (*Gazella spekei*)
294 75c Gerenuk (*Lythocranius walleri*)
295 1s20 Soemmerring's Gazelle (*Gazella
soemmeringi*)
296 1s50 Waterbuck (*Cobus ellipsyprymnus*)
296a 3s Lesser Kudu (*Strepsiceros imberbis*)
296b 5s Hunter's Hartebeest (*Damaliscus
hunteri*)
Set of 8   7.00   5.00

1960

Nos. 293 and 295 overprinted **Somaliland Independence
26 June 1960**
354† 50c Speke's Gazelle 7.50   5.50
355† 1s20 Soemmerring's Gazelle 15.00   5.50
(353/5 *Set of* 3)   28.00   15.00

364 10c Giraffe (stylised)
365 15c Common Zebra
366 25c Black Rhinoceros
367 3s Leopard
Set of 4   1.10   75

1964

418† 1s African Elephant 1.00   25

1965

431† 20c Gazelle sp.   10   10
432† 60c Giraffe   20   10
435† 1s80 Common Zebra   75   25

1967

451 35c Oribi (*Ourebia*)
452 60c Kirk's Dik-Dik (*Rynchotragus*)
453 1s Gerenuk (*Lythocranius walleri*)
454 1s80 Soemmerring's Gazelle (*Gazella
soemmeringi*)
Set of 4   1.00   80

1968

481 1s50 Waterbuck (*Kobus ellypsiprymnus*)
482 1s80 Speke's Gazelle (*Gazella spekei*)
483 2s Lesser Kudu (*Strepsiceros imberbis*)
484 5s Hunter's Hartebeest (*Damaliscus
hunteri*)
485 10s Dibatag (*Ammodorcas clarkei*)
Set of 5   6.00   3.00

1969

498†	40c Black Rhinoceros	5	5
499†	80c African Elephant	15	15
500†	1s Waterbuck	25	15
	(498/501 *Set of* 4)	80	60

1971

529	35c White Rhinoceros
530	1s Cheetah
531	1s30 Common Zebra
532	1s80 Lion, Dromedary

Set of 4   1.60   80

1972

544†	5c Dromedary	10	10

1977

605	50c Hunting Dog (*Licaon pictus*)
606	75c Lesser Bushbaby (*Galago sen.*\
	gallarum)

607	1s African Ass (*Equus asinus somaliensis*)	
608	1s50 Aardwolf (*Proteles cristatus*)	
609	2s Greater Kudu (*Strepsiceros*	
	strepsiceros)	
610	3s Giraffe (*Giraffa reticulata*)	
	Set of 6 2.75 1.50	

1984

720	1s North African Crested Porcupine	
	(*Hystriz cristata*)	
721	1s50 White-tailed Mongoose (*Ichneumia*	
	albicauda)	
722	2s Banded Mongoose (*Mungos mungo*)	
723	4s Ratel (*Mellivora capensis*)	
	Set of 4 1.10 1.00	

EXPRESS LETTER STAMPS

1950

E255	40c Grant's Gazelle		
E256	80c Grant's Gazelle		
	Set of 2 2.50 1.25		

SOMALILAND PROTECTORATE
East Africa
1938 16 annas = 1 rupee
1951 100 cents = 1 shilling

1938

97†	4a Lesser Kudu	1.75	2.40
98†	6a Lesser Kudu	1.10	3.00
99†	8a Lesser Kudu	1.75	3.75
100†	12a Lesser Kudu	2.00	4.50

1942

109†	4a Lesser Kudu	12	35
110†	6a Lesser Kudu	20	35
111†	8a Lesser Kudu	25	35
112†	12a Lesser Kudu	35	45

1951
Nos. 109/12 surcharged

128†	20c on 4a Lesser Kudu	12	15
129†	30c on 6a Lesser Kudu	25	35
130†	50c on 8a Lesser Kudu	30	25
131†	70c on 12a Lesser Kudu	35	40

SORUTH
Indian subcontinent
12 pies =1 anna; 16 annas = 1 rupee

A. Junagadh

1929

50†	½a Lion	3.25	8
54†	4a Lion	9.00	6.50

OFFICIAL STAMPS

1929
Nos. 50 and 54 overprinted **SARKARI**

O2†	½a Lion	30	8
O6†	4a Lion	1.00	40

B. Union of Saurashtra

1949
No. 50 surcharged **POSTAGE & REVENUE ONE ANNA**

58†	1a on ½a Lion	4.25	1.50

OFFICIAL STAMPS

1949
No. O6 surcharged **ONE ANNA**

O16†	1a on 4a Lion	£140	17.00

SOUTH AFRICA
Southern Africa
1926 12 pence = 1 shilling; 20 shillings = 1 pound
1961 100 cents = 1 rand

1926

114†	½d Springbok (black and green)	70	25
120†	1s Black Wildebeest, Blue Wildebeest	5.50	1.50

Nos. 114 and 120 are inscribed in either English or Afrikaans.

1943
As No. 114 but colour changed

105†	½d Springbok (green)	80	1.10

Inscribed in either English or Afrikaans.

1953

147†	1s3d Springbok	2.25	15

1954

151	½d Warthog
152	1d Black Wildebeest
153	1½d Leopard
154	2d Mountain Zebra
155	3d White Rhinoceros
156	4d African Elephant
157	4½d Hippopotamus
158	6d Lion
159	1s Greater Kudu
160	1s3d Springbok
161	1s6d Gemsbok
162	2s6d Nyala
163	5s Giraffe
164	10s Sable Antelope

Set of 14   45.00   7.25

STAMP MONTHLY
– finest and most informative magazine for all collectors. Obtainable from your newsagent or by postal subscription – details on request

1961

As Nos. 151/4, 158, 160/1, 163/4, but face values in cents and rands

185†	½c Warthog	10	10
186†	1c Black Wildebeest	10	5
187†	1½c Leopard	10	12
188†	2c Mountain Zebra	10	12
191†	5c Lion	20	20
194†	12½c Springbok	1.40	1.40
195†	20c Gemsbok	2.50	2.50
196†	50c Giraffe	10.00	10.00
197†	1r Sable Antelope	22.00	19.00

1975

391†	15c Lion	2.25	2.00

1976

404	3c Cheetah (*Acinonyx jubatus*)		
405	10c Black Rhinoceros (*Diceros bicornis*)		
406	15c Blesbok (*Damaliscus dorcas dorcas*)		
407	20c Mountain Zebra (*Equus zebra zebra*)		
	Set of 4	3.50	2.75

OFFICIAL STAMPS

1926

Nos. 114 and 120 overprinted OFFICIAL OFFISIEEL

O8†	½d Springbok	90	1.25
O40†	1s Black Wildebeest, Blue Wildebeest ..	4.00	6.50

SOUTH AUSTRALIA
Australia
12 pence = 1 shilling
20 shillings = 1 pound

1894

253†	2½d Red Kangaroo (violet)		4.00	45
266†	2½d Red Kangaroo (blue) ..	4.50	45	5.50	45

OFFICIAL STAMPS

1901

No. 266 overprinted O.S.

O83†	2½d Red Kangaroo (blue)	5.00	70

SOUTH GEORGIA
South Atlantic
1963 12 pence =1 shilling; 20 shillings = 1 pound
1971 100 pence =1 pound

1963

1†	½d Reindeer	65	50
3†	2d Sperm Whale	70	30
5†	3d South American Fur Seal ('Fur Seal') ..	90	35
6†	4d Fin Whale	90	50
7†	5½d Southern Elephant-Seal ('Elephant Seal')	90	50
10†	1s Leopard Seal	1.00	70
13†	5s Southern Elephant-Seal, South American Fur Seal ('Elephant & Fur Seal')	22.00	16.00
15†	£1 Blue Whale	£130	£100

1971

Nos. 1/13 surcharged

53†	½p on ½d Reindeer	80	80
55†	1½p on 5½d Southern Elephant-Seal	1.40	1.60
21†	2p on 2d Sperm Whale	70	40
58†	3p on 3d South American Fur Seal	2.50	2.00
59†	4p on 4d Fin Whale	10.00	8.00
62†	7½p on 1s Leopard Seal	9.00	10.00
65†	25p on 5s Southern Elephant-Seal, South American Fur Seal	9.00	12.00

1972

36	5p Southern Elephant-Seal		
37	10p Southern Elephant-Seal		
	Set of 2	2.25	1.75

SOUTH KASAI
Central Africa
100 centimes =1 franc

1961

1 1f Leopard
2 1f50 Leopard
3 3f50 Leopard
4 8f Leopard
5 10f Leopard

Set of 5   80   80

SOUTH KOREA
See under Korea

SOUTH VIETNAM
See under Vietnam

SOUTH WEST AFRICA
Southern Africa
1926 12 pence =1 shilling, 20 shillings =1 pound
1961 100 cents = 1 rand

1923
Nos. 114 and 120 of South Africa overprinted **South West Africa**
or **Suidwes Afrika**

45†	½d Springbok	.. ..	1.60	2.75
51†	1s Black Wildebeest, Blue Wildebeest	..	17.00	28.00

1927
Nos. 114 and 120 of South Africa overprinted **S.W.A.**

58†	½d Springbok	.. ..	1.50	2.50
64†	1s Black Wildebeest, Blue Wildebeest	..	22.00	26.00

1931

81†	1s3d Eland	.. ..	7.50	11.00
82†	2s6d Mountain Zebra, Blue Wildebeest	..	18.00	22.00

Inscribed in either English or Afrikaans.

1954

163†	2s6d Lion	.. ..	6.50	1.50
164†	5s Gemsbok	.. ..	15.00	7.00
165†	10s African Elephant	.. ..	40.00	32.00

1976

290 4c Large-toothed Rock Hyrax (*Procavia welwitschii*)
291 10c Kirk's Dik-Dik (*Madoqua kirki*)
292 15c Kuhl's Tree Squirrel (*Funisciurus congicus*)

Set of 3   3.25   1.75

1978

312†	10c Grant's Desert Golden Mole (*Eremitalpa granti namibensis*)	.. ..	40	30

1980

338 4c Killer Whale
339 5c Humpback Whale
340 10c Black Right Whale ('Southern Right Whale')
341 15c Sperm Whale
342 20c Fin Whale
343 25c Blue Whale

Set of 6   3.00   2.75

STAMP MONTHLY
– finest and most informative magazine for all collectors. Obtainable from your newsagent or by postal subscription – details on request

1983

345 5c Impala (*Aepyceros petersi*)
346 10c Topi (*Damaliscus lunatus*)
347 15c Roan Antelope (*Hippotragus equinus*)
348 20c Sable Antelope (*Hippotragus niger*)
Set of 4 1.40 80

415† 10c Common Zebra 12 15
417† 25c African Buffalo 30 35

OFFICIAL STAMPS

1927
No. 114 of South Africa overprinted **OFFICIAL South West Africa**
or **OFFISEEL Suidwes Afrika**
O1† ½d Springbok 65.00 85.00

1929
No. 114 of South Africa overprinted **OFFICIAL S.W.A.** or
OFFISEEL S.W.A.
O9† ½d Springbok 40 3.00

349 1c Black-backed Jackal (*Canis mesomelas*)
350 2c Hunting Dog (*Lycaon pictus*)
351 3c Brown Hyena (*Hyaena brunnea*)
352 4c Springbok (*Antidorcas marsupialis*)
353 5c Gemsbok (*Oryx gazella*)
354 6c Greater Kudu (*Tragelaphus strepsiceros*)
355 7c Mountain Zebra (*Equus zebra hartmannae*)
356 8c Cape Porcupine (*Hystrix africae-australis*)
357 9c Ratel (*Mellivora capensis*)
358 10c Cheetah (*Acinonyx jubatus*)
358a 11c Blue Wildebeest (*Connochaetes taurinus*)
358b 12c African Buffalo (*Synceros caffer*)
359 15c Hippopotamus (*Hippopotamus amphibius*)
360 20c Eland (*Taurotragus oryx*)
361 25c Black Rhinoceros (*Diceros bicornis*)
362 30c Lion (*Panthera leo*)
363 50c Giraffe (*Giraffa camelopardalis*)
364 1r Leopard (*Panthera pardus*)
365 2r African Elephant (*Loxodonta africana*)
Set of 19 3.50 4.25

SOUTHERN RHODESIA
Central Africa
12 pence = 1 shilling
20 shillings = 1 pound

1935

31 1d Giraffe, African Elephant, Lion, Roan Antelope
32 2d Giraffe, African Elephant, Lion, Roan Antelope
33 3d Giraffe, African Elephant, Lion, Roan Antelope
34 6d Giraffe, African Elephant, Lion, Roan Antelope
Set of 4 20.00 25.00

1953

366 1c Meerkat (*Suricata suricatta*)
367 2c Savanna Monkey (*Cercopithecus pygerythrus*)
368 5c Chacma Baboon (*Papio ursinus*)
Set of 3 12 12

72† 1d Springbok, Leopard 15 5

78†	½d Sable Antelope	.. ..	15	20
85†	9d Lion	.. ..	1.50	1.60

1964

93†	1d African Buffalo ('Buffalo')	.. .. ..	10	5
95†	3d Greater Kudu ('Kudu')	.. ..	10	5

SOUTHERN YEMEN
Arabian Peninsula
1000 fils = 1 dinar

1970

56†	15f Dromedary ('Camel')	.. ..	15	15
58†	35f Arabian Oryx ('Oryx')	.. ..	45	45

SPAIN
South-West Europe
100 centimos = 1 peseta

1971

2095†	2p Lynx (*Lynx pardina*)	.. ..	80	10
2096†	3p Brown Bear (*Ursus arctos*)	.. ..	80	10
2098†	8p Spanish Ibex (*Capra pyrenaica*)	..	1.00	25

1972

2160	1p Pyrenean Desman (*Desmana pyrenaica*)			
2161	2p Chamois (*Rupicapra rupicapra*)			
2162	3p Wolf (*Canis lupus*)			
2163	5p Egyptian Mongoose (*Herpestes ichneumon*)			
2164	7p Small-spotted Genet (*Genetta genetta*)			
		Set of 5	4.00	60

1978

2521†	20p Mediterranean Monk Seal ('Foca Monge')	.. ..	40	25

SPANISH GUINEA
West Africa
100 centimos = 1 peseta

1951

359	5c + 5c Leopard			
360	10c + 5c Leopard			
361	60c + 15c Leopard			
		Set of 3	50	40

1954

66†	40c Dorcas Gazelle	15	15
69†	1p Dorcas Gazelle	80	80

1951

| 388† | 10c + 5c African Elephant | 10 | 10 |
| 390† | 60c African Elephant | 40 | 15 |

1955

88	5c + 5c Dromedary		
89	10c + 5c Dromedary		
90	60c + 15c Dromedary		
		Set of 3	60	40

1955

408	5c + 5c Moustached Monkey		
409	15c + 5c Talapoin		
410	70c Moustached Monkey		
		Set of 3	60	40

1957

120	5c + 5c Scimitar Oryx		
121	15c + 5c Scimitar Oryx		
122	70c Scimitar Oryx		
		Set of 3	50	30

1957

422	10c + 5c African Elephant (*Loxodonta africana*)		
423	15c + 5c African Elephant ('Elefante (Elephas)')		
424	20c African Elephant		
425	70c African Elephant		
		Set of 4	50	30

SPANISH SAHARA
North Africa
100 centimos =1 peseta

1943

130†	5c Dromedary	15	10
132†	50c Dorcas Gazelle	15	10
133†	70c Dromedary	1.40	25
135†	1p80 Dorcas Gazelle	1.40	25

| 61† | 1c Dorcas Gazelle | 10 | 10 |
| 64† | 15c Dorcas Gazelle | 10 | 10 |

STANLEY GIBBONS
STAMP COLLECTING SERIES
Introductory booklets on *How to Start, How to Identify Stamps* and *Collecting by Theme*. A series of well illustrated guides at a low price.
Write for details.

1964

139   10c + 5c Striped Hyena
140   15c + 5c Striped Hyena
141   20c Striped Hyena
142   70c Striped Hyena

Set of 4   50   30

1960

173   10c + 5c Leopard
174   20c + 5c Fennec Fox
175   30c + 10c Leopard
176   50c + 20c Red Fox

Set of 4   75   40

1961

187   10c + 5c Dorcas Gazelle
188   25c + 10c Dorcas Gazelle
189   80c + 20c Dorcas Gazelle

Set of 3   50   20

233   5c Eurasian Red Squirrel
234   1p Barbary Ground Squirrel
235   1p50 Eurasian Red Squirrel

Set of 3   50   20

1969

268   1p Dorcas Gazelle
269   1p50 Dorcas Gazelle
270   2p50 Dorcas Gazelle
271   6p Dorcas Gazelle

Set of 4   60   50

1970

276   50c Fennec Fox
277   2p Fennec Fox
278   2p50 Fennec Fox
279   6p Fennec Fox

Set of 4   60   50

COLLECT BIRDS ON STAMPS

The first Stanley Gibbons thematic catalogue – a few
copies still available at £4.95 (p.+p. £1.30) plus FREE
1983–84 Supplement from:
Stanley Gibbons Publications Ltd, 5, Parkside,
Christchurch Road, Ringwood, Hants BH24 3SH.

1971

285† 1p Dorcas Gazelle 10 10

SUDAN

North-east Africa
1000 milliemes =100 piastres = 1 Sudanese pound

1951

123†	1m Ibex	10	20
125†	3m Giraffe	20	40
138†	20p Nile Lechwe	2.75	40

SRI LANKA

Indian Ocean
100 cents =1 rupee

1981

1958

146 15m Black Rhinoceros
147 3p Black Rhinoceros
148 5p Black Rhinoceros

Set of 3 45 40

718 2r50 Fishing Cat
719 3r Golden Palm Civet ('Golden Palm Cat')
720 4r Indian Spotted Chevrotain ('Mouse
    Deer')
721 5r Rusty-spotted Cat

Set of 4 80 1.00

1967

1983

260 15m Ibex
261 3p Greater Kudu, Lesser Kudu, African
    Elephant
262 55m Klipspringer

Set of 3 65 50

788 50c Bottle-nosed Dolphin ('Bottlenose
    Dolphin')
789 2r Dugong
790 2r50 Humpback Whale
791 10r Sperm Whale ('Great Sperm Whale')

Set of 4 75 90

STAMP MONTHLY

– finest and most informative magazine for all collectors.
Obtainable from your newsagent or by postal subscription – details on request

263 15m Giraffe
264 3p Giraffe
265 55m Giraffe

Set of 3 50 40

OFFICIAL STAMPS

1951
Nos. 123 and 125 overprinted **S.G.**

O47†	1m Ibex	10	40
O49†	3m Giraffe	55	1.25

SUNGEI UJONG
South-east Asia
100 cents =1 dollar

1891

51	2c Tiger (red)		
52	2c Tiger (orange)		
56	3c Tiger (full-face)		
53	5c Tiger (blue)		
	Set of 4	8.00	16.00

1894
As No. 53, but colour changed and surcharged in figures and words

54	1c on 5c Tiger (green)		
55	3c on 5c Tiger (red)		
	Set of 2	1.10	2.25

SURINAM
South America
100 cents =1 gulden

1953

415†	17½c Nine-banded Armadillo ('Kapasie')	3.00	2.40

COLLECT BIRDS ON STAMPS
The first Stanley Gibbons thematic catalogue – a few copies still available at £4.95 (p.+p. £1.30) plus FREE 1983–84 Supplement from:
Stanley Gibbons Publications Ltd, 5, Parkside, Christchurch Road, Ringwood, Hants BH24 3SH.

1969

653†	20c Common Squirrel-Monkey (*Saimiri sciurius*)	60	60
654†	25c Nine-banded Armadillo (*Dasypus novemcinctus*)	75	75
	(652/4 *Set of* 3)	1.60	1.60

SWAZILAND
Southern Africa
1956 12 pence = 1 shilling; 20 shillings =1 pound
1961 100 cents =1 rand
1974 100 cents = 1 lilangeni (plural: emalangeni)

1956

58†	6d Greater Kudu ('Kudu')	30	5
64†	£1 Greater Kudu	16.00	23.00

1961
Nos. 58 and 64 surcharged in new currency

72a†	5c on 6d Greater Kudu	15	15
77a†	2r on £1 Greater Kudu	12.00	12.00

As Nos. 58 and 64, but face values in new currency

83†	5c Greater Kudu	30	10
89†	2r Greater Kudu	14.00	14.00

1969

161†	½c Caracal	5	5
162†	1c Cape Porcupine ('Porcupine')	10	5
164†	3c Lion	30	10

165†	3½c African Elephant ('Elephant')	30	10
166†	5c Bush Pig	30	5
167†	7½c Impala	35	10
168†	10c Chacma Baboon	40	10
169†	12½c Ratel	70	70
170†	15c Leopard	1.25	70
171†	20c Blue Wildebeest	95	80
172†	25c White Rhinoceros ('White Rhino') ..	1.40	1.00
173†	50c Common Zebra ('Burchells Zebra') ..	1.50	2.00
174†	1r Waterbuck	4.00	5.00
175†	2r Giraffe	8.50	10.00
	(161/75 Set of 15)	18.00	19.00

SWEDEN

Northern Europe
100 ore =1 krona

1967

1975

As Nos. 174/5, but face values in new currency
219 1e Waterbuck
220 2e Giraffe

	Set of 2	8.50	8.50

542†	90ore Elk	20	10

1968

Nos. 167 and 169 surcharged
230 3c on 7½c Impala
231 6c on 12½c Ratel

	Set of 2	1.10	1.10

568†	30ore Arctic Hare	30	30
570†	30ore Red Fox	30	30
572†	30ore Stoat	30	30

1972

1980

364†	5c Oribi	5	5
366†	50c Temminck's Ground Pangolin		
	('Pangolin')	80	80
367†	1e Leopard	1.60	1.75
	(364/6 Set of 4)	2.25	2.40

682	95ore Roe Deer	20	15

1973

1981

755†	10ore Grey Seal (*Halichoerus grypus*) ..	10	10
757†	25ore Lynx (*Lynx lynx*)	10	10
758†	55ore European Otter (*Lutra lutra*)	15	10
759†	65ore Wolf (*Canis lupus*)	15	10

374†	30c White Rhinoceros	40	40

**STANLEY GIBBONS
STAMP COLLECTING SERIES**

Introductory booklets on *How to Start, How to Identify Stamps* and *Collecting by Theme*. A series of well illustrated guides at a low price.
Write for details.

1975

846†	55ore West European Hedgehog	20	10

1978

950† 1k15 Brown Bear   30   10

1982

1104† 1k65 Elk   30   30

1983

1162† 2k10 Arctic Fox (*Alopex lagopus*)   40   25

1984

1182† 1k90 Norway Lemming (*Lemmus*
       lemmus)   40   25
1183† 1k90 Musk Ox (*Ovibos moschatus*) . .   40   25

1985

1223† 2k Hazel Dormouse (*Muscardinus*
       avellanarius)   40   30

SWITZERLAND

Central Europe
100 centimes =1 franc

1965

J207	5c + 5c West European Hedgehog
J208	10c +10c Alpine Marmot
J209	20c + 10c Red Deer
J210	30c + 10c Eurasian Badger
J211	50c + 10c Arctic Hare

Set of 5   1.25   95

1966

J212	5c + 5c Stoat
J213	10c + 10c Eurasian Red Squirrel
J214	20c + 10c Red Fox
J215	30c + 10c Brown Hare
J216	50c + 10c Chamois

Set of 5   1.10   85

1967

J217	10c + 10c Roe Deer
J218	20c + 10c Pine Marten
J219	30c + 10c Ibex
J220	50c + 20c European Otter

Set of 4   1.10   75

1976

919† 20c Roe Deer (fawn)   25   10

TANGANYIKA

East Africa
100 cents = 1 shilling

1922

74   5c Giraffe (black and purple)
89   5c Giraffe (black and green)
75   10c Giraffe (black and green)
90   10c Giraffe (black and yellow)
76   15c Giraffe
77   20c Giraffe
78   25c Giraffe (black)
91   25c Giraffe (black and blue)
79   30c Giraffe (black and blue)
92   30c Giraffe (black and purple)
80   40c Giraffe
81   50c Giraffe
82   75c Giraffe
83   1s Giraffe
84   2s Giraffe
85   3s Giraffe
86   5s Giraffe
87   10s Giraffe
88   £1 Giraffe

Set of 19   £150   £180

1961

113†   50c Lion   10   5

OFFICIAL STAMPS

1961
No. 113 overprinted **OFFICIAL**
O6†   50c Lion   10   5

TAIWAN
See under China

STAMP MONTHLY
– finest and most informative magazine for all collectors.
Obtainable from your newsagent or by postal subscription – details on request

TANZANIA

East Africa
100 cents =1 shilling

1965

133†   40c Giraffe   25   20
134†   50c Common Zebra ('Zebra')   25   5

1977

200†   3s Hippopotamus   85   75

205†   5s African Elephant 1.50   2.00

214†   2s Hunter's Hartebeest 1.25   55
215†   3s Red Colobus 2.00   1.00
216†   5s Dugong 2.50   2.00

1978

244†   1s Giraffe, African Buffalo   20   10
246†   5s African Elephant, African Buffalo   ..   75   75
248†   20s African Elephant, Bohar Reedbuck   ..   3.25   3.50

1980

285† 10s Giraffe (on stamp No. 78 of
Tanganyika) 1.50 1.60

307	10c Spring Hare		
308	20c Large-spotted Genet ('Genet')		
309	40c Banded Mongoose ('Mongoose')		
310	50c Ratel		
311	75c Large-toothed Rock Hyrax ('Rock Hyrax')		
312	80c Leopard		
313	1s Impala		
314	1s50 Giraffe		
315	2s Common Zebra ('Zebra')		
316	3s African Buffalo ('Buffalo')		
317	5s Lion		
318	10s Black Rhinoceros ('Rhinoceros')		
319	20s African Elephant ('Elephant')		
320	40s Cheetah		
	Set of 14	7.50	7.50

1981

321† 50c Giraffe 10 5

1982

351	50c Cheetah		
352	1s Golden Jackal ('Wild Dog')		
353	5s Chimpanzee		
354	10s African Elephant		
	Set of 4	2.10	2.25

OFFICIAL STAMPS

1965

No. 134 overprinted **OFFICIAL**

O14† 50c Common Zebra 15 5

1980

Nos. 307/13 and 315/17 overprinted **OFFICIAL**

O54	10c Spring Hare		
O55	20c Large-spotted Genet		
O56	40c Banded Mongoose		
O57	50c Ratel		
O58	75c Large-toothed Rock Hyrax		
O59	80c Leopard		
O60	1s Impala		
O61	2s Common Zebra		
O62	3s African Buffalo		
O63	5s Lion		
	Set of 10	1.25	1.50

THAILAND

South-east Asia
100 satangs =1 baht

1957

385†	5s Sambar	.. .. † ..	10	10
386†	10s Sambar	.. .. † ..	15	10
387†	15s Sambar	.. .. † ..	20	20

1960

405 25s Indian Elephant 30 10

COLLECT BIRDS ON STAMPS

The first Stanley Gibbons thematic catalogue – a few copies still available at £4.95 (p.+p. £1.30) plus FREE 1983–84 Supplement from:
Stanley Gibbons Publications Ltd, 5, Parkside, Christchurch Road, Ringwood, Hants BH24 3SH.

1973

782 20s Schomburgk's Deer (*Cervus schomburgki*)
783 25s Kouprey (*Bos sauveli*)
784 75s Common Goral (*Naemorhedus goral*)
785 1b25 Water Buffalo (*Bubalus bubalis*)
786 1b50 Javan Rhinoceros (*Rhinoceros sondaicus*)
787 2b Thamin (*Cervus eldi*)
788 2b75 Sumatran Rhinoceros (*Dedermocerus sumatrensis*)
789 4b Mainland Serow (*Capricornis sumatraensis*)

Set of 8   3.00   2.00

1974

812 4b Indian Elephant ("Roping an Elephant")   50   30

1975

825 20s Marbled Cat
826 75s Gaur
827 2b75 Indian Elephant ('Asiatic Elephant')
828 3b Clouded Leopard

Set of 4   80   45

1976

913 1b Banteng
914 2b Malayan Tapir ('Malay Tapir')
915 4b Sambar ('Sambar Deer')
916 5b Hog-Deer ('Hog Deer')

Set of 4   1.10   70

1982

1125 1b25 Pileated Gibbon
1126 3b Pigtail Macaque ('Pig-tailed Macaque')
1127 5b Slow Loris
1128 7b Silvered Leaf Monkey

Set of 4   1.75   1.75

TOGO
West Africa
100 centimes = 1 franc

1940

138†	70c African Buffalo	.. ..	20	20
139†	90c African Buffalo	.. ..	35	35
140†	1f African Buffalo	.. ..	15	15
141†	1f25 African Buffalo	.. ..	40	40
142†	1f40 African Buffalo	.. ..	15	15
143†	1f60 African Buffalo	.. ..	30	30
144†	2f African Buffalo	.. ..	30	30

1941
No. 144 surcharged SECOURS NATIONAL *and value*

154†   +3f on 2f African Buffalo 2.25   2.25

1944
No. 139 surcharged

157 3f50 on 90c African Buffalo
158 4f on 90c African Buffalo
159 5f on 90c African Buffalo
160 5f50 on 90c African Buffalo
161 10f on 90c African Buffalo
162 20f on 90c African Buffalo

Set of 6   3.00   3.00

1947

175†	5f Red-fronted Gazelle	. . . .	50	15
176†	6f Red-fronted Gazelle	. . . .	60	45
177†	10f Red-fronted Gazelle	. . . .	70	15
181†	40f African Elephant (air)	. . . .	2.50	1.75

1957

201†	4f Kob ('Le Cobe de Buffon')	. . . . . .	60	25
202†	5f Kob	. . . .	60	25
203†	6f Kob	. . . .	60	25
204†	8f Kob	. . . .	60	25
205†	10f Kob	. . . .	60	25

1959

As Nos. 201/5, but inscribed "REPUBLIQUE DU TOGO"

222†	4f Kob	. . . .	40	15
223†	5f Kob	. . . .	40	20
224†	6f Kob	. . . .	40	20
225†	8f Kob	. . . .	40	15
226†	10f Kob	. . . .	40	15

1963

323†	25f African Buffalo (on stamp No. 140)	. .	40	15

STANLEY GIBBONS
STAMP COLLECTING SERIES

Introductory booklets on *How to Start, How to Identify Stamps* and *Collecting by Theme.* A series of well illustrated guides at a low price.

Write for details.

1964

357†	40f Pygmy Hippopotamus (*Cheropsis liberiensis*)	. . . .	1.25	30
358†	45f African Palm Civet (*Nandinia*)	. . . .	1.40	45
359†	60f Bohar Reedbuck (*Redunca*)	. . . .	2.25	60
360†	85f Olive Baboon (*Papio*)	. . . .	3.00	80

1967

544†	5f Bohar Reedbuck (*Redunca*)	. . . . .	10	10
546†	15f Common Zebra (*Equus burchelli*)	. .	35	15
548†	25f Leopard (*Panthera pardus*)	. . . . .	50	25
550†	45f Lion (*Panthera leo*) (air)	. . . . .	65	40
551†	60f African Elephant (*Proboscidea*)	. . . .	1.50	80

1971

823†	40f Olive Baboon	. . . .	40	20
824†	50f Red-fronted Gazelle (air)	. . . . .	60	25
826†	100f Hippopotamus	. . . .	1.25	50

1972

Nos. 823/4 overprinted **VISITE DU PRESIDENT NIXON EN CHINE FEVRIER** 1972 or surcharged also

878 300f on 40f Olive Baboon

879 50f Red-fronted Gazelle (air)

		Set of 2	4.00	2.50

1973

962†	30f Common Zebra (on stamp No. 546)		40	20

1974

1036 20f Leopard (*Panthera pardus*)
1037 30f Giraffe (*Giraffinae*)
1038 40f African Elephant (*Probiscidea*)

1039 90f Lion (*Panthera leo*) (air)
1040 100f Black Rhinoceros (*Diceros*)
                                    Set of 5   2.40   1.40

1975

1078 30f Bush Hare
1079 40f Eurasian Beaver
1080 90f Red Deer
1081 100f Wild Boar
                                    Set of 4   2.40   1.40

1977

1218† 60f Western Black-and-White Colobus
      (*Colobus*)   45   25
1219† 90f Chimpanzee (*Pan*)   60   30
1220† 100f Leopard (*Panthera pardus*)   75   35
1221† 200f African Manatee (*Trichechus*) .. 1.50   70

1978

1315† 100f Warthog 1.10   55

1984

1722 45f African Manatee (*Trichechus
      senegalensis*)
1723 70f African Manatee (*Trichechus
      senegalensis*)

1724 90f African Manatee (*Trichechus
      senegalensis*) (*air*)
1725 105f African Manatee (*Trichechus
      senegalensis*)
                                    Set of 4   95   1.10
MS1726 Two sheets (a) 1000f Olive Colobus
      (*Colobus verus*); (b) 1000f Lesser
      Bushbaby (*Galago senegalensis*) 7.00   7.50

TONGA
South Pacific
100 seniti = 1 pa'anga

1977

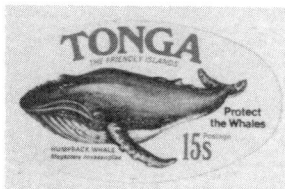

628 15s Humpback Whale
629 22s Humpback Whale
630 31s Humpback Whale
631 38s Humpback Whale
632 64s Humpback Whale

633 11s Sei Whale, Fin Whale (air)
634 17s Sei Whale, Fin Whale
635 18s Sei Whale, Fin Whale
636 39s Sei Whale, Fin Whale
637 50s Sei Whale, Fin Whale
                                    Set of 10   8.50   7.00

1978

690† 15s Humpback Whale   30   30
691† 18s Insular Flying Fox   35   35
694† 60s Humpback Whale 1.10   1.10

695†	17s Humpback Whale (air)	35	35
696†	22s Insular Flying Fox	40	40
699†	45s Humpback Whale	85	85

OFFICIAL STAMPS

1977

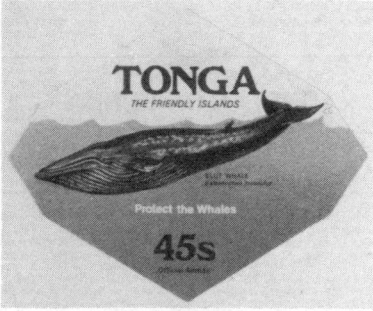

O160	45s Blue Whale
O161	65s Blue Whale
O162	85s Blue Whale
		Set of 3	5.50	4.75

1978

As Nos. 690/9, but inscribed "OFFICIAL MAIL"

O184†	40s Humpback Whale	70	70
O185†	50s Insular Flying Fox	95	95
		(O184/6 Set of 3)	3.25	3.25

TRENGGANU
South-east Asia
100 cents = 1 dollar

1957

94†	10c Tiger (sepia)	15	5
94a†	10c Tiger (purple)	25	5

COLLECT BIRDS ON STAMPS
The first Stanley Gibbons thematic catalogue – a few copies still available at £4.95 (p.+p. £1.30) plus FREE 1983–84 Supplement from:
Stanley Gibbons Publications Ltd, 5, Parkside, Christchurch Road, Ringwood, Hants BH24 3SH.

TRIESTE
Southern Europe
100 paras = 1 dinar

Zone B Yugoslav Military Government

1954

As Nos. 765/9 of Yugoslavia overprinted **STT VUJNA**

B119†	2d European Souslik	10	10
B120†	5d Lynx	10	10
B121†	10d Red Deer	15	10
B122†	15d Brown Bear	20	15
B123†	17d Chamois	20	15

TRINIDAD AND TOBAGO
West Indies
100 cents = 1 dollar

1971

392	3c Red Brocket ('Brocket-Deer')
393	5c Collared Peccary ('Quenk')
394	6c Paca ('Lappe')
395	30c Brazilian Agouti ('Agouti')
396	40c Ocelot
		Set of 5	4.25	4.00

1975

459†	25c Common Vampire Bat (Desmodus rotundus)	25	20

1978

521 15c Tayra
522 25c Ocelot
523 40c Brazilian Tree Porcupine ('The
     Porcupine')
524 70c Tamandua ('Yellow Tamandua')
                              Set of 4   1.50   1.25

1933

163† 5li + 1li Leopard 24.00   30.00

TRISTAN DA CUNHA
South Atlantic
1954 12 pence = 1 shilling; 20 shillings =1 pound
1961 100 cents =1 rand
1971 100 pence =1 pound

1954

25† 2s6d Southern Elephant-Seal ("Elephant
     Seal at Gough Island") 22.00   14.00

1960

41† 10s Black Right Whale ('Atlantic Right
     Whale') 48.00   50.00

1961
As No. 41, but face value in new currency
54† 1r Black Right Whale 48.00   60.00

1975

200 2p Killer Whale
201 3p Rough-toothed Dolphin
202 5p Black Right Whale ('Atlantic Right
     Whale')
203 20p Fin Whale ('Finback Whale')
                              Set of 4   3.75   3.75

TRIPOLITANIA
North Africa
100 centesimi =1 lira

1929

64† 50c + 20c Dorcas Gazelle 2.00   2.50

1930

80† 2li55 + 45c Blackbuck 7.00   5.50

1932

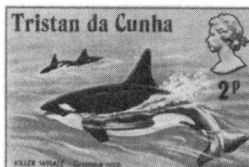

151† 1li75 + 25c Lion 8.50   9.00
153† 10li + 2li Dorcas Gazelle 42.00   48.00

1978

255† 5p Southern Elephant-Seal ('Elephant
      Seal')   30   30
256† 10p Afro-Australian Fur Seal ('Fur Seal')   40   40

TUNISIA
North Africa
1000 milliemes =1 dinar

1968

678† 5m Golden Jackal (*Canis aurens*)   20   8
679† 8m North African Crested Porcupine
      (*Hystrix cristata*)   25   12
680† 10m Dromedary (*Camelus dromedarius*) .   45   15
681† 15m Dorcas Gazelle (*Gazella dorcas*) ..   50   25
682† 20m Fennec Fox (*Fennecus zerda*)   ..   55   35
683† 25m Algerian Hedgehog (*Aethechinus*
      algirus)   65   35
685† 60m Wild Boar (*Sus scrofa*) 1.00   70
                    (678/85 *Set of* 8)   4.00   2.00

1980

962† 50m Barbary Sheep (*Ammotragus lervia*)   20   10

TURKEY
South-east Europe and Asia Minor
1922 40 paras = 1 kurus =1 piastre
1947 100 kurus = 1 lira

1922

A84† 10pi Wolf 10.00   40

1967

2191 50k Fallow Deer ('Alageyik')
2192 60k Wild Goat ('Yabankecisi')
2193 100k Brown Bear ('Ayi')
2194 130k Wild Boar ('Yabandomuzu')
                    Set of 4   2.75   1.50

1970

2331† 250k Roe Deer ('Karaca')   80   45

STANLEY GIBBONS
STAMP COLLECTING SERIES

Introductory booklets on *How to Start, How to Identify
Stamps* and *Collecting by Theme.* A series of well illus-
trated guides at a low price.
Write for details.

1979

2682†	5li + 1li Goitred Gazelle (*Gazella subgutturosa*)	50	25
2683†	5li + 1li Mouflon (*Ovis amon orientalis*)	50	25

748 95c Sperm Whale
749 $1.10 Cuvier's Beaked Whale ('Goosebeak Whale')
750 $2 Blue Whale
751 $2.20 Humpback Whale
752 $3 Long-finned Pilot Whale ('Longfin Pilot Whale')

Set of 8	13.00	14.00
MS753 $3 Fin Whale	4.00	4.50

1984

Nos. 748/9 and MS753 overprinted **19th UPU CONGRESS, HAMBURG, WEST GERMANY 1874–1984**
810 95c Sperm Whale
811 $1.10 Cuvier's Beaked Whale

Set of 2	3.25	3.75
MS812 $3 Fin Whale	3.75	3.00

TURKS AND CAICOS ISLANDS
West Indies
100 cents = 1 dollar

1979

537†	55c Rough-toothed Dolphin	85	60
538†	$1 Humpback Whale	1.50	1.50

1981

663†	$1 Common Dolphin ("Diving with Dolphins")	1.25	1.25

1983

745 50c Minke Whale ('Piked Whale')
746 65c Black Right Whale ('Right Whale')
747 70c Killer Whale

821† $1.10 Koala ('Koala Bear')	1.75	1.90
MS822 $2 Eastern Grey Kangaroo ('Grey Kangaroo')	3.25	3.50

TUVA
Central Asia
1927 100 kopecks = 1 rouble
1935 100 kopecks = 1 tugrik
1936 100 kopecks = 1 aksha

1927

16†	2k Red Deer	80	45
17†	3k Common Goral	1.00	50

STAMP MONTHLY
– finest and most informative magazine for all collectors. Obtainable from your newsagent or by postal subscription – details on request

1934

| 50† | 20k Corsac Fox | . . . . | 4.50 | 2.00 |

1936

86†	12k Brown Bear	. . . .	2.75	75
88†	20k Brown Bear (blue)	. . . .	2.75	75
90†	30k Bactrian Camel	. . . .	2.00	75

1938
As Nos. 70 and 88, but colours changed

| 115† | 5k Sable (green) | . . . . | 30.00 |
| 118† | 20k Brown Bear (red) | . . . . | 90.00 |

51†	1k Yak	. . . .	80	60
55†	25k Argali	. . . .	1.50	60
56†	50k Yak	. . . .	1.50	60
58†	1t Yak . .	. . . .	2.00	1.25
59†	2t Roe Deer	. . . .	2.00	1.25

1935

68	1k Eurasian Badger
69	3k Eurasian Red Squirrel
70	5k Sable (red)
71	10k Corsac Fox
72	25k European Otter
73	50k Lynx
74	1t Elk
75	2t Yak
76	3t Bactrian Camel
77	5t Brown Bear

Set of 10 12.00 6.50

COLLECT BIRDS ON STAMPS

The first Stanley Gibbons thematic catalogue – a few copies still available at £4.95 (p.+p. £1.30) plus FREE 1983–84 Supplement from:
Stanley Gibbons Publications Ltd, 5, Parkside, Christchurch Road, Ringwood, Hants BH24 3SH.

UBANGI–SHARI
Central Africa
100 centimes = 1 franc

A. Ubangi – Shari – Chad

1915
Nos. 1/7 and 21/2 of Middle Congo overprinted
OUBANGUI – CHARI – TCHAD

1†	1c Leopard	. . . .	10	10
2†	2c Leopard	. . . .	10	10
3†	4c Leopard	. . . .	10	10
4†	5c Leopard (green and blue)	. . . .	10	10
19†	5c Leopard (yellow and blue)	. . . . .	15	15
5†	10c Leopard (red and blue)	. . . . . .	15	15
20†	10c Leopard (green)	. . . . . .	10	10
5a†	15c Leopard	. . . .	40	40
6†	20c Leopard	. . . .	60	60

1916
No. 5 surcharged with large cross and **5c** *in black*

| 17 | 10c + 5c Leopard | . . . . | 60 | 60 |

No. 5 surcharged with small cross and **5c** *in red*

| 18 | 10c + 5c Leopard | . . . . | 15 | 15 |

B. Ubangi – Shari

1922
Nos. 1/7 of Middle Congo in new colours overprinted
OUBANGUI – CHARI

24†	1c Leopard	. . . .	10	10
25†	2c Leopard	. . . .	15	15
26†	4c Leopard	. . . .	20	20
27†	5c Leopard	. . . .	30	30
28†	10c Leopard	. . . .	40	40
29†	15c Leopard	. . . .	60	60
30†	20c Leopard	. . . .	2.25	2.25

1924

Nos. 24/30 further overprinted **AFRIQUE EQUATORIALE**
FRANCAISE

42†	1c Leopard	. . . .	10	10
43†	2c Leopard	. . . .	10	10
44†	4c Leopard	. . . .	10	10
45†	5c Leopard	. . . .	10	10
46†	10c Leopard (green)	. . . .	10	10
47†	10c Leopard (red and blue)	. . . .	10	10
48†	15c Leopard	. . . .	10	10
49†	20c Leopard	. . . .	15	15

307	80c Hunting Dog	
308	1s Lion	
309	1s50 Gorilla ('Mountain Gorilla')	
310	2s Common Zebra	
311	2s70 Leopard	
312	3s50 Black Rhinoceros	
313	5s Waterbuck ('Defassa Waterbuck')	
314	10s African Buffalo ('African Black Buffalo')	
315	20s Hippopotamus	
316	40s African Elephant	

Set of 14   4.00   3.00

UGANDA

East Africa
100 cents = 1 shilling

1977

186†	3s Hippopotamus	80	90

191†	5s African Elephant	1.60	1.90

201†	2s Hunter's Hartebeest	1.25	55
202†	3s Red Colobus	1.50	1.10
203†	5s Dugong	2.25	1.75

1979

303	10c Impala
304	20c Large-spotted Genet
305	30c Thomson's Gazelle
306	50c Lesser Bushbaby ('Bush Baby')

1983

406	5s African Elephant
407	10s African Elephant
408	30s African Elephant
409	70s African Elephant

Set of 4   80   85

MS410 300s Grevy's Zebra ('Zebra') (latin name
wrong) 1.75   1.90

418†	70s Lion	35	40

Nos. 303, 305/9 and 313 surcharged

421	100s on 10c Impala
422	135s on 1s Lion
423	175s on 30c Thomson's Gazelle
424	200s on 50c Lesser Bushbaby
425	400s on 80c Hunting Dog
426	700s on 5s Waterbuck
427	1000s on 1s50 Gorilla

Set of 7   10.00   10.00

As Nos. 308/12 and 315/16, but with different face values

433	100s Lion
434	135s Gorilla
435	175s Common Zebra
436	200s Leopard
437	400s Black Rhinoceros
438	700s African Elephant
439	1000s Hippopotamus

Set of 7   7.00   10.00

STAMP MONTHLY

– finest and most informative magazine for all collectors.
Obtainable from your newsagent or by postal subscription – details on request

POSTAGE DUE STAMPS

1985

D24	5s Lion		
D25	10s African Buffalo		
D26	20s Kob ('Uganda Kob')		
D27	40s African Elephant ('Elephant')		
D28	50s Common Zebra ('Zebra')		
D29	100s Black Rhinoceros ('Rhinoceros')		
		Set of 6	55	65

UMM AL QIWAIN
Arabian Peninsula
1964 100 naye paise = 1 rupee
1967 100 dirhams = 1 riyal

1964

1†	1np Mountain Gazelle	10	10
3†	3np Striped Hyena	10	10
10†	40np Mountain Gazelle	30	10
12†	70np Striped Hyena	60	10

1965
Designs as Nos. 1 and 3, but inscribed "AIR MAIL"

34†	15np Mountain Gazelle	15	10
36†	35np Striped Hyena	25	10

1967
Nos. 1, 3, 10, 12, 34 and 36 with currency names changed by overprinting

80†	1d on 1np Mountain Gazelle	10	10
82†	3d on 3np Striped Hyena	10	10
89†	40d on 40np Mountain Gazelle	30	20
91†	70d on 70np Striped Hyena	45	35
98†	15d on 15np Mountain Gazelle	10	10
100†	35d on 35np Striped Hyena	20	20

OFFICIAL STAMPS

1965
Designs as Nos. 1 and 3, but inscribed "ON STATE'S SERVICE"

O49†	25np Mountain Gazelle	15	10
O51†	50np Striped Hyena	30	10

STANLEY GIBBONS
STAMP COLLECTING SERIES
Introductory booklets on *How to Start, How to Identify Stamps* and *Collecting by Theme*. A series of well illustrated guides at a low price.
Write for details.

1967
Nos. O49 and O51 with currency names changed by overprinting

O107†	25d on 25np Mountain Gazelle	20	15
O109†	50d on 50np Striped Hyena	35	25

Appendix
The following stamps have either been issued in excess of postal needs, or have not been made available to the public in reasonable quantities at face value. Miniature sheets, imperforate stamps etc., are excluded from this section.

1971
Wild Animals (Tiger, Gorilla, Zebra, Brown Bear, African Elephant). Postage 10, 15, 20, 25d; Air 5r.

UNITED NATIONS

C. Vienna International Centre, Austria
100 groschen = 1 shilling

1984

V41†	3s50 Common Zebra	35	35

UNITED STATES OF AMERICA
North America
100 cents = 1 dollar

1898

293†	4c American Bison ("Indian Hunting Buffalo")	75.00	10.00

1922

700†	30c American Bison	13.00	10

1956

1080† 3c Pronghorn ('Pronghorn Antelope') .. 25 10

1958

1121 4c Red Deer 10 10

1970

1378† 6c African Elephant 30 15

1382 6c American Bison 15 10

1971

1430† 8c Polar Bear 40 15

1972

1469† 8c Northern Fur Seal ('Fur Seal') 30 15
1472† 8c American Bighorn ('Bighorn Sheep') 30 15

1978

MS1726 13c Elk ('Moose'); 13c Least Chipmunk
('Chipmunk'); 13c Red Fox; 13c
Common Racoon ('Raccoon') 2.00 2.00
No. MS1726 also shows four bird designs.

1981

1856 18c American Bighorn
1857 18c Puma
1858 18c Common Seal
1859 18c American Bison
1860 18c Brown Bear
1861 18c Polar Bear
1862 18c Red Deer
1863 18c Elk
1864 18c White-tailed Deer
1865 18c Pronghorn
                                Set of 10 2.75 50

1896† 18c American Badger 30 20
1897† 18c Brown Bear 30 20

STAMP MONTHLY

– finest and most informative magazine for all collectors.
Obtainable from your newsagent or by postal subscription – details on request

1982

1926	20c American Bighorn	35	10

1983

2063	20c Reindeer	30	10

1984

2093	20c American Black Bear	35	30

UPPER VOLTA
West Africa
100 centimes = 1 franc

1962

99†	5f African Buffalo ('Buffles')	30	15
100†	10f Lion ('Couple de Lions')	35	25
101†	15f Waterbuck ('Cob Defassa')	50	40
104†	85f Kob ('Cob de Buffon')	2.40	1.75

1965

168†	85f Lion	1.75	80

1966

176†	5f Warthog ('Phacochere')	15	10
178†	8f Savanna Monkey ('Singe Vert')	15	15
179†	10f Dromedary ('Dromedaire')	30	15
180†	15f Leopard ('Panthere')	45	30
181†	20f African Buffalo ('Buffle')	50	30
182†	25f Pygmy Hippopotamus ('Hippopotame')	70	35
187†	85f African Elephant ('Elephant')	1.60	1.00

1972

396†	65f Dromedary	80	40

1978

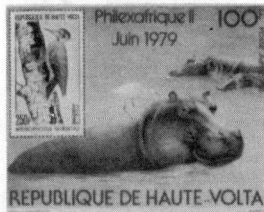

499†	100f Hippopotamus	1.10	80

1979

528 30f Kob (*Kobus kob*)
529 40f Roan Antelope (*Hippotragus equinus*)
530 60f Caracal (*Felis caracal*)
531 100f African Elephant (*Loxodonta africana*)
532 175f Hartebeest (*Alcelaphus buselaphus*)
533 250f Leopard (*Panthera pardus*)
    Set of 6   4.00   2.25

1980

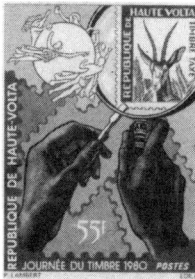

547 55f Red-fronted Gazelle (on stamp as No.
    D95)   35   30

1981

609 5f Topi ('Le Damalisque')
610 15f Waterbuck ('Cob Defassa')
611 40f Roan Antelope (*Hippotragus equinus*)
612 60f Dorcas Gazelle (*Gazella dorcas*)
613 70f African Elephant (*Elephantus*)
    Set of 6   1.25   80

OFFICIAL STAMPS

1963

O112 1f African Elephant
O113 5f African Elephant
O114 10f African Elephant
O115 15f African Elephant
O116 25f African Elephant
O117 50f African Elephant
O118 60f African Elephant
O119 85f African Elephant
O120 100f African Elephant
O121 200f African Elephant
    Set of 10   7.00   7.00

POSTAGE DUE STAMPS

1962

D95   1f Red-fronted Gazelle
D96   2f Red-fronted Gazelle
D97   5f Red-fronted Gazelle
D98   10f Red-fronted Gazelle
D99   20f Red-fronted Gazelle
D100 50f Red-fronted Gazelle
    Set of 6   1.75   1.75

Appendix
The following stamps have either been issued in excess of postal needs, or have not been made available to the public in reasonable quantities at face value. Miniature sheets, imperforate stamps etc., are excluded from this section.

1973
African Wildlife (Giraffe, Elephant, Leopard, Lion). 100, 150, 200, 250f.
A further values shows a crocodile.

URUGUAY

South America
100 centesimos = 1 peso

1954

1034†	8c Southern Sealion	50	10
1043†	4p Southern Sealion	14.00	6.00

1970

1417†	50p Capybara (*Hydrochoerus hydrochaeris*)	75	40
1418†	100p Mulita Armadillo (*Dasypus hibrydus*)	1.25	60
1419†	150p Puma (*Felis concolor*)	1.90	1.00
1420†	200p Coypu (*Myocastor coypus*)	2.40	1.50
1421†	250p South American Fur Seal (*Arctocephalus australis*)	3.75	2.00

1976

1630†	50c Geoffroy's Cat (*Felis geoffroyi paraguae*)	50	30

VENEZUELA

South America
100 centimos = 1 bolivar

1963

1766	5c White-tailed Deer (*Odocoileus virginianus*)	

1767	10c Collared Peccary (*Tagassu tajacu*)		
1768	35c Widow Monkey (*Callicebus torquatus*)		
1769	50c Giant Otter (*Pteronura brasiliensis*)		
1770	1b Puma (*Felis concolor*)		
1771	3b Capybara (*Hydrochoerus hydrochoeris*)		
1772	5c Spectacled Bear (*Tremarctos ornatus*) (air)		
1773	40c Paca (*Cuniculus paca*)		
1774	50c Pale-throated Sloth (*Bradypus trydactilus*)		
1775	55c Giant Anteater (*Myrmecophaga tridactyla*)		
1776	1b50 Brazilian Tapir (*Tapirus terrestris*)		
1777	2b Jaguar (*Felis onca*)		
	Set of 12	20.00	12.00

1965

Nos. 1770/1 and 1776/7 surcharged **RESELLADO VALOR** and new value

1848†	25c on 1b Puma	40	20
1849†	25c on 3b Capybara	30	20
1885†	25c on 1b50 Brazilian Tapir (air)	60	20
1886†	25c on 2b Jaguar	60	30

VIETNAM

South-east Asia

South Vietnam

100 cents = 1 piastre

1971

S385	9p Hog-Deer		
S386	30p Tiger		
	Set of 2	1.00	60

1973

S449	5p Water Buffalo ('Con Trau')		
S450	10p Water Buffalo ('Con Trau')		
	Set of 2	40	25

North Vietnam

100 xu = 1 dong

1961

N158 12x Sambar (*Rusa unicolor*)
N159 20x Sun Bear (*Helarctos malynus*)
N160 50x Indian Elephant (*Elephas maximus indicus*)
N161 1d Crested Gibbon (*Hylobates leucogenys*)
          Set of 4   14.00   7.00

1964

N316 12x Spotted Deer (*Pseudaxis axis*)
N317 12x Malayan Tapir (*Tapirus indicus*)
N318 12x Tiger (*Panthera tigris*)
N319 20x Water Buffalo (*Bubalus bubalis*)
N320 30x Sumatran Rhinoceros (*Rhinoceros bicornis*)
N321 40x Banteng (*Bibos banteng*)
          Set of 6   11.00   5.50

1965

N366 12x Yellow-throated Marten (*Martes flavigula*)
N367 12x Owston's Palm Civet (*Chrotogale ovvstoni*)
N368 12x Chinese Pangolin (*Manis pentadactyla*)
N369 12x Francois' Monkey (*Presbytis delacouri*)

N370 20x Red Giant Flying Squirrel (*Petaurista lylei*)
N371 50x Lesser Slow Loris (*Nycticebus pygmaeus*)
          Set of 6   8.00   5.50

1967

N472 12x Dhole (*Cuon rutilans*)
N473 12x Binturong (*Arctictis binturong*)
N474 12x Hog-Badger (*Arctonyx collaris*)
N475 20x Large Indian Civet (*Viverra zibetha*)
N476 40x Bear Macaque (*Macaca speciosa*)
N477 50x Clouded Leopard (*Neofelis nebulosa*)
          Set of 6   8.00   5.00

1973

N724 12x Dhole (*Cuon alpinus*)
N725 30x Leopard (*Panthera pardus*)
N726 50x Leopard Cat (*Felis bengalensis*)
N727 1d European Otter (*Lutra lutra*)
          Set of 4   2.50   1.00

N736 12x Lesser Malay Chevrotain (*Tragulus javanicus*)
N737 30x Mainland Serow (*Capricornis sumatraensis*)
N738 50x Wild Boar (*Sus scrofa*)
N739 1d Siberian Musk Deer (*Moschus moschiferus*)
          Set of 4   2.00   1.00

STAMP MONTHLY

– finest and most informative magazine for all collectors. Obtainable from your newsagent or by postal subscription – details on request

1976

N850 12x Masked Palm Civet (*Paguma larvata*)
N851 12x Belly-banded Squirrel (*Callosciurus erythraeus*)
N852 20x Rhesus Macaque (*Macaca mulatta*)
N853 30x Chinese Porcupine (*Hystrix hodgsoni*)
N854 40x Racoon-Dog (*Nyctereutes procyonoides*)
N855 50x Asiatic Black Bear (*Selenarctos thibetanus*)
N856 60x Leopard (*Panthera pardus*)
N857 1d Malayan Flying Lemur (*Cynocephalus variegatus*)

Set of 8   3.50   1.50

Vietnam Republic
100 xu = 1 dong

1981

396 12x Bear Macaque (*Macaca speciosa*)
397 12x Crested Gibbon (*Hylobates concolor*)
398 20x Asiatic Black Bear (*Selenarctos thibetanus*)
399 30x Dhole (*Cuon alpinus*)
400 40x Wild Boar (*Sus scrofa*)
401 50x Sambar (*Cervus unicolor*)
402 60x Leopard (*Panthera pardus*)
403 1d Tiger (*Panthera tigris*)

Set of 8   2.75   2.75

435 30x European Bison (*Bison bonasus*)
436 30x Orang-Utan (*Pongo pymaeus*)
437 40x Hippopotamus (*Hippopotamus amphibius*)

438 40x Red Kangaroo (*Macropus rubra*)
439 50x Giraffe (*Giraffa camelopardis*)
440 50x Javan Rhinoceros (*Rhinoceros sondaicus*)
441 60x Common Zebra (*Equus burchelli*)
442 1d Lion (*Panthera leo*)

Set of 8   3.00   3.00

WALLIS AND FUTUNA ISLANDS
South Pacific
100 centimes = 1 franc

1984

449 90f Killer Whale (*Orcina orca*) 1.10   80

POSTAGE DUE STAMPS

1930
Nos. D179/91 of New Caledonia overprinted
ILES WALLIS et FUTUNA

D85 2c Sambar
D86 4c Sambar
D87 5c Sambar
D88 10c Sambar
D89 15c Sambar
D90 20c Sambar
D91 25c Sambar
D92 30c Sambar
D93 50c Sambar
D94 60c Sambar
D95 1f Sambar
D96 2f Sambar
D97 3f Sambar

Set of 13   1.60   1.60

WEST BERLIN
See under Germany

WEST GERMANY
See under Germany

WEST IRIAN
South-east Asia
100 sen = 1 rupiah

1963
Nos. 724 and 727 of Indonesia surcharged **IRIAN BARAT** *and value*

1† 1s on 70s Banteng   10   10
2† 2s on 90s Sumatran Rhinoceros   10   10

1968

31†	50s Common Phalanger (*Phalangeridae*)	55	55
33†	1r Common Forest Wallaby (*Macropodidae*)	1.10	1.10

YEMEN

Arabia
1964 40 bogaches = 1 rial
1975 100 fils = 1 riyal

1964

290†	½b Hamadryas Baboon	15	10
293†	1b Lion	30	15
294†	1½b Mountain Gazelle	35	15
295†	4b Mountain Gazelle (air)	55	30
297†	20b Lion	2.75	1.50

1966

386†	½b Brown Hare	25	20
390†	4b Dromedary	60	40

1982

667†	25f Common Rabbit	60	25
672†	125f Red Deer	2.25	1.25

POSTAGE DUE STAMPS

1964

As No. 294, but inscribed "POSTAGE DUE"

D298†	4b Mountain Gazelle	1.25	50

YEMEN PEOPLE'S DEMOCRATIC REPUBLIC

Arabia
1000 fils = 1 dinar

1981

261	50f Sand Fox (*Vulpes ruppelli*)	
262	90f Leopard (*Panthera pardus nimr*)	
263	250f Ibex (*Capra ibex*)	
	Set of 3	2.50 2.25

YUGOSLAVIA

South-east Europe
100 paras = 1 dinar

1954

765†	2d European Souslik (*Citellus citellus*)	20	10
766†	5d Lynx (*Lynx lynx*)	35	15
767†	10d Red Deer (*Cervus elaphus montanus*)	60	25
768†	15d Brown Bear (*Ursus arctos bosniensis*)	80	30
769†	17d Chamois (*Rupicapra rupicapra balcanica*)	1.40	30

1960

956 15d West European Hedgehog (*Erinaceus europaeus*)
957 20d Eurasian Red Squirrel (*Sciurus vulgaris*)
958 25d Pine Marten (*Martes martes*)
959 30d Brown Hare (*Lepus europaeus*)
960 35d Red Fox (*Vulpes vulpes*)
961 40d Eurasian Badger (*Meles meles*)
962 55d Wolf (*Canis lupus*)
963 80d Roe Deer (*Capreolus capreolus*)
964 100d Wild Boar (*Sus scrofa*)

Set of 9 2.40 2.00

1967

1296† 1d20 Red Deer (*Cervus elaphus montanus*) 25 25

1976

1732† 8d Muskrat (*Ondatra zibethica*) 60 60

1978

1857† 1d50 Eurasian Red Squirrel 15 15
1859† 2d Red Deer 20 20

1980

1932† 10d Common Dolphin (*Delphinus delphis*) 45 40

1981

2006 13d Lynx 40 40

1982

2038† 15d Mediterranean Monk Seal 45 40

1983

2091† 23d70 Chamois 40 30

ZAIRE

Central Africa
100 kuta = 1 zaire

1974

825 1k Leopard
826 2k Leopard
827 3k Leopard
828 4k Leopard
829 5k Leopard
830 14k Leopard

Set of 6 1.40 90

1975

863	1k Okapi
864	2k Okapi
865	3k Okapi
866	4k Okapi
867	5k Okapi

| | Set of 5 | 60 | 40 |

1977

Nos. 656 and 773 of Congo (Kinshasa) surcharged
REPUBLIQUE DU ZAIRE

| 895† | 2k on 9.6k Leopard .. .. | 10 | 10 |
| 897† | 10k on 10s Savanna Monkey .. .. .. | 30 | 30 |

1979

| 954† | 4k African Elephant .. .. | 10 | 10 |
| 957† | 17k Lion .. .. | 15 | 15 |

1980

988†	10k African Elepnant (on Belgian Congo No. 22)	15	10
990†	40k African Elephant (on Belgian Congo No. 140)	30	15
991†	150k Chimpanzee (on Belgian Congo No. 228)	80	40
992†	200k Leopard (on Belgian Congo No. 261)	1.25	55
MS994	10z Leopard	6.00	6.00

| 1046† | 145k Chimpanzee, Lesser Kudu, White Rhinoceros .. .. | 90 | 50 |

1982

1120	1z Lion
1121	1z70 African Buffalo ('Buffles')
1122	3z50 African Elephant ('Elephants')
1123	6z50 Topi ('Antilopes Topis')
1124	8z Hippopotamus ('Hippopotames')
1125	10z Savanna Monkey ('Grivets')
1126	10z Leopard

| | Set of 7 | 10.00 | 8.50 |

1984

1172†	10k Giant Eland ('Elans de Derby') ..	10	10
1174†	3z Serval	15	15
1175†	10z White Rhinoceros ('Rhinoceros Blancs')	50	40
1176†	15z Lion	75	60
1177†	37z50 Warthog ('Phacocheres')	2.10	1.60

1209	2z Okapi
1210	3z Okapi
1211	8z Okapi
1212	10z Okapi

| | Set of 4 | 1.40 | 1.25 |
| **MS**1213 | 50z Okapi .. .. | 2.40 | 2.25 |

COLLECT BIRDS ON STAMPS

The first Stanley Gibbons thematic catalogue – a few copies still available at £4.95 (p.+p. £1.30) plus FREE 1983–84 Supplement from:
Stanley Gibbons Publications Ltd, 5, Parkside, Christchurch Road, Ringwood, Hants BH24 3SH.

ZAMBIA
Central Africa
1964 12 pence =1 shilling; 20 shillings =1 pound
1968 100 ngwee = 1 kwacha

1964

104† 2s6d African Elephant 50 35

1968

140† 2k Eland 4.00 3.00

1969

148† 10n Waterbuck ('Defassa Waterbuck') .. 30 5

1972

168 4n Cheetah
169 10n Lechwe
170 15n North African Crested Porcupine
    ('Porcupine')
171 25n African Elephant ('Elephant')
                        Set of 4   3.75   3.75

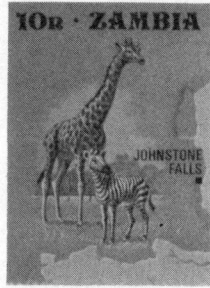

MS176   10n Giraffe, Common Zebra; 10n Black
        Rhinoceros; 10n Hippopotamus,
        Common Duiker; 10n Lion 7.00   9.00
    Each design includes part of a map showing Zambian National
Parks, the four forming a composite design.

1974

226† 1n Black Rhinoceros ('Rhinoceros') .. 10 5
231† 8n Sitatunga 15 5
232† 9n African Elephant 20 5
233† 10n Temminck's Ground Pangolin ('Giant
        Pangolin') 20 5

1978

275 8n African Elephant ('Elephant')
276 18n Lechwe ('Kafue Lechwe')
277 28n Warthog
278 32n Cheetah
                        Set of 4   1.25   1.50

1979
No. 232 surcharged
279† 8n on 9n African Elephant 10 8

STANLEY GIBBONS
STAMP COLLECTING SERIES
Introductory booklets on *How to Start, How to Identify
Stamps* and *Collecting by Theme.* A series of well illus-
trated guides at a low price.
Write for details.

ZIL ELWANNYEN SESEL
Indian Ocean
100 cents = 1 rupee

1980

288† 32n Common Zebra, African Elephant,
African Buffalo, Giraffe, Waterbuck   . .   45   50

1982

367† 28n African Buffalo   40   40

1983

388 12n Giraffe ('Thornicroft's Giraffe')
389 28n Blue Wildebeest ('Cookson's
     Wildebeest')
390 35n Lechwe ('Black Lechwe')
391 1k Yellow-backed Duiker
                        Set of 4   1.60   2.00

1985

425 12n Chacma Baboon
426 20n Diademed Monkey ('Moloney's
     Monkey')
427 45n Diademed Monkey ('Blue Monkey')
428 1k Savanna Monkey ('Vervet Monkey')
                        Set of 4   1.10   1.75

12† 1r50 Seychelles Flying Fox ('Flying Fox,
     Roussette')   35   35

22† 5r Sperm Whale 1.10   1.10

ZIMBABWE
Central Africa
100 cents = 1 dollar

1980

581† 9c White Rhinoceros ('Rhinoceros')   . .   10   10
582† 11c Lion   10   12
583† 13c Warthog   12   15
584† 15c Giraffe   15   20
585† 17c Common Zebra ('Zebra')   20   25

Mammal Species Section

This Section contains two parts.

The **Index** contains two alphabetic lists, by English name or by systematic (zoological) name, of every wild mammal family or species which has appeared on stamps. Against each entry is the numerical code for identification in the Systematic Listing.

In the **Systematic Listing** the mammals are grouped in the families recognised by zoologists. To aid identification each family is given a numeral, as is each species within that family. Elephants, for example, are family No. 82 with the Indian Elephant as species No. 2 within that family. The numerical code for the Indian Elephant would, therefore, be 82-2, the first figure identifying the family and the second the species.

Index

I. By English Name

A

Aardvark, see 87-1 AARDVARK
Aardwolf, see 66-1 HYENAS
Abbott's Duiker, see 97-36 CATTLE, ANTELOPE, SHEEP, GOATS
Abyssinian Hare, see 128-15 RABBITS, HARES
Addax, see 97-56 CATTLE, ANTELOPE, SHEEP, GOATS
Addra Gazelle, see 97-83 CATTLE, ANTELOPE, SHEEP, GOATS
African Ass, see 83-1 HORSES
African Brush-tailed Porcupine, see 111-10 OLD-WORLD PORCUPINES
African Buffalo, see 97-21 CATTLE, ANTELOPE, SHEEP, GOATS
African Civet, see 65-15 CIVETS, MONGOOSES
African Clawless Otter, see 64-64 WEASELS, BADGERS, OTTERS
African Elephant, see 82-1 ELEPHANTS
African Golden Cat, see 67-1 CATS
African Linsang, see 65-1 CIVETS, MONGOOSES
African Manatee, see 81-3 MANATEES
African Mole-Rats, see 125 AFRICAN MOLE-RATS
African Palm Civet, see 65-21 CIVETS, MONGOOSES
Afro-Australian Fur Seal, see 68-6 EARED SEALS, SEALIONS
Agile Mangabey, see 57-16 OLD-WORLD MONKEYS
Algerian Hedgehog, see 25-7 HEDGEHOGS, MOONRATS
Alpine Marmot, see 100-147 SQUIRRELS
Amazon Manatee, see 81-1 MANATEES
American Anteaters, see 19 AMERICAN ANTEATERS
American Badger, see 64-38 WEASELS, BADGERS, OTTERS
American Beaver, see 103-1 BEAVERS
American Bighorn, see 97-119 CATTLE, ANTELOPE, SHEEP, GOATS
American Bison, see 97-22 CATTLE, ANTELOPE, SHEEP, GOATS
American Black Bear, see 61-3 BEARS
American Manatee, see 81-2 MANATEES
American Mink, see 64-15 WEASELS, BADGERS, OTTERS
American Opossums, see 3 AMERICAN OPOSSUMS
Andean Hog-nosed Skunk, see 64-49 WEASELS
Angolan Black-and-White Colobus, see 57-48 OLD-WORLD MONKEYS
Angwantibo, see 53-5 LORISES, BUSHBABIES
Anoa, see 97-13 CATTLE, ANTELOPE, SHEEP, GOATS
Antelope, see 97 CATTLE, ANTELOPE, SHEEP, GOATS
Apes, see 58 APES
Arabian Oryx, see 97-55 CATTLE, ANTELOPE, SHEEP, GOATS

Arabian Tahr, see 97-108 CATTLE, ANTELOPE, SHEEP, GOATS
Arctic Fox, see 60-8 DOGS, FOXES
Arctic Hare, see 128-23 RABBITS, HARES
Argali, see 97-118 CATTLE, ANTELOPE, SHEEP, GOATS
Argentine Grey Fox, see 60-24 DOGS, FOXES
Armadillos, see 21 ARMADILLOS
Asiatic Black Bear, see 61-2 BEARS
Asiatic Wild Ass, see 83-5 HORSES
Atlantic Hump-backed Dolphin, see 72-4 MARINE DOLPHINS
Atlantic White-sided Dolphin, see 72-15 MARINE DOLPHINS
Aye-Aye, see 52-1 AYE-AYE

B

Babirusa, see 88-8 PIGS
Back-striped Mouse, see 106-672 MICE, RATS, VOLES, GERBILS, HAMSTERS
Bactrian Camel, see 91-3 CAMELS, LLAMAS
Badgers, see 64 WEASELS, BADGERS, OTTERS
Bahaman Hutia, see 118-5 HUTIAS
Baird's Tapir, see 84-1 TAPIRS
Banded Duiker, see 97-39 CATTLE, ANTELOPE, SHEEP, GOATS
Banded Mongoose, see 65-60 CIVETS, MONGOOSES
Bandicoots, see 10 BANDICOOTS
Banteng, see 97-16 CATTLE, ANTELOPE, SHEEP, GOATS
Barbary Ape, see 57-12 OLD-WORLD MONKEYS
Barbary Ground Squirrel, see 100-135 SQUIRRELS
Barbary Sheep, see 97-116 CATTLE, ANTELOPE, SHEEP, GOATS
Bat-eared Fox, see 60-35 DOGS, FOXES
Beaked Whales, see 76 BEAKED WHALES
Bear Macaque, see 57-1 OLD-WORLD MONKEYS
Bearded Seal, see 70-9 EARLESS SEALS
Bears, see 61 BEARS
Beavers, see 103 BEAVERS
Beech Marten, see 64-19 WEASELS, BADGERS, OTTERS
Beecroft's Hyrax, see 86-2 HYRAXES
Beira Antelope, see 97-69 CATTLE, ANTELOPE, SHEEP, GOATS
Belly-banded Squirrel, see 100-86 SQUIRRELS
Bharal, see 97-117 CATTLE, ANTELOPE, SHEEP, GOATS
Binturong, see 65-28 CIVETS, MONGOOSES
Black Colobus, see 57-53 OLD-WORLD MONKEYS
Black Lemur, see 50-4 LARGE LEMURS
Black Mangabey, see 57-15 OLD-WORLD MONKEYS
Black Rhinoceros, see 85-5 RHINOCEROSES
Black Right Whale, see 79-2 RIGHT WHALES
Black Spider Monkey, see 56-29 NEW-WORLD MONKEYS
Black Wildebeest, see 97-57 CATTLE, ANTELOPE, SHEEP, GOATS
Black-backed Jackal, see 60-5 DOGS, FOXES
Black-handed Spider Monkey, see 56-28 NEW-WORLD MONKEYS
Blackbuck, see 97-78 CATTLE, ANTELOPE, SHEEP, GOATS
Blesbok, see 97-61 CATTLE, ANTELOPE, SHEEP, GOATS
Blue Duiker, see 97-30 CATTLE, ANTELOPE, SHEEP, GOATS
Blue Whale, see 78-4 RORQUALS
Blue Wildebeest, see 97-58 CATTLE, ANTELOPE, SHEEP, GOATS
Bobak Marmot, see 100-141 SQUIRRELS
Bohar Reedbuck, see 97-48 CATTLE, ANTELOPE, SHEEP, GOATS
Bongo, see 97-4 CATTLE, ANTELOPE, SHEEP, GOATS
Bonin Islands Flying Fox, see 30-59 FRUIT BATS, FLYING FOXES

F

Falkland Island Wolf, see 60-22 DOGS, FOXES
Fallow Deer, see 94-10 DEER
False Killer Whale, see 72-27 MARINE DOLPHINS
Fat Dormouse, see 107-1 DORMICE
Feather-tailed Possum, see 13-5 PYGMY POSSUMS
Fennec Fox, see 60-21 DOGS, FOXES
Fin Whale, see 78-5 RORQUALS
Finless Porpoise, see 73-6 PORPOISES
Fishing Cat, see 67-26 CATS
Flat-headed Cat, see 67-19 CATS
Flying Foxes, see 30 FRUIT BATS, FLYING FOXES
Flying Lemurs, see 29 FLYING LEMURS
Forest Dormouse, see 107-5 DORMICE
Four-striped Grass Mouse, see 106-670 MICE, RATS, VOLES,
    GERBILS, HAMSTERS
Four-toed Elephant-Shrew, see 129-12 ELEPHANT-SHREWS
Foxes, see 60 DOGS, FOXES
Francois' Monkey, see 57-64 OLD-WORLD MONKEYS
Fruit Bats, see 30 FRUIT BATS, FLYING FOXES

G

Galapagos Fur Seal, see 68-4 EARED SEALS, SEALIONS
Gambian Sun Squirrel, see 100-76 SQUIRRELS
Garden Dormouse, see 107-3 DORMICE
Gaur, see 97-17 CATTLE, ANTELOPE, SHEEP, GOATS
Gelada, see 57-25 OLD-WORLD MONKEYS
Gemsbok, see 97-54 CATTLE, ANTELOPE, SHEEP, GOATS
Geoffrey's Cat, see 67-9 CATS
Gerbils, see 106 MICE, RATS, VOLES, GERBILS, HAMSTERS
Gerenuk, see 97-80 CATTLE, ANTELOPE, SHEEP, GOATS
Giant Anteater, see 19-1 AMERICAN ANTEATERS
Giant Armadillo, see 21-6 ARMADILLOS
Giant Eland, see 97-3 CATTLE, ANTELOPE, SHEEP, GOATS
Giant Forest Hog, see 88-7 PIGS
Giant Ground Pangolin, see 98-2 PANGOLINS
Giant Otter, see 64-63 WEASELS, BADGERS, OTTERS
Giant Panda, see 63-2 PANDAS
Giraffe, see 95-2 GIRAFFE, OKAPI
Gliding Phalangers, see 14 RINGTAILS, GLIDING
    PHALANGERS
Goats, see 97 CATTLE, ANTELOPE, SHEEP, GOATS
Goitred Gazelle, see 97-92 CATTLE, ANTELOPE, SHEEP,
    GOATS
Golden Jackal, see 60-2 DOGS, FOXES
Golden Langur, see 57-66 OLD-WORLD MONKEYS
Golden Lion Tamarin, see 55-16 MARMOSETS, TAMARINS
Golden Moles, see 24 GOLDEN MOLES
Golden Palm Civet, see 65-25 CIVETS, MONGOOSES
Gorilla, see 58-10 APES
Grant's Desert Golden Mole, see 24-3 GOLDEN MOLES
Grant's Gazelle, see 97-86 CATTLE, ANTELOPE, SHEEP,
    GOATS
Greater Dwarf Lemur, see 49-4 MOUSE-LEMURS, DWARF
    LEMURS
Greater Glider, see 14-18 RINGTAILS, GLIDING PHALANGERS
Greater Horseshoe Bat, see 36-22 HORSESHOE BATS
Greater Kudu, see 97-9 CATTLE, ANTELOPE, SHEEP, GOATS
Greater Malay Chevrotain, see 92-4 CHEVROTAINS
Greater Mascarene Flying Fox, see 30-49 FRUIT BATS,
    FLYING FOXES
Greater Trinidadian Murine Opossum, see 3-34 AMERICAN
    OPOSSUMS
Greater White-nosed Monkey, see 57-40 OLD-WORLD
    MONKEYS
Grevy's Zebra, see 83-4 HORSES
Grey Fox, see 60-12 DOGS, FOXES
Grey Gentle Lemur, see 50-7 LARGE LEMURS
Grey Seal, see 70-8 EARLESS SEALS
Grey Whale, see 77-1 GREY WHALE
Grey-headed Flying Fox, see 30-58 FRUIT BATS, FLYING
    FOXES
Guadeloupe Racoon, see 62-7 RACOONS
Guanaco, see 91-1 CAMELS, LLAMAS

Guinea Baboon, see 57-21 OLD-WORLD MONKEYS
Gunther's Dik-Dik, see 97-65 CATTLE, ANTELOPE, SHEEP,
    GOATS

H

Hairy-nosed Otter, see 64-62 WEASELS, BADGERS, OTTERS
Haitian Solenodon, see 22-2 SOLENODONS
Hamadryas Baboon, see 57-20 OLD-WORLD MONKEYS
Hamsters, see 106 MICE, RATS, VOLES, GERBILS,
    HAMSTERS
Hares, see 128 RABBITS, HARES
Harp Seal, see 70-7 EARLESS SEALS
Hartebeest, see 97-59 CATTLE, ANTELOPE, SHEEP, GOATS
Harvest Mouse, see 106-617 MICE, RATS, VOLES, GERBILS,
    HAMSTERS
Hazel Dormouse, see 107-2 DORMICE
Hedgehogs, see 25 HEDGEHOGS, MOONRATS
Hendee's Woolly Monkey, see 56-31 NEW-WORLD MONKEYS
Hippopotamus, see 90-1 HIPPOPOTAMUSES
Hispaniolan Hutia, see 118-11 HUTIAS
Hog Badger, see 64-35 WEASELS, BADGERS, OTTERS
Hog-Deer, see 94-15 DEER
Horses, see 83 HORSES
Horseshoe Bats, see 36 HORSESHOE BATS
Hottentot Mole-Rat, see 125-2 AFRICAN MOLE-RATS
Hourglass Dolphin, see 72-18 MARINE DOLPHINS
House Rat, see 106-764 MICE, RATS, VOLES, GERBILS,
    HAMSTERS
Huidobria Otter, see 64-61 WEASELS, BADGERS, OTTERS
Humpback Whale, see 78-6 RORQUALS
Hunter's Hartebeest, see 97-62 CATTLE, ANTELOPE, SHEEP,
    GOATS
Hunting Dog, see 60-34 DOGS, FOXES
Hutias, see 118 HUTIAS
Hyenas, see 66 HYENAS
Hyraxes, see 86 HYRAXES

I

Ibex, see 97-114 CATTLE, ANTELOPE, SHEEP, GOATS
Impala, see 97-77 CATTLE, ANTELOPE, SHEEP, GOATS
Indian Crested Porcupine, see 111-8 OLD-WORLD
    PORCUPINES
Indian Elephant, see 82-2 ELEPHANTS
Indian Flying Fox, see 30-28 FRUIT BATS, FLYING FOXES
Indian Muntjac, see 94-4 DEER
Indian Palm Squirrel, see 100-45 SQUIRRELS
Indian Rhinoceros, see 85-2 RHINOCEROSES
Indian Spotted Chevrotain, see 92-3 CHEVROTAINS
Indo-Pacific Hump-backed Dolphin, see 72-3 MARINE
    DOLPHINS
Indri, see 51-4 LEAPING LEMURS
Indus Dolphin, see 71-5 RIVER DOLPHINS
Insular Flying Fox, see 30-72 FRUIT BATS, FLYING FOXES
Iriomote Cat, see 67-11 CATS
Irrawaddy Dolphin, see 72-26 MARINE DOLPHINS

J

Jaguar, see 67-30 CATS
Jaguarundi, see 67-28 CATS
Jamaican Long-tongued Bat, see 40-40 NEW-WORLD LEAF-
    NOSED BATS
Japanese Macaque, see 57-5 OLD-WORLD MONKEYS
Japanese Serow, see 97-101 CATTLE, ANTELOPE, SHEEP,
    GOATS
Javan Mongoose, see 65-46 CIVETS, MONGOOSES
Javan Pig, see 88-5 PIGS
Javan Rhinoceros, see 85-1 RHINOCEROSES
Jentink's Duiker, see 97-27 CATTLE, ANTELOPE, SHEEP,
    GOATS
Jerboas, see 110 JERBOAS
Juan Fernandez Fur Seal, see 68-5 EARED SEALS, SEALIONS
Jungle Cat, see 67-6 CATS

K

Kangaroos, see 15 KANGAROOS, WALLABIES
Kerguelen Fur Seal, see 68-3 EARED SEALS, SEALIONS
Killer Whale, see 72-28 MARINE DOLPHINS
Kinkajou, see 62-13 RACOONS
Kirk's Dik-Dik, see 97-66 CATTLE, ANTELOPE, SHEEP, GOATS
Klipspringer, see 97-64 CATTLE, ANTELOPE, SHEEP, GOATS
Koala, see 16-1 KOALA
Kob, see 97-42 CATTLE, ANTELOPE, SHEEP, GOATS
Kouprey, see 97-20 CATTLE, ANTELOPE, SHEEP, GOATS
Kuhl's Tree Squirrel, see 100-59 SQUIRRELS

L

L'Hoest's Monkey, see 57-36 OLD-WORLD MONKEYS
Large Indian Civet, see 65-18 CIVETS, MONGOOSES
Large Lemurs, see 50 LARGE LEMURS
Large-spotted Genet, see 65-10 CIVETS, MONGOOSES
Large-toothed Rock Hyrax, see 86-5 HYRAXES
Leadbeater's Possum, see 14-1 RINGTAILS, GLIDING PHALANGERS
Leaping Lemurs, see 51 LEAPING LEMURS
Least Chipmunk, see 100-199 SQUIRRELS
Lechwe, see 97-43 CATTLE, ANTELOPE, SHEEP, GOATS
Leopard Cat, see 67-3 CATS
Leopard Seal, see 70-12 EARLESS SEALS
Leopard, see 67-31 CATS
Lesser Bushbaby, see 53-7 LORISES, BUSHBABIES
Lesser Egyptian Jerboa, see 110-4 JERBOAS
Lesser Kudu, see 97-5 CATTLE, ANTELOPE, SHEEP, GOATS
Lesser Malay Chevrotain, see 92-2 CHEVROTAINS
Lesser Mouse-Lemur, see 49-2 MOUSE-LEMURS, DWARF LEMURS
Lesser Panda, see 63-1 PANDAS
Lesser Slow Loris, see 53-3 LORISES, BUSHBABIES
Lichtenstein's Hartebeest, see 97-60 CATTLE, ANTELOPE, SHEEP, GOATS
Lion, see 67-29 CATS
Liontail Macaque, see 57-10 OLD-WORLD MONKEYS
Little Coatimundi, see 62-12 RACOONS
Llamas, see 91 CAMELS, LLAMAS
Long-eared Jerboa, see 110-27 JERBOAS
Long-fingered Possum, see 14-20 RINGTAILS, GLIDING PHALANGERS
Long-finned Pilot Whale, see 72-31 MARINE DOLPHINS
Long-haired Spider Monkey, see 56-26 NEW-WORLD MONKEYS
Long-nosed Echidna, see 1-2 SPINY ANTEATERS, ECHIDNAS
Long-tailed Chinchilla, see 117-6 VISCACHAS, CHINCHILLAS
Long-tailed Pangolin, see 98-6 PANGOLINS
Lord Derby's Flying Squirrel, see 104-2 SCALY-TAILED SQUIRRELS
Lorises, see 53 LORISES, BUSHBABIES
Lynx, see 67-13 CATS

M

Mainland Serow, see 97-102 CATTLE, ANTELOPE, SHEEP, GOATS
Malagasy Civet, see 65-29 CIVETS, MONGOOSES
Malay Civet, see 65-17 CIVETS, MONGOOSES
Malayan Flying Lemur, see 29-1 FLYING LEMURS
Malayan Pangolin, see 98-3 PANGOLINS
Malayan Tapir, see 84-2 TAPIRS
Manatees, see 81 MANATEES
Mandrill, see 57-24 OLD-WORLD MONKEYS
Maned Wolf, see 60-31 DOGS, FOXES
Marbled Cat, see 67-16 CATS
Marbled Polecat, see 64-16 WEASELS, BADGERS, OTTERS
Marine Dolphins, see 72 MARINE DOLPHINS
Marine Otter, see 64-56 WEASELS
Marmosets, see 55 MARMOSETS, TAMARINS
Marsh Deer, see 94-24 DEER
Marsupial Cats, see 6 MARSUPIAL MICE, MARSUPIAL CATS
Marsupial Mice, see 6 MARSUPIAL MICE, MARSUPIAL CATS

Masked Palm Civet, see 65-26 CIVETS, MONGOOSES
Matschie's Tree Kangaroo, see 15-51 KANGAROOS, WALLABIES
Mediterranean Monk Seal, see 70-14 EARLESS SEALS
Meerkat, see 65-39 CIVETS, MONGOOSES
Melon-headed Whale, see 72-21 MARINE DOLPHINS
Mexican Bulldog Bat, see 38-2 BULLDOG BATS
Mice, see 106 MICE, RATS, VOLES, GERBILS, HAMSTERS
Minke Whale, see 78-1 RORQUALS
Moles, see 27 MOLES, SHREW-MOLES, DESMANS
Mona Monkey, see 57-38 OLD-WORLD MONKEYS
Mongoose-Lemur, see 50-5 LARGE LEMURS
Mongooses, see 65 CIVETS, MONGOOSES
Moonrats, see 25 HEDGEHOGS, MOONRATS
Mouflon, see 97-122 CATTLE, ANTELOPE, SHEEP, GOATS
Mountain Gazelle, see 97-85 CATTLE, ANTELOPE, SHEEP, GOATS
Mountain Goat, see 97-103 CATTLE, ANTELOPE, SHEEP, GOATS
Mountain Nyala, see 97-2 CATTLE, ANTELOPE, SHEEP, GOATS
Mountain Reedbuck, see 97-47 CATTLE, ANTELOPE, SHEEP, GOATS
Mountain Tapir, see 84-3 TAPIRS
Mountain Viscacha, see 117-3 VISCACHAS, CHINCHILLAS
Mountain Zebra, see 83-8 HORSES
Mouse-Lemurs, see 49 MOUSE-LEMURS, DWARF LEMURS
Moustached Monkey, see 57-29 OLD-WORLD MONKEYS
Mule Deer, see 94-22 DEER
Mulita Armadillo, see 21-12 ARMADILLOS
Murine Opossum, see 3-26 AMERICAN OPUSSUMS
Musk Deer, see 93 MUSK DEER
Musk Ox, see 97-105 CATTLE, ANTELOPE, SHEEP, GOATS
Muskrat, see 106-440 MICE, RATS, VOLES, GERBILS, HAMSTERS

N

Narwhal, see 74-2 WHITE WHALES
Natal Red Hare, see 128-2 RABBITS, HARES
New Caledonian Flying Fox, see 30-77 FRUIT BATS, FLYING FOXES
New Guinea Marsupial Cat, see 6-28 MARSUPIAL MICE, MARSUPIAL CATS
New-World Leaf-nosed Bats, see 40 NEW-WORLD LEAF-NOSED BATS
New-World Monkeys, see 56 NEW-WORLD MONKEYS
New-World Porcupines, see 112 NEW-WORLD PORCUPINES
Night Monkey, see 56-5 NEW-WORLD MONKEYS
Nile Lechwe, see 97-44 CATTLE, ANTELOPE, SHEEP, GOATS
Nine-banded Armadillo, see 21-15 ARMADILLOS
North African Crested Porcupine, see 111-6 OLD-WORLD PORCUPINES
Northern Coati, see 62-9 RACOONS
Northern Fur Seal, see 68-9 EARED SEALS, SEALIONS
Northern Pika, see 127-1 PIKAS
Northern Sealion, see 68-11 EARED SEALS, SEALIONS
Norway Lemming, see 106-409 MICE, RATS, VOLES, GERBILS, HAMSTERS
Numbat, see 7-1 NUMBAT
Nyala, see 97-1 CATTLE, ANTELOPE, SHEEP, GOATS

O

Ocelot, see 67-18 CATS
Okapi, see 95 GIRAFFE, OKAPI
Old-World Monkeys, see 57 OLD-WORLD MONKEYS
Old-World Porcupines, see 111 OLD-WORLD PORCUPINES
Olive Baboon, see 57-18 OLD-WORLD MONKEYS
Olive Colobus, see 57-54 OLD-WORLD MONKEYS
Orang-Utan, see 58-7 APES
Oribi, see 97-70 CATTLE, ANTELOPE, SHEEP, GOATS
Oriental Small-clawed Otter, see 64-65 WEASELS, BADGERS, OTTERS
Ornate Tree Kangaroo, see 15-48 KANGAROOS, WALLABIES

Otters, see 64 WEASELS, BADGERS, OTTERS
Owl-faced Monkey, see 57-35 OLD-WORLD MONKEYS
Owston's Palm Civet, see 65-32 CIVETS, MONGOOSES

P

Paca, see 116-1 PACAS, AGOUTIS
Pacas, see 116 PACAS, AGOUTIS
Pale-throated Sloth, see 20-2 SLOTHS
Pallas's Cat, see 67-14 CATS
Pallas's Pika, see 127-8 PIKAS
Pampas Deer, see 94-25 DEER
Pandas, see 63 PANDAS
Pangolins, see 98 PANGOLINS
Patas Monkey, see 57-47 OLD-WORLD MONKEYS
Peale's Dolphin, see 72-17 MARINE DOLPHINS
Peccaries, see 89 PECCARIES
Pel's Flying Squirrel, see 104-3 SCALY-TAILED SQUIRRELS
Peruvian Guemal, see 94-26 DEER
Phalangers, see 12 PHALANGERS
Phayre's Flying Squirrel, see 100-230 SQUIRRELS
Philippine Tarsier, see 54-3 TARSIERS
Pigs, see 88 PIGS
Pigtail Macaque, see 57-7 OLD-WORLD MONKEYS
Pikas, see 127 PIKAS
Pileated Gibbon, see 58-5 APES
Pine Marten, see 64-20 WEASELS, BADGERS, OTTERS
Platypus, see 2-1 PLATYPUS
Polar Bear, see 61-5 BEARS
Polecat, see 64-12 WEASELS, BADGERS, OTTERS
Porpoises, see 73 PORPOISES
Potto, see 53-4 LORISES, BUSHBABIES
Prehensile-tailed Hutia, see 118-9 HUTIAS
Proboscis Monkey, see 57-60 OLD-WORLD MONKEYS
Pronghorn, see 96-1 PRONGHORN
Puku, see 97-45 CATTLE, ANTELOPE, SHEEP, GOATS
Puma, see 67-8 CATS
Pygmy Chimpanzee, see 58-8 APES
Pygmy Glider, see 13-6 PYGMY POSSUMS
Pygmy Hippopotamus, see 90-2 HIPPOPOTAMUSES
Pygmy Hog, see 88-3 PIGS
Pygmy Possums, see 13 PYGMY POSSUMS
Pyrenean Desman, see 27-3 MOLES, SHREW-MOLES,
   DESMANS

Q

Queensland Hairy-nosed Wombat, see 17-2 WOMBATS

R

Rabbit-Bandicoots, see 11 RABBIT-BANDICOOTS
Rabbits, see 128 RABBITS, HARES
Racoon-Dog, see 60-30 DOGS, FOXES
Racoons, see 62 RACOONS
Ratel, see 64-33 WEASELS, BADGERS, OTTERS
Rats, see 106 MICE, RATS, VOLES, GERBILS, HAMSTERS
Red Brocket, see 94-28 DEER
Red Colobus, see 57-49 OLD-WORLD MONKEYS
Red Deer, see 94-12 DEER
Red Forest Duiker, see 97-31 CATTLE, ANTELOPE, SHEEP,
   GOATS
Red Fox, see 60-20 DOGS, FOXES
Red Fruit Bat, see 40-129 NEW-WORLD LEAF-NOSED BATS
Red Giant Flying Squirrel, see 100-217 SQUIRRELS
Red Howler, see 56-24 NEW-WORLD MONKEYS
Red Kangaroo, see 15-41 KANGAROOS, WALLABIES
Red Uakari, see 56-17 NEW-WORLD MONKEYS
Red and White Flying Squirrel, see 100-213 SQUIRRELS
Red-fronted Gazelle, see 97-88 CATTLE, ANTELOPE, SHEEP,
   GOATS
Reedbuck, see 97-46 CATTLE, ANTELOPE, SHEEP, GOATS
Reindeer, see 94-21 DEER
Rhesus Macaque, see 57-6 OLD-WORLD MONKEYS

Rhinoceroses, see 85 RHINOCEROSES
Ribbon Seal, see 70-6 EARLESS SEALS
Right Whales, see 79 RIGHT WHALES
Ring-tailed Lemur, see 50-1 LARGE LEMURS
Ringed Seal, see 70-2 EARLESS SEALS
Ringtails, see 14 RINGTAILS, GLIDING PHALANGERS
Risso's Dolphin, see 72-29 MARINE DOLPHINS
River Dolphins, see 71 RIVER DOLPHINS
Roan Antelope, see 97-50 CATTLE, ANTELOPE, SHEEP,
   GOATS
Rodriguez Flying Fox, see 30-62 FRUIT BATS, FLYING FOXES
Roe Deer, see 94-34 DEER
Rorquals, see 78 RORQUALS
Ross Seal, see 70-11 EARLESS SEALS
Rough-toothed Dolphin, see 72-1 MARINE DOLPHINS
Royal Antelope, see 97-76 CATTLE, ANTELOPE, SHEEP,
   GOATS
Rufescent Bandicoot, see 10-12 BANDICOOTS
Ruffed Lemur, see 50-9 LARGE LEMURS
Russian Desman, see 27-2 MOLES, SHREW-MOLES,
   DESMANS
Rusty-spotted Cat, see 67-20 CATS
Ryukyu Rabbit, see 128-1 RABBITS, HARES

S

Sable Antelope, see 97-52 CATTLE, ANTELOPE, SHEEP,
   GOATS
Sable, see 64-23 WEASELS, BADGERS, OTTERS
Saiga, see 97-98 CATTLE, ANTELOPE, SHEEP, GOATS
Salt's Dik-Dik, see 97-68 CATTLE, ANTELOPE, SHEEP,
   GOATS
Sambar, see 94-18 DEER
Sand Fox, see 60-18 DOGS, FOXES
Sand Gazelle, see 97-87 CATTLE, ANTELOPE, SHEEP,
   GOATS
Savanna Monkey, see 57-26 OLD-WORLD MONKEYS
Scaly-tailed Squirrels, see 104 SCALY-TAILED SQUIRRELS
Schomburgk's Deer, see 94-16 DEER
Scimitar Oryx, see 97-53 CATTLE, ANTELOPE, SHEEP,
   GOATS
Sea Cows, see 80 SEA COWS
Sea Otter, see 64-67 WEASELS, BADGERS, OTTERS
Sealions, see 68 EARED SEALS, SEALIONS
Sei Whale, see 78-2 RORQUALS
Serval, see 67-22 CATS
Servaline Genet, see 65-9 CIVETS, MONGOOSES
Seychelles Flying Fox, see 30-66 FRUIT BATS, FLYING FOXES
Sheep, see 97 CATTLE, ANTELOPE, SHEEP, GOATS
Short-finned Pilot Whale, see 72-30 MARINE DOLPHINS
Short-nosed Echidna, see 1-1 SPINY ANTEATERS, ECHIDNAS
Short-tailed Chinchilla, see 117-5 VISCACHAS, CHINCHILLAS
Shrew-Moles, see 27 MOLES, SHREW-MOLES, DESMANS
Shrews, see 26 SHREWS
Siberian Chipmunk, see 100-206 SQUIRRELS
Siberian Flying Squirrel, see 100-220 Squirrels
Siberian Musk Deer, see 93-2 MUSK DEER
Siberian Weasel, see 64-13 WEASELS, BADGERS, OTTERS
Sika Deer, see 94-14 DEER
Silvered Leaf Monkey, see 57-62 OLD-WORLD MONKEYS
Simian Jackal, see 60-7 DOGS, FOXES
Sitatunga, see 97-8 CATTLE, ANTELOPE, SHEEP, GOATS
Six-banded Armadillo, see 21-2 ARMADILLOS
Slender Loris, see 53-1 LORISES, BUSHBABIES
Sloth Bear, see 61-7 BEARS
Sloths, see 20 SLOTHS
Slow Loris, see 53-2 LORISES, BUSHBABIES
Small Indian Mongoose, see 65-40 CIVETS, MONGOOSES
Small-spotted Genet, see 65-4 CIVETS, MONGOOSES
Smith's Red Hare, see 128-1 RABBITS, HARES
Snow Leopard, see 67-33 CATS
Snub-nosed Monkey, see 57-58 OLD-WORLD MONKEYS
Soemmerring's Gazelle, see 97-90 CATTLE, ANTELOPE,
   SHEEP, GOATS

II. By Zoological Name

Both elements of the zoological name are covered in this section.

Systematic Listing

17 WOMBATS
17-1   Common Wombat *(Vombatus ursinus)*
Australia 561

17-2   Queensland Hairy-nosed Wombat *(Lasiorhinus kreffti)*
Australia 784

17-3   Southern Hairy-nosed Wombat *(Lasiorhinus latifrons)*
Laos 780

19 AMERICAN ANTEATERS
19-1   Giant Anteater *(Myrmecophaga tridactyla)*
Argentine Republic 1817
Brazil 1958
Colombia 1008
Costa Rica 673
Ecuador 1160
French Guiana 58 59 60 61 83 62 84 104 63 81 82 89 90
91 92 95
Guyana 764
Venezuela 1775

19-2   Collared Anteater *(Tamandua mexicana)*
Belize 351 366
British Honduras 259

19-3   Tamandua *(Tamandua tetradactyla)*
Costa Rica 670
Guyana 763
Nicaragua 1947
Trinidad and Tobago 524

20 SLOTHS
20-2   Pale-throated Sloth *(Bradypus tridactylus)*
Venezuela 1774

20-3   Brown-throated Sloth *(Bradypus variegatus)*
Panama **MS**1388

20-4   Two-toed Sloth *(Choloepus didactylus)*
Colombia 1005 1078
Ecuador 1295
Guyana 759

21 ARMADILLOS
21-2   Six-banded Armadillo *(Euphractus sexcinctus)*
Guyana 762 1202

21-6   Giant Armadillo *(Priodontes maximus)*
France 2047

21-12   Mulita Armadillo *(Dasypus hydridus)*
Uruguay 1418

21-15   Nine-banded Armadillo *(Dasypus novemcinctus)*
British Honduras 188
Colombia 1009
Costa Rica 672
Ecuador 1291
Grenada 316 507 602 767
Guyana 498
Surinam 415 654

22 SOLENODONS
22-1   Cuban Solenodon *(Solenodon cubanus)*
Cuba 1057c 2766 3043

22-2   Haitian Solenodon *(Solenodon paradoxus)*
Dominican Republic 1306 1581

24 GOLDEN MOLES
24-3   Grant's Desert Golden Mole *(Eremitalpa granti)*
South West Africa 312

25 HEDGEHOGS, MOONRATS
25-7   Algerian Hedgehog *(Erinaceus algirus)*
Libya 878
Tunisia 683

25-9   East European Hedgehog *(Erinaceus concolor)*
Albania 813
Bulgaria 1374

25-10   West European Hedgehog *(Erinaceus europaeus)*
Czechoslovakia 1686
Denmark 613.
Germany (East Germany) E703
Great Britain 1039
Hungary 1272
Luxembourg 853
Netherlands 1241
Sweden 846
Switzerland J207
Yugoslavia 956

25-11   South African Hedgehog *(Erinaceus frontalis)*
Malawi 705

25-14   Daurian Hedgehog *(Hemiechinus dauuricus)*
Mongolia 1566

25-16   Brandt's Hedgehog *(Paraechinus hypomelas)*
Afghanistan 888

26 SHREWS
26-3   Eurasian Common Shrew *(Sorex araneus)*
Bulgaria 3128
Germany (East Germany) E610

26–65   Eurasian Water Shrew *(Neomys fodiens)*
Mongolia 1568

27 MOLES, SHREW-MOLES, DESMANS
27-2   Russian Desman *(Desmana moschata)*
Russia 4283

27-3   Pyrenean Desman *(Galemys pyrenaicus)*
Spain 2160

29 FLYING LEMURS
29-1   Malayan Flying Lemur *(Cynocephalus variegatus)*
Malaysia 191
Vietnam (North Vietnam) N857

30 FRUIT BATS, FLYING FOXES
30-1   Straw-coloured Fruit Bat *(Eidolon helvum)*
Mozambique 1010

30-28   Indian Flying Fox *(Pteropus giganteus)*
Maldive Islands 459 464

30-49   Greater Mascarene Flying Fox *(Pteropus niger)*
Mauritius 559

30-58   Grey-headed Flying Fox *(Pteropus poliocephalus)*
New Hebrides 187 F202

30-59   Bonin Islands Flying Fox *(Pteropus pselaphon)*
Japan 1372

30-62   Rodriguez Flying Fox *(Pteropus rodricensis)*
Great Britain (Jersey) 221

30-66   Seychelles Flying Fox *(Pteropus seychellensis)*
Seychelles 175a 236 414 490 518 519 520 521
Zil Elwannyen Sesel 12

30-72   Insular Flying Fox *(Pteropus tonganus)*
Niuafo'ou 43
Tonga 691 696 O185

30-77   New Caledonian Flying Fox *(Pteropus vetulus)*
New Caledonia 600 D703 D704 D705 D706 D707 D708
D709 D710 D711

30-150/7   Tube-nosed Bat sp. *(Nyctimene sp.)*
Papua New Guinea 399

36   HORSESHOE BATS
36-22   Greater Horseshoe Bat *(Rhinolophus ferrumequinum)*
Bulgaria 3129

38   BULLDOG BATS
38-2   Mexican Bulldog Bat *(Noctilio leporinus)*
Antigua 746

40   NEW-WORLD LEAF-NOSED BATS
40-12   Waterhouse's Leaf-nosed Bat *(Macrotus waterhousei)*
Cayman Islands 522

40-40   Jamaican Long-tongued Bat *(Monophyllus redmani)*
Cuba 1054

40-129   Red Fruit Bat *(Stenoderma rufum)*
Chile 381i 382i 383i

40-136   Buffy Flower Bat *(Erophylla sezekorni)*
Bahamas 626

41   VAMPIRE BATS
41-1   Common Vampire Bat *(Desmodus rotundus)*
Trinidad and Tobago 459

46   VERPERTILIONID BATS
46-260   Common Long-eared Bat *(Plecotus auritus)*
Bulgaria 3130
Germany (East Germany) E611

49   MOUSE-LEMURS, DWARF LEMURS
49-2   Lesser Mouse-Lemur *(Microcebus murinus)*
Malagasy Republic 491

49-4   Greater Dwarf Lemur *(Cheirogaleus major)*
Malagasy Republic 261 264

50   LARGE LEMURS
50-1   Ring-tailed Lemur *(Lemur catta)*
Great Britain (Jersey) 60
Madagascar and Dependencies 327
Malagasy Republic 409

50-4   Black Lemur *(Lemur macaco)*
Malagasy Republic 410 413

50-5   Mongoose-Lemur *(Lemur mongoz)*
Malagasy Republic 31

50-7   Grey Gentle Lemur *(Hapalemur griseus)*
Malagasy Republic 29

50-9   Ruffed Lemur *(Varecia variegata)*
Malagasy Republic 30 489

50-14   Weasel-Lemur *(Lepilemur mustelinus)*
Malagasy Republic 262 263

51   LEAPING LEMURS
51-2   Diadem Sifaka *(Propithecus diadema)*
Malagasy Republic 32

51-3   Verreaux's Sifaka *(Propithecus verreauxi)*
Malagasy Republic 34 490

51-4   Indri *(Indri indri)*
Comoro Islands **MS**213
Malagasy Republic 33 143 493

52   AYE-AYE
52-1   Aye-Aye *(Daubentonia madagascariensis)*
Comoro Islands 215
Malagasy Republic 187 492

53   LORISES, BUSHBABIES
53-1   Slender Loris *(Loris tardigradus)*
Ceylon 562

53-2   Slow Loris *(Nycticebus coucang)*
Thailand 1127

53-3   Lesser Slow Loris *(Nycticebus pygmaeus)*
Vietnam (North Vietnam) N371

53-4   Potto *(Perodicticus potto)*
Central African Republic 255
Congo (Brazzaville) 338
Ivory Coast 228
Malagasy Republic **MS**494
Rio Muni 81
Rwanda 864

53-5   Angwantibo *(Arctocebus calabariensis)*
Central African Republic 254

53-7   Lesser Bushbaby *(Galago senegalensis)*
Central African Republic 252
Kenya 23
Somalia 606
Toga **MS**1726
Uganda 306 424

53-8   Thick-tailed Bushbaby *(Otolemur crassicaudatus)*
Malawi 496
Mozambique 675

53-10   Western Needle-clawed Bushbaby *(Euoticus elegantulus)*
Central African Republic 253
Fernando Poo 301

53-11   Eastern Needle-clawed Bushbaby *(Euoticus inustus)*
Rwanda 862

53-12   Demidoff's Galago *(Galagoides demidoff)*
Belgian Congo 342
Congo (Kinshasa) 381
Ghana 1045
Katanga 26

54   TARSIERS
54-1   Western Tarsier *(Tarsius bancanus)*
Sarawak 172

54-3   Philippine Tarsier *(Tarsier syrichta)*
Philippines 1088

55   MARMOSETS, TAMARINS
55-16   Golden Lion Tamarin *(Leontopithecus rosalia)*
Brazil 1589
Great Britain (Jersey) 324

56   NEW-WORLD MONKEYS
56-3   White-throated Capuchin *(Cebus capucinus)*
Costa Rica 654

56-5   Night Monkey *(Aotus trivirgatus)*
Cuba 1678

56-8   Widow Monkey *(Callicebus torquatus)*
Venezuela 1768

56-10   Common Squirrel-Monkey *(Saimiri sciureus)*
Guyana 758
Surinam 653

56-17   Red Uakari *(Cacajao rubicundus)*
Peru 1245 1246

56-24   Red Howler *(Alouatta seniculus)*
Guyana 757

56-26   Long-haired Spider Monkey *(Ateles belzebuth)*
Colombia 1007 1079

56-28   Black-handed Spider Monkey *(Ateles geoffroyi)*
Costa Rica 1212
El Salvador 1662

56-29   Black Spider Monkey *(Ateles paniscus)*
El Salvador 1181

56-30   Woolly Spider Monkey *(Brachyteles arachnoides)*
Brazil 2089 2090

56-31   Hendee's Woolly Monkey *(Lagothrix flavicauda)*
Peru 1588

57   OLD-WORLD MONKEYS
57-1   Bear Macaque *(Macaca arctoides)*
China (People's Republic) 2968
Vietnam 396
Vietnam (North Vietnam) N476

57-3   Taiwan Macaque *(Macaca cyclopis)*
China (Taiwan) 807 1278 1279

57-4   Crab-eating Macaque *(Macaca fascicularis)*
Philippines 1516

57-5   Japanese Macaque *(Macaca fuscata)*
Japan 1315

57-6   Rhesus Macaque *(Macaca mulatta)*
Afghanistan 600
Hong Kong 245 246
Vietnam (North Vietnam) N852

57-7   Pigtail Macaque *(Macaca nemestrina)*
Thailand 1126

57-10   Liontail Macaque *(Macaca silenus)*
India 1097

57-12   Barbary Ape *(Macaca sylvanus)*
Algeria 801
Gibraltar 169

57-14   White-cheeked Mangabey *(Cercocebus albigena)*
Gabon 401

57-15   Black Mangabey *(Cercocebus aterrimus)*
Congo (Kinshasa) 778

57-16   Agile Mangabey *(Cercocebus galeritus)*
Kenya 215

57-17   White-collared Mangabey *(Cercocebus torquatus)*
Gabon 513
Ghana 1044

57-18   Olive Baboon *(Papio anubis)*
Dahomey 356
French Territory of the Afars and the Issas 603
Guinea 658
Rwanda 866
Togo 360 823 878

57-19   Yellow Baboon *(Papio cynocephalus)*
Congo (Kinshasa) 776
Liberia 1240
Rwanda 104

57-20   Hamadryas Baboon *(Papio hamadryas)*
Guinea-Bissau 735
Yemen 290

57-21   Guinea Baboon *(Papio papio)*
Mauritania 168

57-22   Chacma Baboon *(Papio ursinus)*
Bophuthatswana 7
Lesotho 333 469 612
South West Africa 368
Swaziland 168
Zambia 425

57-24   Mandrill *(Mandrillus sphinx)*
Burundi 1032 1056 1080
Central African Republic 824
Cuba 2506
Guinea-Bissau 738
Poland 2584
Rio Muni 18 20
Russia 5395

57-25   Gelada *(Theropithecus gelada)*
Ethiopia 929
Guinea-Bissau 737

57-26   Savanna Monkey *(Cercopithecus aethiops)*
Bophuthatswana 10
Congo (Kinshasa) 773
French Territory of the Afars and the Issas 659
Kenya 33
Liberia 1087
Rwanda 456 865
St. Kitts-Nevis 385 386 387 388
South West Africa 367
Upper Volta 178
Zaire 897 1125
Zambia 428

57-29   Moustached Monkey *(Cercopithecus cephus)*
Cameroun 309 316 319
Congo (Kinshasa) 774
Fernando Poo 293 295
Gabon 514
Spanish Guinea 408 410

57-31   Diana Monkey *(Cercopithecus diana)*
Central African Empire 505
Congo (Kinshasa) 780
Guinea-Bissau 741
Liberia 627

57-35   Owl-faced Monkey *(Cercopithecus hamlyni)*
Congo (Kinshasa) 779

57-36   L'Hoest's Monkey *(Cercopithecus lhoesti)*
Congo (Kinshsa) 782

57-37   Diademed Monkey *(Cercopithecus mitis)*
Mozambique 679
Nigeria 472
Zambia 426 427

57-38   Mona Monkey *(Cercopithecus mona)*
Gabon 515
Ghana 637
Grenada 317 510
Rwanda 863

57-39   De Brazza's Monkey *(Cercopithecus neglectus)*
Congo (Brazzaville) 339
Congo (Kinshasa) 775

57-40   Greater White-nosed Monkey *(Cercopithecus
nictitans)*
Fernando Poo 292 294

57-45   Talapoin *(Miopithecus talapoin)*
Spanish Guinea 409

57-47   Patas Monkey *(Erythrocebus patas)*
Mali 858
Mauritania 173

57-48   Angolan Black-and-White Colobus *(Colobus
angolensis)*
Burundi 1042 1066

57-49   Red Colobus *(Colobus badius)*
Central African Republic 256
Hungary 2935
Kenya 99
Tanzania 215
Uganda 202

57-50   Eastern Black-and-White Colobus *(Colobus guereza)*
Belgian Congo 345
Burundi 11 15
Congo (Kinshasa) 384
Ethiopia 643
Germany (East Germany) E561
Guinea-Bissau 740
Ivory Coast 757
Katanga 29
Ruanda-Urundi 205 209
Rwanda 58 61 861

57-52   Western Black-and-White Colobus *(Colobus
polykomos)*
Congo (Kinshasa) 781
Great Britain (Jersey) 59
Ivory Coast 236
Togo 1218

57-53   Black Colobus *(Colobus satanas)*
Cameroun 940

57-54   Olive Colobus *(Procolobus verus)*
Ghana 811
Ivory Coast 614
Togo **MS**1726

57-58   Snub-nosed Monkey *(Pygathrix roxellana)*
China (People's Republic) 2121 2122 2123

57-60   Proboscis Monkey *(Nasalis larvatus)*
Indonesia 1489
Japanese Occupation of North Borneo J4 J23
North Borneo 306 323 338

57-62   Silvered Leaf Monkey *(Presbytis cristata)*
Thailand 1128

57-64   Francois' Monkey *(Presbytis francoisi)*
Vietnam (North Vietnam) N369

57-66   Golden Langur *(Presbytis geei)*
Bhutan 521 522 523 524
India 1096

58   APES
58-1   Crested Gibbon *(Hylobates concolor)*
Vietnam 397
Vietnam (North Vietnam) N161

58-4   Common Gibbon *(Hylobates lar)*
Laos 273
Poland 2151
Singapore 177

58-5   Pileated Gibbon *(Hylobates pileatus)*
Thailand 1125

58-7   Orang-Utan *(Pongo pygmaeus)*
Comoro Islands 212
Germany (East Germany) E1746
Germany (West Berlin) **MS**B332
Great Britain (Jersey) 218
Indonesia 800
Japanese Occupation of North Borneo J7 J26 J32a
Labuan 112 113 D3
Malaysia 197
North Borneo 98 99 130a 296 309 326 341 403 D38
Sabah 420
Sarawak 189
Singapore 225
Vietnam 436

58-8   Pygmy Chimpanzee *(Pan paniscus)*
Burundi 1185 1209
Congo (Brazzaville) 340
Congo (Kinshasa) 777

58-9   Chimpanzee *(Pan troglodytes)*
Angola 835
Belgian Congo 228
Benin 761
Bulgaria 1612
Burundi 625 649
Congo (Brazzaville) 623
Cuba 1167 2596
Czechoslovakia 1292
French West Africa 82
Gabon 278
Ghana **MS**985
Guinea 689 690 691 692 871 951 952 953 975 976 977
Guinea-Bissau 739

Ivory Coast 618
Liberia 226 954 1292 O239
Mali 686
Niger Republic 455
Poland 2150
Rwanda 859
Senegal 710 **MS**716
Sierra Leone 745 746 747 748
Tanzania 353
Togo 1219
Zaire 991 1046

58-10   Gorilla *(Gorilla Gorilla)*
Belgian Congo 343
Burundi 9 13 629 653 680
Cameroun 858 976
Central African Empire 555
Congo (Brazzaville) 337
Congo (Kinshasa) 382
Czechoslovakia 2595
Equatorial Guinea 60
Gabon 212 676
Great Britain (Jersey) 220
Guinea-Bissau 736
Japan 1660
Katanga 27
Liberia 1295
Rio Muni 33
Ruanda – Urundi 203 207
Rwanda 60 369 370 371 372 373 374 375 376 860 1169
    1170 1171 1172 1173 1174 1175 1176
Uganda 309 427 434

60   DOGS, FOXES
60-2   Golden Jackal *(Canis aureus)*
Albania 815
Bulgaria 2579
Burundi 1192 1216
Ifni 136 137 138 139
Kampuchea 538
Mauritania 537 815
Tanzania 352
Tunisia 678

60-3   Coyote *(Canis latrans)*
El Salvador 1180
Kampuchea 535

60-4   Wolf *(Canis lupus)*
Albania 817
Bulgaria 2575
Comoro Islands 214
Czechoslovakia 1115
Greenland 130
Hungary 3017
Kampuchea 541
Mongolia 554, 931
Norway 644
Poland 1613 2232 2491
Portugal 1798
Rumania 3889
Spain 2162
Sweden 759
Turkey A84
Yugoslavia 962

60-5   Black-backed Jackal *(Canis mesomelas)*
Burundi 1045 1069 1085 1394 1407
Lesotho **MS**473 615
Rwanda 1050
South West Africa 349

60-7   Simian Jackal *(Canis simensis)*
Ethiopia 928

60-8   Arctic Fox *(Alopex lagopus)*
Iceland 582
Mongolia 1392
Russia 865 3452 5009
Sweden 1162

60-11   Cape Fox *(Vulpes chama)*
Ciskei 31

60-12   Grey Fox *(Vulpes cinereoargentateus)*
Costa Rica 671

60-13   Corsac Fox *(Vulpes corsac)*
Tuva 50 71

60-18   Sand Fox *(Vulpes rueppelli)*
Yemen People's Democratic Republic 261

60-20   Red Fox *(Vulpes vulpes)*
Albania 812
Bulgaria 2576
Czechoslovakia 1616
Finland 1037
Germany (East Germany) E670 E1263 E1988
Germany (West Berlin) B296
Germany (West Germany) 1437
Hungary 1276 2205 3018
Ireland 463
Kampuchea 539
Korea (North Korea) N1253
Liberia 1086
Mongolia 389 926
Niger Republic 453
Poland 1615 2256 2754
Portugal 1797
Rumania 2857 3886 4238
Russia 3453 3454 5008
St. Pierre et Miquelon 376 379 432
Spanish Sahara 176
Sweden 570
Switzerland J214
United States of America **MS**1726
Yugoslavia 960

60-21   Fennec Fox *(Vulpes zerda)*
Algeria 373 490
Burundi 1048 1072 1088
French Somali Coast 457
Ifni 74 75 76
Mauritania 136
Morocco 657
Spanish Sahara 174 276 277 278 279
Tunisia 682

60-22   Falkland Island Wolf *(Dusicyon australis)*
Falkland Islands 424

60-24   Argentine Grey Fox *(Dusicyon griseus)*
Chile 1009

60-30   Racoon-Dog *(Nyctereutes procyonoides)*
Bulgaria 2244
Korea (North Korea) N370
Vietnam (North Vietnam) N854

60-31   Maned Wolf *(Chrysocyon brachyurus)*
Argentine Republic 1815
Brazil 1959
Germany (East Germany) E2243
Kampuchea 540

60-32   Bush Dog *(Speothos venaticus)*
Peru 1191

60-33   Dhole *(Cuon alpinus)*
Bhutan 72 75 112 224
Korea (North Korea) N1255
Vietnam 399
Vietnam (North Vietnam) N472 N724

60–34   Hunting Dog *(Lycaon pictus)*
Afghanistan 959
Bophuthatswana 16
Burundi 632 656 683
Ethiopia 1166
Ghana 813
Ivory Coast 235
Kampuchea 537
Mozambique 680
Rhodesia 531
Rwanda 103 1056
Somalia 605
South West Africa 350
Uganda 307 425

60-35   Bat-eared Fox *(Otocyon megalotis)*
Botswana 396
Burundi 1198 1222
Kenya 31

61   BEARS
61-1   Spectacled Bear *(Tremarctos ornatus)*
Ecuador 1162
Great Britain (Jersey) 75
Peru 1190
Venezuela 1772

61-2   Asiatic Black Bear *(Selenarctos thibetanus)*
Afghanistan 761
Bhutan 68 78 115 205 256
Cuba 1174
Hungary 3157
Korea (North Korea) N372
Korea (South Korea) 677
Mongolia 850
Russia 3852
Vietnam 398
Vietnam (North Vietnam) N855

61-3   American Black Bear *(Ursus americanus)*
United States of America 2093

61-4   Brown Bear *(Ursus arctos)*
Albania 675 970 971 972 973 974 975 976 977
ndorra F230
Bulgaria 1095
Cuba 2600
Czechoslovakia 994 1617
Finland 519
Hungary 1718 3019 3159
Italy 1178
Korea (North Korea) N1256
Liberia 1088 1092
Mongolia 555 845 848 851 932 1142
Poland 1617
Rumania 2428 2479 2855 3333 3890 4235 4738
Russia 2534 3309
Spain 2096
Sweden 950
Trieste B122
Turkey 2193
Tuva 77 86 88 118
United States of America 1860 1897
Yugoslavia 768

61-5   Polar Bear *(Thalarctos maritimus)*
Bulgaria 1614
Canada 447 705
Chad 482
Czechoslovakia 1291
Germany (East Germany) E292
Greenland 6 6a 7 14 23 37 38 56 57 58 59 71 144
Hungary 1722 3158
Mongolia 358 1142 1394 1395 1396 1397
Norway 167 168 169 170 171 172 173 745 819 820 823
824
Poland 2579
Russia 584 585 586 587 687 2058a 3002 4725
United States of America 1430 1861

61-6   Sun Bear *(Helarctos malayanus)*
Germany (East Germany) E1341
Labuan 115
Laos 272
North Borneo 104 134 392 D42
Sabah 409
Vietnam (North Vietnam) N159

61-7   Sloth Bear *(Melursus ursinus)*
Bangladesh 101
Mongolia 849

62   RACOONS
62-6   Common Racoon *(Procyon lotor)*
Bahamas 628
Cuba 1169
El Salvador 1182
Nicaragua 1949
San Marino 1122
United States of America **MS**1726

62-7   Guadeloupe Racoon *(Procyon minor)*
France 2002

62-9   Northern Coati *(Nasua narica)*
Canal Zone 194
El Salvador 1184

62–12   Little Coatimundi *(Nasuella olivacea)*
Ecuador 1205

62-13   Kinkajou *(Potos flavus)*
Belize 355 370
British Honduras 263 286
Ecuador 1203
El Salvador 1185
Nicaragua 1951

63   PANDAS
63-1   Lesser Panda *(Ailurus fulgens)*
Belgium 1782
Germany (East Germany) E2242
Hungary 3155
India 473
Nepal 323

63-2   Giant Panda *(Ailuropoda melanoleuca)*
China (People's Republic) 1812 1813 2116 2117 2118 2498
2499 2500 2501 2502 2503 3062
Cuba 2602
Hungary 3156
Japan 1662
Korea (North Korea) N1354
Laos **MS**502
Mongolia 846 847 1091 1092 1093 1094 1095 1096 1097
Netherlands 1447
Nicaragua **MS**2295
Russia 3001

64 WEASELS, BADGERS, OTTERS

64-3 Stoat *(Mustela erminea)*
Andorra F279
Cuba **MS**2897
Czechoslovakia 1684
Finland 644
Germany (West Berlin) B294
Germany (West Germany) 1435
Ireland 461
Mongolia 394
Poland 2963
Rumania 2556
Russia 3456
Sweden 572
Switzerland J212

64-4 Steppe Polecat *(Mustela eversmanni)*
Hungary 3278
Korea (North Korea) N203

64-8 European Mink *(Mustela lutreola)*
Finland 1036
Germany (East Germany) E1264 E2388
Korea (North Korea) N435
Russia 3458 5010

64-10 Weasel *(Mustela nivalis)*
Bulgaria 2577
Germany (East Germany) E609
Poland 2962

64-12 Polecat *(Mustela putorius)*
Germany (East Germany) E2387

64-13 Siberian Weasel *(Mustela sibirica)*
Korea (North Korea) N202
Mongolia 771

64-15 American Mink *(Mustela vison)*
Mongolia 777
St. Pierre et Miquelon 408

64-16 Marbled Polecat *(Vormela peregusna)*
Bulgaria 1375

64-18 Yellow-throated Marten *(Martes flavigula)*
Korea (North Korea) N557
Russia 2063b 3851
San Marino 1125
Vietnam (North Vietnam) N366

64-19 Beech Marten *(Martes foina)*
Albania 811
Bulgaria 1376
Germany (East Germany) E2389
Hungary 1274 3279
Mongolia 393
Poland 2964

64-20 Pine Marten *(Martes martes)*
Czechoslovakia 1687
Finland 643
Hungary 3276
Switzerland J218
Yugoslavia 958

64-23 Sable *(Martes zibellina)*
Afghanistan 901
China (People's Republic) 3185 3186
Mongolia 171 388 880
Poland 2269

Russia 2063 3308 3457 4435 5012 5466
Tuva 70 115

64-24 Tayra *(Eira barbara)*
Belize 357 372
British Honduras 265
Panama 1385
Trinidad and Tobago 521

64-29 Zorilla *(Ictonyx striatus)*
French Territory of the Afars and the Issas 643
Lesotho 331
Rwanda 1053

64-32 Wolverine *(Gulo gulo)*
Finland 575
Mongolia 776

64-33 Ratel *(Mellivora capensis)*
Brundi 1194 1218
Mozambique 676
Somalia 723
South West Africa 357
Swaziland 169 231
Tanzania 312 O57

64–34 Eurasian Badger *(Meles meles)*
Albania 674
Belgium 2373
Bulgaria 1377
Czechoslovakia 1612
Germany (West Berlin) B312
Germany (West Germany) 1456
Great Britain 638 1043
Hungary 3277
Italy 1834
Korea (South Korea) 676
Liechtenstein 285
Mongolia 774
Poland 1616
Rumania 2860
Russia 4437
Switzerland J210
Tuva 68
Yugoslavia 961

64-35 Hog-Badger *(Arctonyx collaris)*
Vietnam (North Vietnam) N474

64-38 American Badger *(Taxidea taxus)*
United States of America 1896

64-40 Chinese Ferret-Badger *(Melogale moschata)*
Korea (North Korea) N371

64-43 Striped Skunk *(Mephitis mephitis)*
Chile 381d 382d 383d

64-49 Andean Hog-nosed Skunk *(Conepatus chinga)*
Chile 1000

64-56 Marine Otter *(Lutra felina)*
Chile 1003

64-58 European Otter *(Lutra lutra)*
Albania 673
Bulgaria 1378
Denmark 616
Finland 628
Germany (West Berlin) B311
Germany (West Germany) 1455
Great Britain 1042
Hungary 1275 3274
Japan 1356

Korea (North Korea) N204
Liechtenstein 632
Monaco 982
Mongolia 174 390
Morocco 532
Poland 2494 2966
Sweden 758
Switzerland J220
Tuva 72
Vietnam (North Vietnam) N727

64-61   Huidobria Otter *(Lutra provocax)*
Chile 381a 382a 383a

64-62   Hairy-nosed Otter *(Lutra sumatrana)*
Indonesia 716 717 718
Riau-Lingga Archipelago 24 29 30 31

64-63   Giant Otter *(Pteronura brasiliensis)*
Brazil 1546
Peru 1186
Venezuela 1769

64-64   African Clawless Otter *(Aonyx capensis)*
Botswana 394
Burundi 1036 1060
Ghana 979

64-65   Oriental Small-clawed Otter *(Aonyx cinerea)*
Philippines 1519

64-66   Zaire Clawless Otter *(Aonyx congica)*
Rwanda 1054

64-67   Sea Otter *(Enhydra lutris)*
Russia 3968

65   CIVETS, MONGOOSES
65-1   African Linsang *(Poiana richardsoni)*
Fernando Poo 300

65-4   Small-spotted Genet *(Genetta genetta)*
Spain 2164

65-9   Servaline Genet *(Genetta servalina)*
Gabon 403
Rwanda 1051

65-10   Large-spotted Genet *(Genetta tigrina)*
French Territory of the Afars and the Issas 604
Malawi 706
Tanzania 308 O55
Uganda 304

65-15   African Civet *(Viverra civetta)*
Burundi 1038 1062
Cameroun 975
Congo (Brazzaville) 964
Ethiopia 930

65-17   Malay Civet *(Viverra tangalunga)*
Philippines 1515

65-18   Large Indian Civet *(Viverra zibetha)*
Hong Kong 411
Vietnam (North Vietnam) N475

65-21   African Palm Civet *(Nandinia binotata)*
Liberia 350 376 394 536 547 O363 O401
Togo 358

65-23   Common Palm Civet *(Paradoxurus hermaphroditus)*
Laos 331 332

65-25   Golden Palm Civet *(Paradoxurus zeylonensis)*
Sri Lanka 719

65-26   Masked Palm Civet *(Paguma larvata)*
Vietnam (North Vietnam) N850

65-28   Binturong *(Arctictis binturong)*
Laos 170
Vietnam (North Vietnam) N473

65-29   Mlagasy Civet *(Fossa fossa)*
Malagasy Republic 411

65-32   Owston's Palm Civet *(Chrotogale owstoni)*
Vietnam (North Vietnam) N367

65-39   Meerkat *(Suricata suricatta)*
South West Africa 366

65-40   Small Indian Mongoose *(Herpestes auropunctatus)*
Antigua 744
Jamaica 365 366 367
St. Vincent 650

65-45   Egyptian Mongoose *(Herpestes ichneumon)*
Spain 2163

65-46   Javan Mongoose *(Herpestes javanicus)*
Laos 168

65-60   Banded Mongoose *(Mungos mungo)*
Rwanda 1052
Somalia 722
Tanzania 309 O56

65-65   White-tailed Mongoose *(Ichneumia albicauda)*
French Territory of the Afars and the Issas 641
Somalia 721

66   HYENAS
66-1   Aardwolf *(Proteles cristatus)*
Somalia 608

66-2   Spotted Hyena *(Crocuta crocuta)*
Angola 839
Bophuthatswana 12
Botswana 348
Burundi 627 651 1397 1410
Dahomey 355
Mauritania 166 592
Mozambique 682
Rwanda 462
Senegal 713 **MS**716

66-3   Brown Hyena *(Hyaena brunnea)*
Botswana 398
Rhodesia 530
South West Africa 351

66-4   Striped Hyena *(Hyaena hyaena)*
Afghanistan 601
Burundi 1184 1208
Cuba 1164
French Territory of the Afars and the Issas 662
Guinea 447 448
Iraq 829 O986
Jordan 811
Mauritania 165
Morocco 377
Spanish Sahara 139 140 141 142
Umm Al Qiwain 3 12 36 82 91 100 O51 O109

67   CATS

67-1   African Golden Cat *(Felis aurata)*
Gabon 402
Rio Muni 82
Rwanda 1055
Sierra Leone 658 659

67-3   Leopard Cat *(Felis bengalensis)*
Korea (North Korea) N555 N1251
Laos 166
Philippines 1518
Vietnam (North Vietnam) N726

67-5   Caracal *(Felis caracal)*
Burundi 634 658 685
Ciskei 33
Djibouti 747
French Territory of the Afars and the Issas 590
India 828
Israel 375
Laos 514
Morocco 427
Swaziland 161
Upper Volta 530

67-6   Jungle Cat *(Felis chaus)*
Laos 517

67-8   Puma *(Felis concolor)*
Argentine Republic 948 O957
Belize 359 374
British Honduras 267
Canada 886
Costa Rica 1211
Cuba 2417
Ecuador 1163
Monaco 534
Nicaragua 1948
Paraguay 930 931 932 933
United States of America 1857
Uruguay 1419
Venezuela 1770 1848

67-9   Geoffrey's Cat *(Felis geoffroyi)*
Uruguay 1630

67-11   Iriomote Cat *(Felis iriomotensis)*
Japan 1348

67-13   Lynx *(Felis lynx)*
Afghanistan 724
Albania 725
Czechoslovakia 1114 1614 2678
Finland 576
Germany (East Germany) E474
Guinea–Bissau 861
Hungary 3016
Korea (North Korea) N554 N1252
Mongolia 556 927 1227
Poland 1614 2237 2435
Portugal 1619
Rumania 2429 2480 2853 3885 4239 4819
Russia 3732
Spain 2095
Sweden 757 ·
Trieste B120
Tuva 73
Yugoslavia 766 2006

67-14   Pallas's Cat *(Felis manul)*
Mongolia 392 1226

67-16   Marbled Cat *(Felis marmorata)*
Thailand 825

67-18   Ocelot *(Felis pardalis)*
Comoro Islands 218
Costa Rica 651
Grenada 551
Guatemala 1128
Guyana 499
Mexico 1454
Nicaragua 1950
Trinidad and Tobago 396 522

67-19   Flat-headed Cat *(Felis planiceps)*
Laos 516

67-20   Rusty-spotted Cat *(Felis rubiginosus)*
Sri Lanka 721

67-22   Serval *(Felis serval)*
Botswana 395
Burundi 1051 1075 1091
Congo (Brazzaville) 436
Gambia 356
Rwanda 1049
Senegal 584
Sierra Leone 656 657
Zaire 1174

67-23   Wild Cat *(Felis silvestris)*
Albania 816
Andorra F325
Bulgaria 2578 2942
Czechoslovakia 1683
Germany (West Berlin) B310
Germany (West Germany) 1454
Hungary 2207 3275
Laos 512
Lesotho 468
Libya 881

67-26   Fishing Cat *(Felis viverrinus)*
Laos 513
Sri Lanka 718

67-28   Jaguarundi *(Felis yagouarundi)*
Panama 1386

67-29   Lion *(Panthera leo)*
Afghanistan 899
Angola 497
Barbuda 379 380 381 382
Bechuanaland 180
Belgian Congo 230
Benin 624 638 835
Biafra 4 16b
Bophuthatswana 11
Botswana 218 253
Bulgaria 1615
Burundi 25 91 613 637 668 1348 1385 1398
Cameroun 357 358
Central African Empire 462
Central African Republic 393 825 976
Chad 133
Congo (Brazzaville) 333 363 364 385
Cuba 1161 2420 2599
Chechoslovakia 2203 2596
Dahomey 319
Eritrea 59 60 61 62 63
Ethiopia 192 205 522
French Equatorial Africa 289
Germany (East Germany) E145 E2037
Germany (West Germany) 1206
Ghana 587
Guinea 327 330 656 665 880 884 886 957 958 959 981 982
    983
Guinea–Bissau 858

Hungary 3020 3360
India 476 826
Ivory Coast 340
Japan 1661
Kenya 17 35
Kenya, Uganda and Tanganyika 112 123 150ba 170 172
   175 367 O4 O7
Korea (North Korea) N1259
Kuwait 937 938
Liberia 952 1244 1377
Malawi 568 651
Mali 967
Mauritania 420 421 445 446 539 543
Mongolia 1232
Mozambique Company 293 307
Niger Republic 111 112 117 454 482
Nigeria 172
Rhodesia 561
Rio Muni 71
Ruanda-Urundi 230
Rumania 3202
Rwanda 69 107 465 1124
Senegal 493 573 682 D339 D340 D341 D342 D343 D344
   D345 D346
Sierra Leone 662 663
Singapore 228
Somalia 3 4 5 6 7 8 9 12 13 13a 14 15 16 17 18 24 25 26
   27 28 36 38 39 40 41 42 43 70 71 72 73 74 75 178 186
   270 271 272 273 274 532
Soruth 50 54 O2 O6 58 O16
South Africa 158 191 391
South West Africa 163 362
Southern Rhodesia 31 32 33 34 85
Swaziland 164
Tanganyika 113 O6
Tanzania 317 O63
Togo 550 1039
Tripolitania 151
Uganda 308 418 422 433 D24
Upper Volta 100 168
Vietnam 442
Yemen 293 297
Zaire 957 1120 1176
Zambia **MS**176
Zimbabwe 582

67-30   Jaguar *(Panthera onca)*
Argentine Republic 1818
Belize 756 757 758 759 **MS**760
Bolivia 362 363
Brazil 1479 2084
British Honduras 248
Costa Rica 650
Dominica 859
Ecuador 1204
Nicaragua 1956 **MS**2503
Poland 2581
Venezuela 1777 1886

67-31   Leopard *(Panthera pardus)*
Afghanistan 764
Angola 487
Bangladesh 103
Belgian Congo 261 262 263 269c
Biafra 8
Bophuthatswana 2 8
Bulgaria 1816
Burundi 24 620 644 675
Cameroun 16 17 18 19 22 30 31 32 33 34 34a 35 46 47 48
   49 50 51 52 63 860
Central African Empire 552
Central African Republic 233
Ceylon 564
Chad 1 2 3 4 5 6 7 19 20 21 22 23 24 25 26

Comoro Islands 209 401
Congo (Brazzaville) 335 385 644
Congo (Kinshasa) 655 656
Cuba 1157 2416 2418 2597
Czechoslovakia 1295
Dahomey 354
Equatorial Guinea 63
Ethiopia 183 200 642
French Congo 36 37 38 39 40 41
Fujeira 7 16 45 91 129 O54 O164
Gabon 280
Gambia 359
Germany (East Germany) E2038
Ghana 492
Guinea 328 331 653 659 875
Guinea-Bissau 862
Hungary 3361
India 827
Iraq 830 O985
Korea (North Korea) N556 N1257
Laos 302
Liberia 407 421 955 1294 O435 O449
Malawi 497
Mali 101
Mauritania 170
Middle Congo 1 2 3 4 21 5 22 6 7 18 20 36 37 38 39 40 41
   42 43 44 45
Mongolia 854 1230
Morocco 405
Mozambique Company 295
Niger Republic 455
Nigeria 177a 224
Nyasaland Protectorate 114 115 116 117 118 119 120 121
   122 130 130a 131 131a 132 132a 133 133a 134 135 136
   137 138 160 174
Rio Muni 49 52 55 67
Ruanda-Urundi 131 132 133 149 229
Rwanda 68
Sierra Leone 660 661 801
Singapore 226 227
Somalia 367
South Africa 153 187
South Kasai 1 2 3 4 5
South West Afric 364
Southern Rhodesia 72
Spanish Guinea 359 360 361
Spanish Sahara 173 175
Swaziland 170 367
Tanzania 312 O59
Togo 548 1036 1220
Tripolitania 163
Ubangi-Shari 1 2 3 4 19 5 20 5a 6 17 18 24 25 26 27 28 29
   30 42 43 44 45 46 47 48 49
Uganda 311 436
Upper Volta 180 533
Vietnam 402
Vietnam (North Vietnam) N725 N856
Yemen People's Democratic Republic 262
Zaire 825 826 827 828 829 830 895 992 **MS**994 1126

67-32   Tiger *(Panthera tigris)*
Afghanistan 964
Bangladesh 27 52 53 54 67 106 234 O6 O17
Bhopal O344
Bhutan 71 73
Bulgaria 1611
China (People's Republic) 2866 2867 2868
China (Taiwan) 766 975 976 1067
Comoro Islands **MS**220
Congo (Brazzaville) 364 453
Cuba 1165 2419 2603
Federated Malay States 1 2 3 4 5 6 7 8 9 10 15 28 52 53
   55 54 16b 58 34 35 57 36a 38 60 39c 61 62 63 64 41a
   42 43a 65 66 67 68 45 70 71 72 73 74a 75 77 79 81

Germany (East Germany) E1751 E2039
Guinea–Bissau 857
Hong Kong 302 303
Hungary 1720
India 475 603 721 730 799 1105
Indonesia 1491
Johore 160
Kedah 97 109 109a
Kelantan 88 89 101
Korea (North Korea) N369 N1258 N1563 **MS**N1564
Korea (South Korea) 280 678 887 1424
Laos 274 704 705 706 707
Liberia **MS**1089
Malacca 44 55
Malaysia 190
Mongolia 1228
Negri Sembilan 2 3 4 5 6 7 8 9 10 11 12 13 14 15 16 17 18
    19 73 74
Nepal 321
Niger Republic 483
Pahang 11 12 13 14 15 16 17 18 19 20 21 22 25 28 80 81
Penang 49 60
Perak 57 58 59 60 61 62 63 64 65 66 67 68 69 70 71 77 78
    79 80 81 151 152
Perlis 34 35
Poland 2154
Portugal 1944
Rumania 3201
Russia 2043 2059b 3005 3854 4727
San Marino 1123
Selangor 49 50 51 52 53 54 55 56 57 58 59 60 66a 66b 67
    121 122 134
Senegal 551 552
Singapore 225
Sungei Ujong 51 52 56 53 54 55
Trengganu 94 94a
Vietnam 403
Vietnam (North Vietnam) N318
Vietnam (South Vietnam) S386

67-33 Snow Leopard *(Panthera uncia)*
Afghanistan 520 963
Bhutan 69 77 114 204 255 **MS**525a
Germany (East Germany) E2040
Great Britain (Jersey) 325
Guinea–Bissau 863
Mongolia 1229
Nepal 449
Pakistan 621 622
Russia 3465 5397

67-34 Clouded Leopard *(Neofelis nebulosa)*
Guinea–Bissau 859
Indonesia 1517
Laos 515
North Borneo 299 393
Sabah 410
Thailand 828
Vietnam (North Vietnam) N477

67-35 Cheetah *(Acinonyx jubatus)*
Burundi 89 97 622 646 677 1395 1408
Central African Republic **MS**977
Chad 558
Cuba 2508
Czechoslovakia 2309
Ethiopia 1168
French Somali Coast 433
Fujeira 100
Great Britain (Jersey) 73
Guinea–Bissau 860
Hungary 3359
Israel 474
Kenya 32

Kenya, Uganda and Tanganyika 191
Liberia 1377
Libya 883
Mali 743 859
Mauritania 167
Mongolia 391 1231
Mozambique 681
Niger Republic 737
Nigeria 176 223 344
Poland 2147
Portugal 1945
Rhodesia 532
Somalia 196 197 198 530
South Africa 404
South West Africa 358
Tanzania 320 351
Zambia 168 278

68 EARED SEALS, SEALIONS
68-1 South American Fur Seal *(Arctocephalus australis)*
Chile 381f 382f 383f
Falkland Islands 184 296
South Georgia 5 13 58 65
Uruguay 1421

68-3 Kerguelen Fur Seal *(Arctocephalus gazella)*
Argentine Republic **MS**1685
British Antarctic Territory 42 43 100 116
French Southern and Antarctic Territories 8 9 14 100 125
    131
Poland 2673

68-4 Galapagos Fur Seal *(Arctocephalus galapagoensis)*
Ecuador 1527

68-5 Juan Fernandez Fur Seal *(Arctocephalus philippi)*
Chile 994

68-6 Afro-Australian Fur Seal *(Arctocephalus pusillus)*
Tristan Da Cunha 256

68-9 Northern Fur Seal *(Callorhinus ursinus)*
Russia 2350b 3375 4284
United States of America 1469

68-10 Californian Sealion *(Zalophus californianus)*
Ecuador 1207 1529 1883
Galapagos Islands 1

68-11 Northern Sealion *(Eumetopias jubata)*
Korea (North Korea) N1921
Mongolia 1397

68-12 Southern Sealion *(Otaria byronia)*
Falkland Islands 161 184 289 290 320 494
Uruguay 1034 1043

69 WALRUS
69-1 Walrus *(Odobenus rosmarus)*
Canada 472
Greenland 72 132 134
Hungary 3367
Korea (North Korea) N1834
Mongolia 1393
Russia 3970 4726

70 EARLESS SEALS
70-2 Ringed Seal *(Phoca hispida)*
Finland 629
St. Pierre et Miquelon 470

70-5   Common Seal *(Phoca vitulina)*
Iceland 585
Monaco 970 979
Newfoundland 26 38 43 59a
United States of America 1858

70-6   Ribbon Seal *(Histriophoca fasciata)*
Russia 3971

70-7   Harp Seal *(Pagophilus groenlandicus)*
Greenland 8 9 10 17 18 19
Newfoundland 217 263

70-8   Grey Seal *(Halichoerus grypus)*
Germany (East Germany) E1750
Newfoundland 75 143
Poland 2582
Sweden 755

70-9   Bearded Seal *(Erignathus barbatus)*
Ireland 564

70-10   Crabeater Seal *(Lobodon carcinophagus)*
Argentine Republic **MS**1858
British Antarctic Territory 118 137
French Southern and Antarctic Territories 184 187
New Zealand 1328

70-11   Ross Seal *(Ommatophoca rossi)*
British Antarctic Territory 117

70-12   Leopard Seal *(Hydrurga leptonyx)*
Argentine Republic **MS**1858
Australian Antarctic Territory 27
British Antarctic Territory 113
French Southern and Antarctic Territories 7 152 153
South Georgia 10 62

70-13   Weddell Seal *(Leptonychotes weddelli)*
Argentine Republic **MS**1858
British Antarctic Territory 40 114
French Southern and Antarctic Territories 101
Mongolia 1318

70-14   Mediterranean Monk Seal *(Monachus monachus)*
Algeria 800
Bulgaria 1251
Italy 1548
Mauritania 418 419 440 444
Portugal 1928
Spain 2521
Yugoslavia 2038

70-16   Caribbean Monk Seal *(Monachus tropicalis)*
Antigua **MS**747
Cuba 2643

70-18   Southern Elephant-Seal *(Mirounga leonina)*
Argentine Republic **MS**1685
Australian Antarctic Territory 11 57
British Antarctic Territory 115
French Southern and Antarctic Territories 10 12 27 132
Russia 4788
South Georgia 7 13 55 65 36 37
Tristan Da Cunha 25 255

71   RIVER DOLPHINS
71-2   Boutu *(Inia geoffrensis)*
Cook Islands 957

71-3   White Flag Dolphin *(Lipotes vexillifer)*
China (People's Republic) 3030 3031

71-5   Indus Dolphin *(Platanista minor)*
Pakistan 581 582

72   MARINE DOLPHINS
72-1   Rough-toothed Dolphin *(Steno bredanensis)*
Maldive Islands 1004
Tristan Da Cunha 201
Turks and Caicos Islands 537

72-3   Indo-Pacific Hump-backed Dolphin *(Sousa chinensis)*
Maldive Islands 1005

72-4   Atlantic Hump-backed Dolphin *(Sousa teuszi)*
Ghana 1036 **MS**1037 1094 **MS**1095

72-6   Striped Dolphin *(Stenella coeruleoalba)*
Dominica 661
Maldive Islands **MS**1008

72-7   Spotted Dolphin *(Stenella dubia)*
Cuba 2987
Grenadines of Grenada **MS**541
Marshall Islands 27

72-8   Spinner Dolphin *(Stenella longirostris)*
Ghana 1035 1093
Grenadines of St. Vincent 164

72-9   Common Dolphin *(Delphinus delphis)*
Anguilla 145 146
Argentine Republic 829
Bahamas 629
Bulgaria 1253Cook Islands 952
Cuba 2985
Grenada 1235
Korea (North Korea) N298
Marshall Islands 25
Portugal 1929
Russia **MS**4421
St. Pierre et Miquelon 473
San Marino 806
Turks and Caicos Islands 663
Yugoslavia 1932

72-11   Bottle-nosed Dolphin *(Tursiops truncatus)*
Antigua 788
Barbuda 667
Cook Islands 954
Cuba 2640 2989
Grenadines of Grenada **MS**551 **MS**638
Grenadines of St Vincent 165
Guinea–Bissau 884
Indonesia 1558
Marshall Islands 28
New Zealand 1177
Senegal 420
Sri Lanka 788

72-15   Atlantic White-sided Dolphin *(Lagenorhynchus acutus)*
Russia 3967

72-17   Peale's Dolphin *(Lagenorhynchus australis)*
Falkland Islands 371

72-18   Hourglass Dolphin *(Lagenorhynchus cruciger)*
Falkland Islands 373

72-20   Dusky Dolphin *(Lagenorhynchus obscurus)*
Falkland Islands 375 494

72-21   Melon-headed Whale *(Peponocephala electra)*
Dominica 842

72-22   Commerson's Dolphin *(Cephalorhynchus commersoni)*
Cook Islands 953
Falkland Islands 372
French Southern and Antarctic Territories 114

72-26   Irrawaddy Dolphin *(Orcaella brevirostris)*
Indonesia 1559

72-27   False Killer Whale *(Pseudorca crassidens)*
Cuba 2988
Ghana 1034
Grenadines of St. Vincent 163

72-28   Killer Whale *(Orcinus orca)*
Australian Antarctic Territory 28
Falkland Islands 376
French Southern and Antarctic Territories 30
Grenada 1232
Guinea–Bissau 886
Mongolia 1321
Portugal 1930
Senegal 513
South West Africa 338
Tristan Da Cunha 200
Turks and Caicos Islands 747
Wallis and Futuna Islands 449

72-29   Risso's Dolphin *(Grampus griseus)*
Cook Islands 947
Cuba 2984
Ghana 1033
Marshall Islands 26

72-30   Short-finned Pilot Whale *(Globicephala macrorhynchus)*
Ghana 1032
Grenadines of Grenada 537
Grenadines of St. Vincent 166

72-31   Long-finned Pilot Whale *(Globicephala melaena)*
Cook Islands 949
Dominica 664
St. Pierre et Miquelon 472
Turks and Caicos Islands 752

73   PORPOISES
73-1   Spectacled Porpoise *(Phocoena dioptrica)*
Antigua 791
Barbuda 670
Falkland Islands 374

73-2   Common Porpoise *(Phocoena phocoena)*
Cook Islands 956

73-5   Dall's Porpoise *(Phocoenoides dalli)*
Grenadines of Grenada 538

73-6   Finless Porpoise *(Neophocaena phocaenoides)*
Maldive Islands 1006

74   WHITE WHALES
74-1   White Whale *(Delphinapterus leucas)*
Cook Islands 951

74-2   Narwhal *(Monodon monoceros)*
Antigua **MS**792
Barbuda **MS**671
Canada 622
Cook Islands 950
Greenland 70
Russia 3969

75   SPERM WHALES
75-1   Pygmy Sperm Whale *(Kogia breviceps)*
Dominica **MS**843
Maldive Islands 1007

75-3   Sperm Whale *(Physeter catodon)*
Argentine Republic 1718
Australia 838
Australian Antarctic Territory 34
British Antarctic Territory 79
Cuba 2986
Equatorial Guinea 72
Fernando Poo 233 235
Grenada 1233
Guinea–Bissau 885
New Zealand 752
Niue 492
Norfolk Island 284
Palau 28
Penrhyn Island 290
St. Pierre et Miquelon 471
St. Vincent 429 532 611
Seychelles 602
South Georgia 3 21
South West Africa 341
Sri Lanka 791
Turks and Caicos Islands 748 810
Zil Elwannyen Sesel 22

76   BEAKED WHALES
76-4   Sowerby's Beaked Whale *(Mesoplodon bidens)*
Cook Islands 955

76-13   True's Beaked Whale *(Mesoplodon mirus)*
Cook Islands 948

76-16   Cuvier's Beaked Whale *(Ziphius cavirostris)*
Cook Islands 946
Cuba 2642
Dominica 839
Turks and Caicos Islands 749 811

77   GREY WHALE
77-1   Grey Whale *(Eschrichtius gibbosus)*
Guinea–Bissau 882
Mexico 1639
Niue 495

78   RORQUALS
78-1   Minke Whale *(Balaenoptera acutorostrata)*
Niue 494
Turks and Caicos Islands 745

78-2   Sei Whale *(Balaenoptera borealis)*
Guinea–Bissau 888
Niue 489
Tonga 633 634 635 636 637

78-4   Blue Whale *(Balaenoptera musculus)*
Australia 840
Brazil 1663
British Antarctic Territory 82 138
Chile 993
French Southern and Antarctic Territories 26 113
Great Britain (Jersey) 278
Grenada 1234
Guinea–Bissau 883
Monaco 1599
Monogolia 1316
Niue 490
Palau 26
Penrhyn Island 294
St. Pierre et Miquelon 541

Seychelles 604
South Georgia 15
South West Africa 343
Tonga O160 O161 O162
Turks and Caicos Islands 750

78-5   Fin Whale *(Balaenoptera physalus)*
Antigua 789
Barbuda 668
British Antarctic Territory 80
Falkland Islands 116 117 118 119 120 121 122 123 124
   125 126 133
Libya 696
Niue 488
Palau 27
Senegal 515
South Georgia 6 59
South West Africa 342
Tonga 633 634 635 636 637
Tristan Da Cunha 203
Turks and Caicos Islands **MS**753 **MS**812

78-6   Humpback Whale *(Megaptera novaeangliae)*
Australia 841
Bermuda 401
British Antarctic Territory 81
Cuba 2641 2990
Dominica 840
Fernando Poo 234 236
French Southern and Antarctic Territories 200 201
Grenada **MS**1236
Grenadines of Grenada 539
New Zealand 1177
Niuafo'ou 44
Niue 493
Norfolk Island 286
Palau 25
Portugal 1931
St. Vincent 430 612
Seychelles 601
South West Africa 339
Sri Lanka 790
Tonga 628 629 630 631 632 690 694 695 699 O184
Turks and Caicos Islands 538 751

79   RIGHT WHALES
79-2   Black Right Whale *(Eubalaena glacialis)*
Australia 839
Dominica 841
Niue 487
Norfolk Island 285
Seychelles 603
South West Africa 340
Tristan Da Cunha 41 54 202
Turks and Caicos Islands 746

79-3   Bowhead Whale *(Balaena mysticetus)*
Antigua 790
Barbuda 669
Canada 937
Greenland 69 136 145
Grenadines of Grenada 540
Guinea–Bissau 887
Niue 491
Russia 4285

80   SEA COWS
80-1   Dugong *(Dugong dugon)*
French Territory of the Afars and the Issas 566
Kenya 100
Palau 20
Papua New Guinea 397
Ryukyu Islands 177
Sri Lanka 789

Tanzania 216
Uganda 203

81   MANATEES
81-1   Amazon Manatee *(Trichechus inunguis)*
Brazil 1767

81-2   American Manatee *(Trichechus manatus)*
Caicos Islands 58
Costa Rica 653
Cuba 2767
Dominican Republic 1411
Guyana 685
Jamaica 543
Panama 1384

81-3   African Manatee *(Trichechus senegalensis)*
Cameroun 317 322
Ghana 814
Ivory Coast 247 615
Mali 685
Mauritania 575
Niger Republic 99 104
Togo 1221 1722 1723 1724 1725

82   ELEPHANTS
82-1   African Elephant *(Loxodonta africana)*
Angola 489
Belgian Congo 22 35 42 66 76 84 97 110 140 346
Benin 762
Biafra 5 16c
Bophuthatswana 18
Botswana D16 D17 D18 D19
Burundi 16 17 21 90 98 626 650 1199 1223 1389 1402
Cameroun 133 134 135 135a 136 137 138 139 140 141
   142 143 144 167 168 170 171 172 173 174 176 177 310
   314 859
Central African Empire 554
Central African Republic 231 820 976 990 991
Congo (Brazzaville) 63 334 533
Congo (Kinshasa) 385
Cuba 2509
Czechoslovakia 1294 2308
Dahomey 530
Eritrea 57 58 206 213
Ethiopia 190 202 519
French Equatorial Africa 290
Gabon 279 851
Gambia 122 124 125 126 127 128 118 130 131 119 133
   134 135 136 17 138 140 141 142 150 151 152a 152b 153
   153a 154 154a 155 156 156a 157 158 159 160 161 185
Ghana 357 589 994 1071
Guinea 206 208 450 451 610 612 666 882 885 887 954 955
   956 969 970 971
Hungary 3364
Ivory Coast 180 181 182 348 349 560 781
Katanga 30
Kenya 10 30 84 92 105
Kenya, Uganda and Tanganyika 169 176 178 223 369 379
   381 O3 O8 O10
Liberia 77 148 149 181 182 220 224 333 413 427 957 1241
   MS1296 1377 O89 O121 O161 O162 O237 O336 O441
   O455
Malawi 629
Mauritania 540 577
Mozambique 797 880
Nicaragua 2168
Niger Republic 114 324 485
Nigeria 173 220
Northern Rhodesia 1 2 3 4 5 6 7 8 9 10 11 12 13 14 15 16
   17 25 26 27 28 29 30 31 32 33 34 35 36 37 38 39 40 41
   42 44 45 61 62 63 64 65 66 67 68 69 70 71 72 73 74

Rhodesia 420
Rio Muni 19 21 69 70
Ruanda – Urundi 21 29 54 210 213 228
Rwanda 62 63 66 105 217 949 1123
San Marino 1129
Senegal 417 711 714 **MS**716
Sierra Leone 178 655 **MS**749 799
Somalia 1 2 10 11 23 33 34 35 37 68 69 270 271 272 273
    274 418 499
South Africa 156
South West Africa 165 365
Southern Rhodesia 31 32 33 34
Spanish Guinea 388 390 422 423 424 425
Sudan 261
Swaziland 165
Tanzania 205 246 248 319 354
Togo 181 551 1038
Uganda 191 316 406 407 408 409 438 D27
United States of America 1378
Upper Volta 187 531 613 O112 O113 O114 O115 O116
    O117 O118 O119 O120 O121
Zaire 954 988 990 1122
Zambia 104 171 232 275 279 288

82-2   Indian Elephant *(Elephas maximus)*
Afghanistan 965
Bangladesh 105
Bulgaria 1610
Cambodia 210
Ceylon 377 394d 480
Congo (Brazzaville) 386 452
Cuba 1158
Czechoslovakia 1294
Germany (East Germany) E287
Hungary 1719
India 309 474
Indian Custodian Forces in Korea K1
Indian Forces in Indo-China N1 N6 N11
Indonesia 1490
Japan 1662
Kampuchea 575
Korea (North Korea) N1356
Laos 521 524 525 526
North Borneo 281 193 219 239 258 D52
Poland 2580
Russia 3000
Sirmoor 22 23 24 25 26 27 28 29
Thailand 405 812 827
Vietnam (North Vietnam) N160

83   HORSES
83-1   African Ass *(Equus africanus)*
Burundi 1041 1065
Chad 559
Ethiopia 517
French Territory of the Afars and Issas 663
Mali 741
Somalia 607

83-2   Common Zebra *(Equus burchelli)*
Belgian Congo 350
Bophuthatswana 101
Botswana 282 D20 D21 D22 D23 D24
Bulgaria 1815
Burundi 18a 19 23 81 85 92 619 643 674 1391 1404
Central African Republic 975 990 991
Congo (Kinshasa) 389
Cuba 1163 1806
Czechoslovakia 2307
Germany (East Germany) E560 E1752
Germany (West Berlin) **MS**B332
Guinea 877
Hungary 1723

Japan 1663
Katanga 34
Kenya 25
Kenya, Uganda and Tanganyika 190 O18
Korea (North Korea) N1352
Liberia 1083 1245 1377
Malawi 499 569
Mali 655
Mozambique Company 290
Nyassa Company 56 57 58 88 89 91 110 111 112 113
    D134 D135
Rhodesia 564
Ruanda – Urundi 139 211 214
Russia 3608
Rwanda 64 67 99 185 189 216 233 234 235 236 237 238
    458 689 806 953 1129 1210 1212 1213 1215 1216
Somalia 365 435 531
South West Africa 415
Swaziland 173
Tanzania 134 315 O14 O61
Togo 546 962
Uganda 310 435 D28
United Nations V41
Vietnam 441
Zambia **MS**176 288
Zimbabwe 585

83-3   Wild Horse *(Equus ferus)*
Afghanistan 961
Belgium 1779
Bulgaria 2902
Czechoslovakia 1296 2597
Laos 627
Mongolia 58 **MS**668 843
Poland 1434 2578
Russia 1239 1240 2059c

83-4   Grevy's Zebra *(Equus grevyi)*
Burundi 1182 1206
Ethiopia 1164
Rumania 3203
Uganda **MS**410

83-5   Asiatic Wild Ass *(Equus hemionus)*
Afghanistan 900
Fujeira 4 13 42 88 97 126 O51 O161
Iran 1853
Israel 472
Russia 4282

83-8   Mountain Zebra *(Equus zebra)*
Angola 493
Poland 2155
South Africa 154 188 407
South West Africa 82 355

84   TAPIRS
84-1   Baird's Tapir *(Tapirus bairdi)*
British Honduras 180a 194
Costa Rica 649
Nicaragua 1108 1954 O1123

84-2   Malayan Tapir *(Tapirus indicus)*
Indonesia 803
Malaysia 195
North Borneo 159 189 214 235 253
Thailand 914
Vietnam (North Vietnam) N317

84-3   Mountain Tapir *(Tapirus roulini)*
Ecuador 1161

84-4   Brazilian Tapir *(Tapirus terrestris)*
Cuba 1171
Grenada 549
Guyana 760
Paraguay 934 935 936
Venezuela 1776 1885

South West Africa 361
Sudan 146 147 148
Tanzania 318
Togo 1040
Uganda 312 437 D29
Zambia **MS**176 226

85   RHINOCEROSES
85-1   Javan Rhinoceros *(Rhinoceros sondaicus)*
Indonesia 801
Khmer Republic 339
Laos 335
Niger Republic 537
Thailand 786
Vietnam 440

85-2   Indian Rhinoceros *(Rhinoceros unicornis)*
Bulgaria **MS**2761
Germany (East Germany) E1748
India 449 460
Maldive Islands 781
Nepal 125

85-3   Sumatran Rhinoceros *(Dicerorhinus sumatrensis)*
Indonesia 725 726 727
North Borneo 282 187 206 221 240 260 398 D53
Sabah 415
Thailand 788
Vietnam (North Vietnam) N320
West Irian 2

85-4   White Rhinoceros *(Ceratotherium simum)*
Belgian Congo 340
Belgium 1778
Bophuthatswana 100
Botswana 347
Burundi 534 535 1031 1055 1079
Comoro Islands 210 402
Congo (Kinshasa) 379 519 523
Cuba 2504
Katanga 24
Mozambique 685
Mozambique Company 292 306
Portugal 1947
Rhodesia 419 560
Rwanda 459
Somalia 529
South Africa 155
Swaziland 172 374
Zaire 1046 1175
Zimbabwe 581

85-5   Black Rhinoceros *(Diceros bicornis)*
Angola 495
Burundi 618 642 673 1387 1400
Cameroun 372 856
Central African Empire 550
Central African Republic 971 972 973 974 975 990
Chad 536 560
Congo (Brazzaville) 622
Czechoslovakia 2311
Ethiopia 188 208c 641
French Equatorial Africa 235 236 237
Germany (East Germany) E289
Guinea 881
Hungary 3362
Kenya 27 92
Kenya, Uganda and Tanganyika 195 367
Liberia 956 1290
Mozambique 798
Rio Muni 50 53 56
Somalia 366 498
South Africa 405

86   HYRAXES
86-1   Tree Hyrax *(Dendrohyrax arboreus)*
Djibouti 820

86-2   Beecroft's Hyrax *(Dendrohyrax dorsalis)*
Ivory Coast 229

86-5   Large-toothed Rock Hyrax *(Procavia capensis)*
Burundi 1190 1214
French Somali Coast 455
Lesotho 329
South West Africa 290
Tanzania 311 O58

87   AARDVARK
87-1   Aardvark *(Orycteropus afer)*
Angola 838
Bophuthatswana 14
Ethiopia 927
French Territory of the Afars and the Issas 660
Ghana 981
Ivory Coast 577
Kenya 22
Mauritania 172
Mozambique 858

88   PIGS
88-1   Bush Pig *(Potamochaerus porcus)*
Bophuthatswana 6
Burundi 1181 1205
Ivory Coast 756
Rio Muni 80
Senegal 586
Swaziland 166

88-3   Pygmy Hog *(Sus salvanius)*
Bhutan 70 76 113 225

88-4   Wild Boar *(Sus scrofa)*
Afghanistan 674 962
Albania 726 946
Austria 1340
Belgium 2367
Bulgaria 1096 2943
Cambodia 208
Cameroun 1008
Cuba 1800
Czechoslovakia 1618 1972
Germany (East Germany) E1990
Hungary 1279 2035 2206 2584 3014
Ifni 158
Italy 1834
Korea (North Korea) N1254
Laos 300 301
Mongolia 557 930 1458
North Borneo 284 208 223 242 263 D55
Poland 1618 2239 2752
Rumania 2355 2426 2477 2854 3335 3888 4237
Russia 3733
San Marino 628 687
Togo 1081
Tunisia 685
Turkey 2194
Vietnam 400

Vietnam (North Vietnam) N738
Yugoslavia 964

88-5   Javan Pig *(Sus verrucosus)*
Philippines 1517

88-6   Warthog *(Phacochoerus aethiopicus)*
Angola 502
Burundi 631 655 682 1392 1405
Central African Empire 460
Central African Republic 391 990
Congo (Brazzaville) 532
Dahomey 353
Djibouti 918
Ethiopia 926
French Somali Coast 432
Guinea 662 873
Ivory Coast 233
Kenya 24
Mauritania 538
Mozambique 683
Niger Republic 487
Rhodesia 562
Rwanda 460
Senegal 230 660 663
South Africa 151 185
Togo 1315
Upper Volta 176
Zaire 1177
Zambia 277
Zimbabwe 583

88-7   Giant Forest Hog *(Hylochoerus meinertzhageni)*
Ivory Coast 232
Mauritania 421 446

88-8   Babirusa *(Babyrousa babyrussa)*
Indonesia 798

89   **PECCARIES**
89-1   White-lipped Peccary *(Tayassu pecari)*
Belize 349 364
British Honduras 257
Costa Rica 655
Dominican Republic 1580
Guyana 496
Panama 1387

89-2   Collared Peccary *(Tayassu tajacu)*
Cuba 1168
Ecuador 1202
Guyana 761
Nicaragua 1953
Trinidad and Tobago 393
Venezuela 1767

90   **HIPPOPOTAMUSES**
90-1   Hippopotamus *(Hippopotamus amphibius)*
Angola 504
Benin 637
Biafra 15
Bophuthatswana 20
Burundi 78 84 95 615 639 670 1390 1403
Cameroun 312 315
Central African Republic 231
Congo (Brazzaville) 336 531 624
Cuba 1170
Dahomey 322
Equatorial Guinea 61
Ethiopia 1309
French West Africa 41
Gabon 275

Ghana 364
Guinea 326 329 655 660 879 963 964 965 972 973 974
Kenya 79
Kenya, Uganda and Tanganyika 193 224 386
Liberia 84 146 147 178 179 172 193 206 476 562 634 O96
    O127 O159 O160 O490
Mozambique 684
Mozambique Company 297
Niger Republic 486
Nigeria 184
Rhodesia 446
Rwanda 101 461
Senegal 362
Sierra Leone 804
Somalia 176 184
South Africa 157
South West Africa 359
Tanzania 200
Togo 826
Uganda 186 315 439
Upper Volta 499
Vietnam 437
Zaire 1124
Zambia **MS**176

90-2   Pygmy Hippopotamus *(Choeropsis liberiensis)*
Germany (East Germany) E1749
Ivory Coast 248 576 617
Liberia 233 1293 1591 1592 1593 1594 O246 O287
Togo 357
Upper Volta 182

91   **CAMELS, LLAMAS**
91-1   Guanaco *(Lama guanicoe)*
Bolivia 511 521
Cuba 1166
Ecuador 1057 1346
Liberia 1085
Russia 3612

91-2   Vicuna *(Vicugna vicugna)*
Argentine Republic 1886
Bolivia 349 350 351
Peru 17 316 778 829 867 921 1188 O326

91-3   Bactrian Camel *(Camelus ferus)*
Burundi 534 535
China (People's Republic) 3016
Czechoslovakia 1293
Korea (North Korea) N1355
Mongolia 136 137 142 147 458 636 1166 1167 1168 1170
    1455 1484
Rumania 3204
Tuva 76 90

91-4   Dromedary *(Camelus dromedarius)*
Ajman 3 12 57 101 110 119 O66 O128
Bahawalpur O2 O15
Burundi 534 535
Chad 377 401
Cuba 1172
Eritrea 199 201 209 222 223 224
Fujeira 8 17 46 92 101 130 O55 O165
Ifni 157 160
Israel 53
Jordan 808 980
Lebanon 995
Libya 880
Mali 209 678 931
Manama 2
Mauritania 169 318
Nyassa Company 34 35 36 37 38 39 40 41 42 51 53 54 55
    72 73 74 75 76 77 80 81 82 83 85 86

Qatar 354
San Marino 1127
Somalia 532 544
Southern Yemen 56
Spanish Sahara 88 89 90 130 133
Tunisia 680
Upper Volta 179 396
Yemen 390

92   CHEVROTAINS
92-1   Water Chevrotain *(Hyemoschus aquaticus)*
Gabon 277 849
Ivory Coast 230
Liberia 623
Rio Muni 72 74

92-2   Lesser Malay Chevrotain *(Tragulus javanicus)*
Indonesia 713 714 715
Laos 333
Malaysia 192
Riau-Lingga Archipelago 23 26 27 28
Vietnam (North Vietnam) N736

92-3   Indian Spotted Chevrotain *(Tragulus meminna)*
Sri Lanka 720

92-4   Greater Malay Chevrotain *(Tragulus napu)*
Philippines 1091

93   MUSK DEER
93-2   Siberian Musk Deer *(Moschus moschiferus)*
Mongolia 177 858
Nepal 124
Russia 4434
Vietnam (North Vietnam) N739

94   DEER
94-1   Chinese Water Deer *(Hydropotes inermis)*
Korea (North Korea) N201

94-4   Indian Muntjac *(Muntiacus muntjak)*
Hong Kong 414
Korea (North Korea) N756

94-9   Spotted Deer *(Cervus axis)*
Bangladesh 102 167 168
Bhopal O345
Ceylon 563
India 508 722
Vietnam (North Vietnam) N316

94-10   Fallow Deer *(Cervus dama)*
Bulgaria 2246 2947
Cuba 2598
Czechoslovakia 1398
Germany (West Berlin) B287
Germany (West Germany) 1418
Hungary 1277 2038 2210
Iran 1855
Israel 471
Italy 1180
Korea (North Korea) N758
Turkey 2191

94-11   Swamp Deer *(Cervus duvauceli)*
India 825 1086
Nepal 322

94-12   Red Deer *(Cervus elaphus)*
Afghanistan 675
Algeria 521

Argentine Republic 1032 1325 1566 O1049
Austria 1341 1361
Bulgaria 1065 1093 1687 **MS**2948
Cuba 1159 **MS**2717
Czechoslovakia 1116 1399 1613 1971 2204 2679
Denmark 516
Dominica 862
Finland 1037
France 1958
Germany (East Germany) E473 E1986
Germany (West Berlin) B288
Germany (West Germany) 1419
Hungary 1280 2040 2128 2209 2585 2587 3380
India 1052
Ireland 464
Italy 1179
Kampuchea 574
Korea (North Korea) N754
Liechtenstein 252
Mongolia 852
Netherlands 971
Poland 1619 2238
Rumania 2322 2434 2485 2856 3334 3336 4234 4284 4569
    4849
Russia 3730 3853 4186 4277
San Marino 630 1120
Switzerland J209
Togo 1080
Trieste B121
Tuva 16
United States of America 1121 1862
Yemen 667
Yugoslavia 767 1296 1859

94-13   Thamin *(Cervus eldi)*
Khmer Republic 341
Singapore 227
Thailand 787

94-14   Sika Deer *(Cervus nippon)*
China (People's Republic) 2995 2996 2997
China (Taiwan) 365 810 1117
Indonesia 689
Japan 293 266 211 267 305 268 1228
Korea (North Korea) N205 N755
Korea (South Korea) 250 285 319 320 551 711
Liberia 1090
Malagasy Republic 324
Russia 2059 3874
Ryukyu Islands 176

94-15   Hog-Deer *(Cervus porcinus)*
Cambodia 209
Thailand 916
Vietnam (South Vietnam) S385

94-16   Schomburgk's Deer *(Cervus schomburgki)*
Thailand 782

94-17   Timor Deer *(Cervus timorensis)*
Mauritius 287 303

94-18   Sambar *(Cervus unicolor)*
Ceylon 419 448
Indonesia 1516
Labuan 63 84 90 111 D1
Laos 334
New Caledonia D179 D180 D181 D182 D183 D184 D185
    D186 D187 D188 D189 D190 D191
North Borneo 69 94a 95 128a 391 D2 D12 D15 D36
Sabah 408
Thailand 385 386 387 915
Vietnam 401
Vietnam (North Vietnam) N158

Wallis and Futuna Islands D85 D86 D87 D88 D89 D90 D91
D92 D93 D94 D95 D96 D97

94-20 Elk *(Alces alces)*
Belgium 1783
Bulgaria 2248
Canada 448
Finland 520
Mongolia 558 1143
Poland 901 1621 2234 2437 2753
Russia 2062 3003
Sweden 542 1104
Tuva 74
United States of America **MS**1726 1863

94-21 Reindeer *(Rangifer tarandus)*
Canada 486
Falkland Islands Dependencies 98 99 100 101
Finland 577 621
Greenland 131
Korea (North Korea) N757
Mongolia 465
Newfoundland 69 130 131 132a 133 134 135 136 137 138
139 140 141 142 156 191 213 225c 259
Norway 262
South Georgia 1 53
United States of America 2063

94-22 Mule Deer *(Odocoileus hemionus)*
Mexico 1453

94-23 White-tailed Deer *(Odocoileus virginianus)*
Costa Rica 652
Cuba 1801
Guatemala 1125
Honduras 885 889 893
United States of America 1864
Venezuela 1766

94-24 Marsh Deer *(Blastocerus dichotomus)*
Brazil 2083

94-25 Pampas Deer *(Ozotoceros bezoarticus)*
Argentine Republic 1816
Brazil 1960

94–26 Peruvian Guemal *(Hippocamelus antisiensis)*
Ecuador 1293

94-27 Chilean Guemal *(Hippocamelus bisulcus)*
Argentine Republic 1887
Chile 381r 382r 383r 995

94-28 Red Brocket *(Mazama americana)*
British Honduras 247
Nicaragua 1955
Trinidad and Tobago 392

94-33 Southern Pudu *(Pudu pudu)*
Chile 1006

94-34 Roe Deer *(Capreolus capreolus)*
Albania 727 **MS**727a 943 1129 1130 1131 1132 1133 1134
1135 1136
Austria 1339
Bulgaria 1092 1686 2946
Cuba 1176
Czechoslovakia 1397
Germany (East Germany) E472 E1989
Germany (West Berlin) B285
Germany (West Germany) 1416
Great Britain 638
Hungary 1278 2042 2208 **MS**2591
Ifni 202

Kampuchea 572
Korea (North Korea) N1560
Liechtenstein 283
Mongolia 464 856 1454 1505
Poland 2236 2755 2867
Rumania 2852 2861 3887 4570
Russia 2536
St. Pierre et Miquelon 433
San Marino 626 682
Sweden 682
Switzerland J217 919
Turkey 2331
Tuva 59
Yugoslavia 963

95 GIRAFFE, OKAPI
95-1 Okapi *(Okapia johnstoni)*
Belgian Congo 191a 192 269 347
Belgium 1780
Burundi 534 535 624 648 679
Central African Republic 823
Congo (Brazzaville) 620
Congo (Kinshasa) 386
Cuba 2505
Germany (East Germany) E2241
Katanga 31
Zaire 863 864 865 866 867 1209 1210 1211 1213 **MS**1214

95-2 Giraffe *(Giraffa camelopardalis)*
Angola 506
Belgian Congo 341
Belgium 1781
Benin 760
Biafra 14
Burundi 79 87 616 640 671 1386 1399
Cameroun 261 295a 320 323 857 928
Central African Empire 553
Central African Republic 821 990 991
Chad 133
Congo (Kinshasa) 380
Cuba 2507
Czechoslovakia 2310
Ethiopia 182 198 520
Germany (East Germany) E811
Germany (West Germany) 1206
Japan 1663
Katanga 25
Kenya 212
Kenya, Uganda and Tanganyika 168 173 194 O2 O6
Liberia 951 1377
Mali 102
Mozambique 799 856
Mozambique Company 286
Niger Republic 107 108 310 346 734 735 842
Nigeria 183 230
Northern Rhodesia 1 2 3 4 5 6 7 8 9 10 11 12 13 14 15 16
17 25 26 27 28 29 30 31 32 33 34 35 36 37 38 39 40 41
42 43 44 45 61 62 63 64 65 66 67 68 69 70 71 72 73 74
Nyassa Company 27 28 29 30 31 32 33 43 44 50 59 60 61
65 66 67 68 69 70 71 78 79 92 93 95 96 97 98 99 D132
D133
Poland 2148
Rhodesia 563
Rwanda 185 189
Somalia 364 432 610
South Africa 163 196
South West Africa 363
Southern Rhodesia 31 32 33 34
Sudan 125 263 264 265 O49
Swaziland 175 220
Tanganyika 74 89 75 90 76 77 78 91 79 92 80 81 82 83 84
85 86 87 88
Tanzania 133 244 285 314 321

Togo 1037
Vietnam 439
Zambia **MS**176 288 388
Zimbabwe 584

96   PRONGHORN
96-1   Pronghorn *(Antilocapra americana)*
United States of America 1080 1865

97   CATTLE, ANTELOPE, SHEEP, GOATS
97-1   Nyala *(Tragelaphus angasi)*
Burundi 1030 1054 1078
Malawi 227 376 567
Mozambique 698
Nyasaland Protectorate 210
South Africa 162

97-2   Mountain Nyala *(Tragelaphus buxtoni)*
Comoro Islands 211
Ethiopia 644

97-3   Giant Eland *(Tragelaphus derbianus)*
Chad 132
French Equatorial Africa 288
Mali 689
Rwanda 638
Senegal 231 712 714 **MS**716
Zaire 1172

97-4   Bongo *(Tragelaphus euryceros)*
Burundi 636 660 687
Cameroun 939
Czechoslovakia 2312
Ghana 1114 1115 1116 1117
Ivory Coast 234
Kenya 213
Liberia 349 375 393 411 425 504 1291 O362 O400 O439
    O453 O506
Mauritania 171
Rwanda 632

97-5   Lesser Kudu *(Tragelaphus imberbis)*
Burundi 1049 1073 1089
Gambia 384
Somalia 177 185 296a 483
Somaliland Protectorate 97 98 99 100 109 110 111 112 128
    129 130 131
Sudan 261
Zaire 1046

97-6   Eland *(Tragelaphus oryx)*
Angola 490
Belgian Congo 350
Burundi 18a 19 23 1033 1057 1081 1393 1406
Congo (Kinshasa) 389
Cuba 1162
Ethiopia 518
Guinea 948 949 950 966 967 968
Katanga 34
Lesotho 470 611
Malawi 380
Mozambique 800
Rhodesia 490
Ruanda-Urundi 211 214
Russia 3612
Rwanda 64 67
South West Africa 81 360
Zambia 140

97-7   Bushbuck *(Tragelaphus scriptus)*
Botswana 238
Burundi 1195 1219

Congo (Brazzaville) 62
Gabon 399
Gambia 357
Ghana 980
Liberia 560 625 638
Malawi 385
Niger Republic 674
Portuguese Guinea 312
Rhodesia 493
Senegal 232
Sierra Leone **MS**805

97-8   Sitatunga *(Tragelaphus spekei)*
Angola 494
Burundi 1046 1070 1086
Gambia 358
Rwanda 634
Senegal 588 589
Zambia 231

97-9   Greater Kudu *(Tragelaphus strepsiceros)*
Angola 505 833
Bophuthatswana 21
Burundi 1189 1213
Chad 134
Djibouti 821
French Equatorial Africa 291
Guinea 876
Hungary 3363
Ivory Coast 780
Kenya 29
Malawi 375 652
Mozambique Company 301 311
Rhodesia 362 376 408 489
Rwanda 635 **MS**639 899
Somalia 609
South Africa 159
South West Africa 354
Southern Rhodesia 95
Sudan 261
Swaziland 58 64 72a 77a 83 89

97-12   Water Buffalo *(Bubalus arnee)*
Albania 882 883 884 885 886
Brazil 2091 2092 2093
Ceylon 561
Cuba 1175
Khmer Republic 343
Philippines 1090
Thailand 785
Vietnam (North Vietnam) N319
Vietnam (South Vietnam) S449 S450

97-13   Anoa *(Bubalus depressicornis)*
Indonesia 799

97-14   Tamarau *(Bubalus mindorensis)*
Philippines 1089

97-16   Banteng *(Bos javanicus)*
Indonesia 722 723 724
Khmer Republic 342
North Borneo 175 287 396
Riau-Lingga Archipelago 25 32
Sabah 413
Thailand 913
Vietnam (North Vietnam) N321
West Irian 1

97-17   Gaur *(Bos gaurus)*
Bangladesh 104
Germany (West Berlin) **MS**B332
India 472
Khmer Republic 344

Laos 303
Malaysia 196
Thailand 826

97-18   Yak *(Bos mutus)*
Afghanistan 523
Bhutan 3 7 61 **MS**525b
Mongolia 132 133 134 135 635
Nepal 293
Tuva 51 56 58 75

97-20   Kouprey *(Bos sauveli)*
Cambodia 159 160 161
Kampuchea 577
Thailand 783

97-21   African Buffalo *(Synceros caffer)*
Angola 498 836
Belgian Congo 344
Benin 636 730
Biafra 16
Bophuthatswana 5
Burundi 10 14 80 86 93 614 638 669 1039 1063 1388 1401
Cameroun 904
Central African Republic 991
Chad 133
Congo (Brazzaville) 530 621
Congo (Kinshasa) 383
Dahomey 318
Ethiopia 191
Gabon 213 840
Guinea 449 452 652 664 878
Ivory Coast 758
Katanga 28
Kenya 26 105
Kenya, Uganda and Tanganyika 197 380
Korea (North Korea) N1353
Liberia 478 561 635 1242 O492
Malawi 635
Mali 99 745
Mozambique 802 876
Niger Republic 114 324
Nigeria 185 471
Rhodesia 360 374
Rio Muni 32 34
Ruanda-Urundi 89 110 204 208
Rwanda 55 56 57 102 218 457 952 1126 1211 1214 1217
Senegal 229
South West Africa 358b 417
Southern Rhodesia 93
Tanzania 244 246 316 O62
Togo 138 139 140 141 142 143 144 154 157 158 159 160
   161 162 323
Uganda 314 D25
Upper Volta 99 181
Zaire 1121
Zambia 288 367

97-22   American Bison *(Bison bison)*
Bularia 1616
Canada 1007
Canal Zone 95
Cuba 1173
Czechoslovakia 1588
Hungary 1717
Russia 3608
United States of America 293 700 1382 1859

97-23   European Bison *(Bison bonasus)*
Bulgaria 2247
Czechoslovakia 1113
France 2046
Germany (East Germany) E291
Hungary 1724 2583

Netherlands 973
Poland 900 1620 2758 2759 2760 2761 2762 2867
Rumania 3605 4287 4571
Russia 2061 3731 4182
Vietnam 435

97-27   Jentink's Duiker *(Cephalophus jentinki)*
Ivory Coast 613
Liberia 624

97-30   Blue Duiker *(Cephalophus monticola)*
Malawi 634

97-31   Red Forest Duiker *(Cephalophus natalensis)*
Malawi 386

97-36   Abbott's Duiker *(Cephalophus spadix)*
Kenya, Uganda and Tanganyika 382

97-37   Yellow-backed Duiker *(Cephalophus sylvicultor)*
Ivory Coast 227 575
Zambia 391

97-39   Banded Duiker *(Cephalophus zebra)*
Burundi 1047 1071 1087
Comoro Islands 216
Liberia 626

97-40   Common Duiker *(Sylvicapra grimmia)*
Bophuthatswana 17
Central African Republic 230
Ethiopia 1311
Malawi 387
Zambia **MS**176

97-41   Waterbuck *(Kobus ellipsiprymnus)*
Angola 503
Burundi 82 88 96
Central African Empire 461
Central African Republic 392 991
Ghana 495
Guinea 874
Kenya 92
Malawi 384
Mali 98
Nigeria 469
Rwanda 464 637
Senegal 233
Singapore 226
Somalia 296 481 500
Swaziland 174 219
Uganda 313 426
Upper Volta 101 610
Zambia 148 288

97-42   Kob *(Kobus kob)*
Belgian Congo 227
Biafra 13
Burundi 1178 1202
Cameroun 311 313 892
Central African Empire 459
Central African Republic 390
Congo (Brazzaville) 529 625
Dahomey 320
Ghana **MS**1118
Guinea 663
Kenya, Uganda and Tanganyika 319
Liberia 477 1243 O491
Nigeria 182 229
Rwanda 631 1082 1133
Togo 201 202 203 204 205 222 223 224 225 226
Uganda D26
Upper Volta 104 528

97-43   Lechwe *(Kobus leche)*
Zambia 169 276 390

97-44   Nile Lechwe *(Kobus megaceros)*
Sudan 138

97-45   Puku *(Kobus vardoni)*
Malawi 378

97-46   Reedbuck *(Redunca arundinum)*
Rhodesia 492

97-47   Mountain Reedbuck *(Redunca fulvorufula)*
Malawi 377 570

97-48   Bohar Reedbuck *(Redunca redunca)*
Burundi 1037 1061
French Somali Coast 447
Guinea 268 269 270 271 272 273 283 284 285 286 287 288
Ifni 130
Tanzania 248
Togo 359 544

97-50   Roan Antelope *(Hippotragus equinus)*
Belgian Congo 339
Benin 635 759
Botswana 543
Burundi 1029 1053 1077
Congo (Kinshasa) 378
Katanga 23
Kenya 214
Malawi 383 498
Niger Republic 114 324
Rhodesia 491 529
Rwanda 633
Senegal 228
South West Africa 347
Southern Rhodesia 31 32 33 34
Upper Volta 529 611

97-52   Sable Antelope *(Hippotragus niger)*
Angola 488 837
Bophuthatswana 102
Botswana 239
Burundi 633 657 684
Ivory Coast 574
Kenya 21
Mozambique 686
Rwanda 633
South Africa 164 197
South West Africa 348
Southern Rhodesia 78

97-53   Scimitar Oryx *(Oryx dammah)*
Chad 131 557
French Morocco 228 301 247 248 305 250 307 316 352
Mali 100
Mauritania 145 573
Niger Republic 738 839
Spanish Sahara 120 121 122

97-54   Gemsbok *(Oryx gazella)*
Angola 496
Burundi 628 652
Ethiopia 521
French Territory of the Afars and the Issas 587
Mali 688
South Africa 161 195
South West Africa 164 353

97-55   Arabian Oryx *(Oryx leucoryx)*
Bahrain **MS**296
Fujeira 2 11 40 86 95 124 O49 O159
Germany (East Germany) E2244

Israel 473
Jordan 826
Oman 270
Qatar 352 534
Southern Yemen 58

97-56   Addax *(Addax nasomaculatus)*
Bahrain **MS**296
Burundi 534 535 1028 1052 1076
Central African Republic 822
Chad 130 556
Germany (East Germany) 1340
Libya 877
Mali 742
Niger Republic 739 843

97-57   Black Wildebeest *(Connochaetes gnou)*
Burundi 1040 1064
Germany (East Germany) E813
Kenya, Uganda and Tanganyika 154
Orange Free State 139 140 141 142 143 144 145 146 147
South Africa 120 O40
South West Africa 51 64

97-58   Blue Wildebeest *(Connochaetes taurinus)*
Angola 500
Burundi 630 654 681 1180 1204 1396 1409
Kenya, Uganda and Tanganyika 154 186 O16
South Africa 120 152 186 O40
South West Africa 51 64 82 358a
Swaziland 171
Zambia 389

97-59   Hartebeest *(Alcelaphus buselaphus)*
Angola 501
Bophuthatswana 103
Dahomey 357
Ethiopia 1167
Ivory Coast 231
Niger Republic 740
Nigeria 470
Poland 2583
Upper Volta 532

97-60   Lichtenstein's Hartebeest *(Alcelaphus lichtensteini)*
Malawi 636

97-61   Blesbok *(Damaliscus dorcas)*
Burundi 1050 1074 1090
Portugal 1946
Russia 5396
South Africa 406

97-62   Hunter's Hartebeest *(Damaliscus hunteri)*
Kenya 98
Somalia 296b 484
Tanzania 214
Uganda 201

97-63 Topi *(Damaliscus lunatus)*
Burundi 617 641 672
Ghana 306
Mali 687
Mozambique 857 878
Niger Republic 114 324
South West Africa 346
Upper Volta 609
Zaire 1123

97-64   Klipspringer *(Oreotragus oreotragus)*
Burundi 1197 1221
Djibouti 718 913
French Somali Coast 459
Lesotho 332

Malawi 381
Sudan 262

97-65   Gunther's Dik-Dik *(Madoqua guentheri)*
Ethiopia 1312

97-66   Kirk's Dik-Dik *(Madoqua kirki)*
Somalia 452
South West Africa 291

97-68   Salt's Dik-Dik *(Madoqua saltiana)*
Burundi 1034 1058 1082
French Territory of the Afars and the Issas 588
Somalia 292

97-69   Beira Antelope *(Dorcatragus megalotis)*
French Territory of the Afars and the Issas 664

97-70   Oribi *(Ourebia ourebi)*
Lesotho 472 613
Somalia 291 451
Swaziland 364

97-71   Steenbok *(Raphiceros campestris)*
Mozambique 678

97-75   Suni *(Neotragus moschatus)*
Malawi 382 633

97-76   Royal Antelope *(Neotragus pygmaeus)*
Ivory Coast 249
Liberia 622

97-77   Impala *(Aepyceros melampus)*
Angola 492
Belgian Congo 348
Burundi 12 20 77 83 94 1201 1225
Congo (Kinshasa) 387 521 526
Guinea 872
Ivory Coast 311 340 780
Katanga 32
Malawi 379 650
Ruanda-Urundi 206 212
Rwanda 59 65 100 219 456 636 **MS**639 1124 1127
South West Africa 345
Swaziland 167 230
Tanzania 313 O60
Uganda 303 421

97-78   Blackbuck *(Antilope cervicapra)*
Bahawalpur O3 O16
Nepal 450
Tripolitania 80

97-79   Springbok *(Antidorcas marsupialis)*
Angola 499 834
Orange Free State 139 140 141 142 143 144 145 146 147
South Africa 114 105 147 160 194 O8
South West Africa 45 58 352 O1 O9
Southern Rhodesia 72

97-80   Gerenuk *(Litocranius walleri)*
Burundi 1043 1067
Ethiopia 197 1310
French Somali Coast 434
Somali 294 453

97-81   Dibatag *(Ammodorcas clarkei)*
Ethiopia 1165
Liberia 1377
Somalia 485

97-82   Edmi Gazelle *(Gazella cuvieri)*
Ifni 201 203

97-83   Addra Gazelle *(Gazella dama)*
Burundi 1044 1068 1084
Ifni 87 88 89 90 91 92
Mauritania 574
Niger Republic 840

97-84   Dorcas Gazelle *(Gazella dorcas)*
Bahrain **MS**296
Israel 376
Libya 873 874 875 882
Mali 857
Mauritania 175
Spanish Sahara 61 64 66 69 132 135 187 188 189 268 269
270 271 285
Tripolitania 64 153
Tunisia 681
Upper Volta 612

97-85   Mountain Gazelle *(Gazella gazella)*
Abu Dhabi 5 6 7 19 20 21 34 65 93
Iraq 831
Jordan 825
Qatar 353
Umm Al Qiwain 1 10 34 80 89 98 O49 O107
Yemen 294 295 D298

97-86   Grant's Gazelle *(Gazella granti)*
Burundi 621 645 676
Central African Republic 976
Eritrea 216 217 218 219 220 221
Italian East Africa 1 8 17
Somalia E255 E256

97-87   Sand Gazelle *(Gazella leptoceros)*
Algeria 450 489
Chad 555
Morocco 335

97-88   Red-fronted Gazelle *(Gazella rufifrons)*
Ghana 225a 391 452
Togo 175 176 177 824 879
Upper Volta 547 D95 D96 D97 D98 D99 D100

97-90   Soemmerring's Gazelle *(Gazella soemmerringi)*
Somalia 295 355 454

97-91   Speke's Gazelle *(Gazella spekei)*
Somalia 293 354 482

97-92   Goitred Gazelle *(Gazella subgutturosa)*
Afghanistan 602 763
Bahrain **MS**296
Jordan 813
Mongolia 1482
Pakistan 600
Turkey 2682

97-93   Thomson's Gazelle *(Gazella thomsoni)*
Burundi 1035 1059 1083
Kenya 20
Kenya, Uganda and Tanganyika 188 O17
Portugal 1945
Uganda 305 423

97-98   Saiga *(Saiga tatarica)*
Mongolia 176
Russia 4281

97-100   Common Goral *(Nemorhaedus goral)*
Korea (North Korea) N438
Korea (South Korea) 1391
Thailand 784
Tuva 17

97-101   Japanese Serow *(Capricornis crispus)*
Japan 658

97-102   Mainland Serow *(Capricornis sumatraensis)*
Khmer Republic 340
Thailand 789
Vietnam (North Vietnam) N737

97-103   Mountain Goat *(Oreamnos americanus)*
Canada 487

97-104   Chamois *(Rupicapra rupicapra)*
Albania 724
Andorra F143 F293
Bulgaria 1094 2945
Czechoslovakia 993 1394 1970
France 1921
Germany (West Berlin) B286
Germany (West Germany) 1417
Liechtenstein 255
Monaco 980
New Zealand 931
Poland 902
Rumania 2432 2483 2858 3332 3604 4236
Slovakia 43 127
Spain 2161
Switzerland J216
Trieste B123
Yugoslavia 769 2091

97-105   Musk Ox *(Ovibos moschatus)*
Canada 478
Germany (East Germany) E1338 E2246
Greenland 73
Sweden 1183

97-106   Takin *(Budorcas taxicolor)*
Bhutan 74 79 116 206

97-108   Arabian Tahr *(Hemitragus jayakari)*
Oman 269

97-110   Wild Goat *(Capra aegagrus)*
Greece 1154
Turkey 2192

97-114   Ibex *(Capra ibex)*
Afghanistan 521
Bulgaria 1613
Czechoslovakia 1395
Ethiopia 645
Germany (East Germany) E1747
Hungary 1721
Israel 374
Italy 1177
Jordan 828
Mongolia 130 131
Nicaragua MS2486
Pakistan 417 418
Russia 4183
Sudan 123 260 O47
Switzerland J219
Yemen People's Democratic Republic 263

97-115   Spanish Ibex *(Capra pyrenaica)*
Spain 2098

97-116   Barbary Sheep *(Ammotragus lervia)*
Algeria 520
Chad 129
Libya 700
Mali 744
Mauritania 135 576
Morocco 336

Niger Republic 105 106
Tunisia 962

97-117   Bharal *(Pseudois nayaur)*
Bhutan MS525c

97-118   Argali *(Ovis ammon)*
Afghanistan 522 960
Mongolia 175 560 857 925 1141 1525
Tuva 55

97-119   American Bighorn *(Ovis canadensis)*
Canada 449 703
Mongolia 1141
United States of America 1472 1856 1426

97-122   Mouflon *(Ovis orientalis)*
Bulgaria 2245 2944
Cyprus 222 231
Czechoslovakia 1396 1969
France 1847
French Southern and Antarctic Territories 198
Germany (East Germany) E290 E1985
Hungary 2039 2211
Liechtenstein 628
Poland 2233
Turkey 2683

97-123   Urial *(Ovis vignei)*
Afghanistan 864
Pakistan 400 401

98   PANGOLINS
98-2   Giant Ground Pangolin *(Manis gigantea)*
Belgian Congo 349
Congo (Brazzaville) 962
Congo (Kinshasa) 388
French West Africa 83
Katanga 33
Kenya 34
Rio Muni 45 47 73 75

98-3   Malayan Pangolin *(Manis javanica)*
Indonesia 719 720 721
Malaysia 193
Philippines 1520
Sarawak 177

98-4   Chinese Pangolin *(Manis pentadactyla)*
China (Taiwan) 809
Hong Kong 412
Laos 270 271
Vietnam (North Vietnam) N368

98-5   Temminck's Ground Pangolin *(Manis temmincki)*
Botswana 397
Mozambique 677
Swaziland 366
Zambia 233

98-6   Long-tailed Pangolin *(Manis tetradactyla)*
Cameroun 906
Ivory Coast 755

100   SQUIRRELS
100-28   Eurasian Red Squirrel *(Sciurus vulgaris)*
Albania 810
Andorra F286 E54
Bulgaria 1373
Cuba 2601
Czechoslovakia 1682
Ecuador 1292

Finland 518
Germany (East Germany) E470
Great Britain 624 1041
Grenada 713
Hungary 1271 3015
Ifni 123 124 125
Italy 1834
Korea (North Korea) N437
Mongolia 775 1565
Rumania 2430 2481 4816
Russia 2063a
Spanish Sahara 233 235
Switzerland J213
Tuva 69
Yugoslavia 957 1857

100-45   Indian Palm Squirrel *(Funambulus palmarum)*
Guinea 960 961 962 978 979 980

100-55   Temminck's Giant Squirrel *(Epixerus ebii)*
Ghana 812
Ivory Coast 616

100-59   Kuhl's Tree Squirrel *(Funisciurus congicus)*
South West Africa 292

100-64   De Winton's Tree Squirrel *(Funisciurus substriatus)*
Ghana 639

100-75   Vincent's Bush Squirrel *(Paraxerus vincenti)*
Mozambique 1007

100-76   Gambian Sun Squirrel *(Heliosciurus gambianus)*
Malawi 704

100-86   Belly-banded Squirrel *(Callosciurus flavimanus)*
Vietnam (North Vietnam) N851

100-135   Barbary Ground Squirrel *(Atlantoxerus getulus)*
Spanish Sahara 234

100-137   Cape Ground Squirrel *(Xerus inauris)*
Ciskei 32

100-139   Unstriped Ground Squirrel *(Xerus rutilus)*
French Territory of the Afars and the Issas 508

100-141   Bobak Marmot *(Marmota bobak)*
Mongolia 559 928

100-147   Alpine Marmot *(Marmota marmota)*
Czechoslovakia 1112
Germany (East Germany) E2386
Liechtenstein 256
Poland 2967
Switzerland J208

100-150   Vancouver Marmot *(Marmota vancouverensis)*
Canada 1006

100-164   European Souslik *(Spermophilus citellus)*
Trieste B119
Yugoslavia 765

100-199   Least Chipmunk *(Tamias minimus)*
United States of America MS1726

100-206   Siberian Chipmunk *(Tamias sibiricus)*
Japan 1150
Korea (North Korea) N439
Korea (South Korea) 1064
Mongolia 772 1569

100-213   Red and White Flying Squirrel *(Petaurista alborufus)*
China (Taiwan) 808

100-217   Red Giant Flying Squirrel *(Petaurista petaurista)*
Vietnam (North Vietnam) N370

100-220   Siberian Flying Squirrel *(Pteromys volans)*
Finland 1035
Mongolia 773

100-230   Phayre's Flying Squirrel *(Hylopetes phayrei)*
Laos 167

103   BEAVERS
103-1   American Beaver *(Castor canadensis)*
Canada 10 26 31 439 473 1037
Hungary 3195
Mongolia 1138
San Marino 1128

103-2   Eurasian Beaver *(Castor fiber)*
Austria 1943
Germany (East Germany) E425
Germany (West Berlin) B313
Germany (West Germany) 1457
Mongolia 853 1138 1480
Poland 903 2965
Russia 2535 4185
Togo 1079

104   SCALY-TAILED SQUIRRELS
104-2   Lord Derby's Flying Squirrel *(Anomalurus derbianus)*
Fernando Poo 302

104-3   Pel's Flying Squirrel *(Anomalurus peli)*
Gabon 400

105   SPRING HARE
105-1   Spring Hare *(Pedetes capensis)*
Tanzania 307 O54

106   MICE, RATS, VOLES, GERBILS, HAMSTERS
106-352   Common Hamster *(Cricetus cricetus)*
Germany (East Germay) E1265
Germany (West Berlin) B295
Germany (West Germany) 1436

106-409   Norway Lemming *(Lemmus lemmus)*
Sweden 1182

106-440   Muskrat *(Ondatra zibethicus)*
Bulgaria 2243
Finland 627
Mongolia 173
Russia 3455
Yugoslavia 1732

106-592   Congo Forest Mouse *(Deomys ferrugineus)*
Central African Republic 113

106-604   Dollman's Tree Mouse *(Prionomys batesi)*
Central African Republic 115

106-617   Harvest Mouse *(Micromys minutus)*
Mongolia 1567

106-670   Four-striped Grass Mouse *(Rhabdomys pumilio)*
Mozambique 1006

106-672   Back-striped Mouse *(Hybomys univittatus)*
Central African Republic 114

106-754   Brown Rat *(Rattus norvegicus)*
Niger Republic 454

106-764   House Rat *(Rattus rattus)*
New Caledonia 676

106-835   Stick-nest Rat *(Leporillus conditor)*
Australia 797

107   DORMICE
107-1   Fat Dormouse *(Glis glis)*
Bulgaria 3132

107-2   Hazel Dormouse *(Muscardinus avellanarius)*
Czechoslovakia 1685
Sweden 1223

107-3   Garden Dormouse *(Eliomys quercinus)*
Finland 1034

107-5   Forest Dormouse *(Dryomys nitedula)*
Bulgaria 3131

110   JERBOAS
110-4   Lesser Egyptian Jerboa *(Jaculus jaculus)*
Morocco 858

110-27   Long-eared Jerboa *(Euchoreutes naso)*
Mongolia 1564

111   OLD-WORLD PORCUPINES
111-4   Cape Porcupine *(Hystrix africaeaustralis)*
Bophuthatswana 13
Lesotho 330 471
South West Africa 356
Swaziland 162

111-6   North African Crested Porcupine *(Hystrix cristata)*
French Territory of the Afars and the Issas 642
Ghana 511
Libya 879
Mauritania 174
Somalia 720
Tunisia 679
Zambia 170

111-7   Chinese Porcupine *(Hystrix hodgsoni)*
Hong Kong 413
Laos 169
Vietnam (North Vietnam) N853

111-8   Indian Crested Porcupine *(Hystrix indica)*
Afghanistan 673

111-10   African Brush-tailed Porcupine *(Atherurus africanus)*
Equatorial Guinea 62

112   NEW-WORLD PORCUPINES
112-5   Brazilian Tree Porcupine *(Coendou prehensilis)*
Guyana 756
Trinidad and Tobago 523

114   CAPYBARA
114-1   Capybara *(Hydrochoerus hydrochaeris)*
Brazil 2084
Uruguay 1417
Venezuela 1771 1849

116   PACAS, AGOUTIS
116-1   Paca *(Cuniculus paca)*
Belize 353 368
British Honduras 261 284 313
Costa Rica 648
El Salvador 1810
Guyana 497
Trinidad and Tobago 394
Venezuela 1773

116-3   Brazilian Agouti *(Dasyprocta aguti)*
Dominica 353
Grenada 762
Guyana 458 767
St. Lucia 571
St. Vincent 648
Trinidad and Tobago 395

117   VISCACHAS, CHINCHILLAS
117-3   Mountain Viscacha *(Lagidium viscaccia)*
Bolivia 356 357 452

117-5   Short-tailed Chinchilla *(Chinchilla brevicaudata)*
Peru 1192

117-6   Long-tailed Chinchilla *(Chinchilla laniger)*
Chile 381j 382j 383j 996

118   HUTIAS
118-3   Brown's Hutia *(Capromys browni)*
Jamaica 512 513 514 515

118-5   Bahaman Hutia *(Capromys ingrahami)*
Bahamas 627

118-6   Bushy-tailed Hutia *(Capromys melanurus)*
Cuba 3047

118-7   Dwarf Hutia *(Capromys nanus)*
Cuba 1720

118-8   Desmarest's Hutia *(Capromys pilorides)*
Cuba 1057a 1057d 2765

118-9   Prehensile-tailed Hutia *(Capromys prehensilis)*
Cuba 1057b

118-11   Hispaniolan Hutia *(Plagiodontia aedium)*
Dominican Republic 1410

118-12   Coypu *(Myocastor coypus)*
Nicaragua 1952
Russia 5011
Uruguay 1420

125   AFRICAN MOLE-RATS
125-2   Hottentot Mole-Rat *(Cryptomys hottentotus)*
Mozambique 1008

127   PIKAS
127-1   Northern Pika *(Ochotona alpina)*
Liberia 1094

127-8   Pallas's Pika *(Ochotona pallasi)*
Mongolia 1563

128   RABBITS, HARES
128-1   Ryukyu Rabbit *(Pentalagus furnessi)*
Japan 1361
Malagasy Republic 321

128-2   Natal Red Hare *(Pronolagus crassicaudatus)*
Lesotho 614
Mozambique 1009

128-4   Smith's Red Hare *(Pronologus rupestris)*
Malawi 703

128-13   Brown Hare *(Lepus capensis)*
Albania 814 947 1155
Austria 1560
Bahrain **MS**296
Bulgaria 1091 1685
Ciskei 30
Czechoslovakia 892 1615 2202
Djibouti 740
Finland 642
Germany (East Germany) E471 E1082
Great Britain 1040
Hungary 1273 2037 2659
Maldive Islands 782
Panama 955
Rumania 2423 2474 2859
Russia 2059a
Switzerland J215
Yemen 386
Yugoslavia 959

128-15   Abyssinian Hare *(Lepus habessinicus)*
French Territory of the Afars and the Issas 605

128-22   Chinese Hare *(Lepus sinensis)*
China (Taiwan) 1035 1036
Korea (North Korea) N436

128-23   Arctic Hare *(Lepus timidus)*
Finland 1037
Ireland 462
Liechtenstein 253
Mongolia 778
Sweden 568
Switzerland J211

128-25   Bush Hare *(Lepus whytei)*
Ghana 470 551 708 **MS**709 1031a
Mauritania 536
Togo 1078

128-39   Common Rabbit *(Oryctolagus cuniculus)*
Albania 1157
Ascension 346
Germany (West Berlin) B293
Germany (West Germany) 1434
Italy 1836
St. Pierre et Miquelon 431
Yemen 662

129   ELEPHANT-SHREWS
129-12   Four-toed Elephant-Shrew *(Petrodromus tetradactylus)*
Mozambique 1005

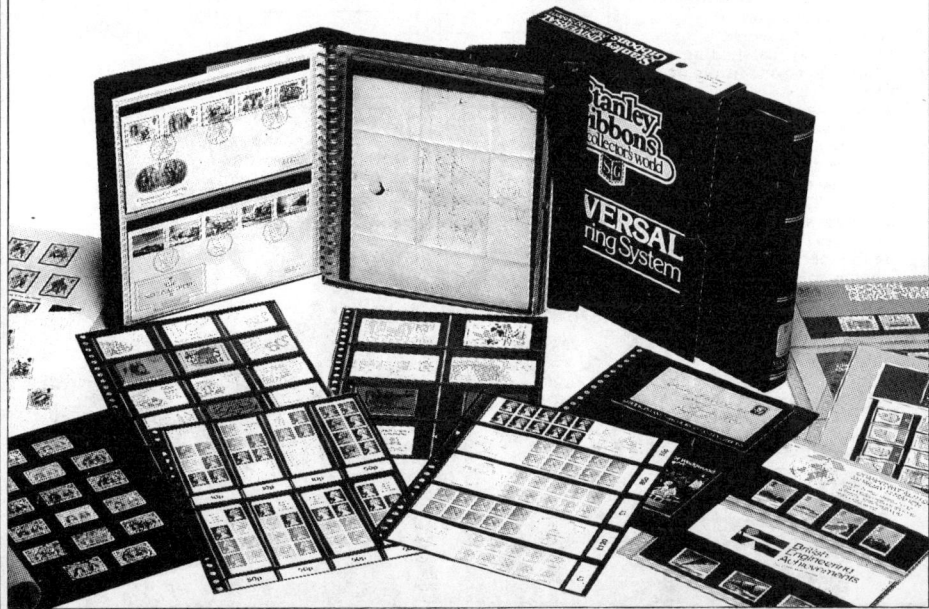

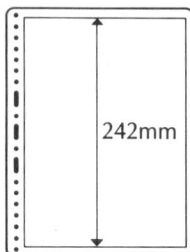

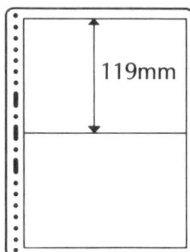

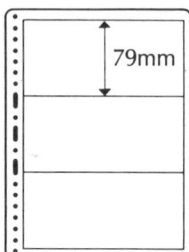

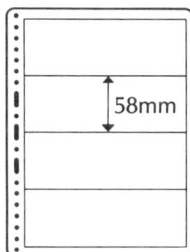

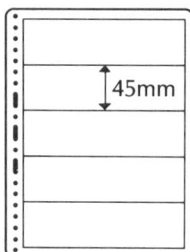

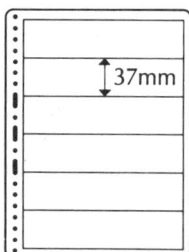

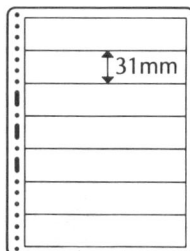

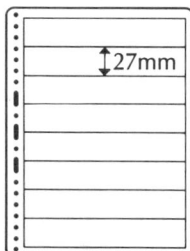

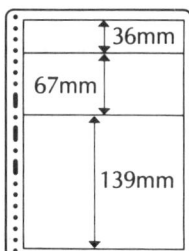